Lecture Notes in Artificial Inte

Subseries of Lecture Notes in Computer Sc
Edited by J. Siekmann

Lecture Notes in Computer Science
Edited by G. Goos and J. Hartmanis

F. von Martial

Coordinating Plans
of Autonomous Agents

Springer-Verlag
Berlin Heidelberg New York
London Paris Tokyo
Hong Kong Barcelona
Budapest

Series Editor

Jörg Siekmann
University of Saarland
German Research Center for Artificial Intelligence (DFKI)
Stuhlsatzenhausweg 3, W-6600 Saarbrücken 11, FRG

Author

Frank von Martial
DETECON GMBH
Aennchenstr. 19, W-5300 Bonn 2, FRG

CR Subject Classification (1991): I.2.11, H.5.3, I.2.8, H.1.2, I.2.1

ISBN 3-540-55615-X Springer-Verlag Berlin Heidelberg New York
ISBN 0-387-55615-X Springer-Verlag New York Berlin Heidelberg

Typesetting: Camera ready by author/editor
Printing and binding: Druckhaus Beltz, Hemsbach/Bergstr.
45/3140-543210 - Printed on acid-free paper

Foreword

mediated.

The use of computers to support collaborative work is an emerging trend that will have a significant impact on how we do our daily work, especially as our work becomes mediated by computerized intelligent assistants that understand our goals and plans. This book represents an important contribution to the field of *Computer-Supported Cooperative Work*. However, this book is also equally important to the area of *Distributed Artificial Intelligence* because of the techniques it develops for agent coordination, specifically multi-agent planning. It considers the issue of how plans that are developed autonomously by individual agents should be restructured when other agent plans are in conflict or when there exist beneficial relationships among them. The basic approach to the recognition of these relationships among agents' plans and their resolution is a distributed one.

This work is not only interesting for the computational techniques developed for plan coordination but also for the formal framework that underlies these techniques. The characterization of plan interactions among agents is built on a formal logical framework based on an event-based characterization of actions. This framework allows for the representation of concurrent actions in multiple agent plans, temporal relationships among actions, and plans at multiple levels of abstraction. Based on this framework, a taxonomy of plan relationships is defined that includes both positive and negative relationships among plans.

Negative relationships are those that may prevent either or both plans from carrying out their intended purpose. The basis for these negative relationships are due to shared resource usage or incompatible actions. Actions are incompatible when the action of one plan creates a logical state of the world which precludes another agent from successfully completing its action. Resource conflicts due to shared resource usage are further broken down into two categories, one involving consumable resources and the other non-consumable resources.

Positive relationships are also broken into categories involving equality, subsumption and favor. An equality relationship indicates the ability of an agent to carry out an action in another agent's plan and is the basis of task sharing. A subsumption relationship indicates that one agent's actions will make unnecessary an action of another agent. A favor relationship indicates one agent has the potential for slightly altering its plan in such a way that the number of actions required by another agent to carry out the intended purpose of its plan is reduced. The formal specification of these relationships among agents' plans and how these relationships can be used to improve overall network problem solving is an important aspect of this work.

The major emphasis in the discussion on resolving negative conflicts is on those caused by shared access to non-consumable resources. The techniques for handling other types of conflicts are more domain-dependent in character and are not treated in detail. In a principled way, the alternative strategies for resolving this type of conflict are detailed based on temporal ordering constraints; additionally, heuristics are specified for choosing the order of resolving multiple conflicts among agents and for choosing among alternative strategies for resolving conflicts. The protocol for exploiting the favor relationship is also explored in detail. Especially interesting is the quantitative heuristics for deciding when the favor relationship should lead to agents restructuring their plans. The techniques for resolving non-consumable resource conflicts and exploiting favor relationships are explained through a number of examples which provide a good understanding.

The distributed negotiation protocols used by agents to recognize and resolve/exploit these plan relationships are some of the most sophisticated strategies yet devised for coordinating agent activities. They exploit the hierarchical nature of plan descriptions to reduce communication among agents, and can work with only partially expanded plan networks. These complex, multi-step, asynchronous protocols are extremely hard to verify for correctness. This work reworks and applies verification techniques, developed for the analysis of low-level network communication protocols, so that they can be used to verify these high-level negotiation protocols.

The final part of this book examines the design of a prototype system that supports collaborative work in the office domain based on the plan coordination techniques developed in early parts of the book. As part of the system, a planning subsystem is described, which is used to generate the activity plans of individual agents.

In summary, this book represents a thorough and deep investigation of an important topic in distributed AI and computer-supported collaborative work. It is clearly written with many examples and background material that should allow readers of both fields to understand it.

University of Massachusetts at Amherst, January 1992   Victor R. Lesser

Preface

The ability to coordinate and negotiate is part of almost any intelligent behavior and, hence, reasoning about coordination is one of its fundamental components. This work deals with the coordination of distributed agents which have planning and communicative competence.

Important issues in this book are:
- How to recognize and reconcile conflicting intentions among a collection of agents.
- How to recognize and take advantage of favorable interactions.
- How to enable individual agents to represent and reason about the actions, plans, and knowledge of other agents in order to coordinate with them.
- When to call a set of plans "coordinated" and what operations are possible to transform uncoordinated plans into coordinated ones.
- How to enable agents to communicate and interact: what communication languages or protocols to use, and what and when to communicate.

We will present a novel approach to coordinate activities of autonomous agents. The intended actions of agents are described as plans. The coordination of plans is triggered by the relations which exist between the actions of different plans. With the help of an explicit model of multiagent plan relations a powerful approach for coordination is realized. Our model covers the whole spectrum from negative to positive relations between plans. Negative relations may prevent one or several of the plans from being executed as intended. Positive relations are all those relations between plans where some benefit to the agents can be derived by combining the plans. The handling of plan relations includes both the operations for conflict resolution and for the utilization of favorable relations and the way agents can interact and negotiate about their relations.

The main contributions of our work include:
- a detailed taxonomy of relations between plans of different agents,
- strategies for coordination and plan modifications based on these relations, and
- a negotiation framework for synchronizing activities.

The reader may also appreciate the thorough introduction to the field of *distributed artificial intelligence* and its subarea *multiagent planning*.

Acknowledgements

I would like to thank Jörg Siekmann for all his help during my research. His enthusiasm animated me very much when launching my research project. He accompanied my work with many constructive suggestions. I would like to express my gratitude to Wolfgang Wahlster for fruitful discussions and helpful comments on drafts of this book.

The research presented here grew mainly out of the author's contribution to the Assisting Computer project of GMD's Institute for Applied Information Technology, which is headed by Peter Hoschka. I would like to thank GMD for providing me with extremely satisfying working conditions. Thomas Kreifelts helped me to sharpen and develop some of my ideas. I am grateful for his many valuable comments on drafts of this book. During the time I worked at GMD he has always been a highly cooperative and friendly group leader. I would like to thank Frank Victor for inspiring me to write this book. Parts of the implementations of this research have been done by Thomas Kreifelts, Edgar Sommer, Frank Victor and Gerd Woetzel. I would like to thank them for their work. Peter Seuffert and Gerd Woetzel have helped me a lot with problems I had with the computing environment. I also owe great debt to Peter Wißkirchen for providing the basis of my research spirit.

I am particularly grateful to Victor Lesser for his valuable contributions to my research. His interest and belief in my work stimulated me very much and his criticism helped me to improve drafts of this book.

Christoph Weidenbach spent considerable time with me discussing mathematical aspects of my work. I would like to thank him for his efforts. I am also grateful to Toru Ishida, who introduced me into the field of Distributed Artificial Intelligence during the time I stayed at NTT in Japan.

My very special thanks go to my wife Suha and our kids Rascha, Simon and Marius for tolerating my not being available to them so often. Although highly motivated to study the mentally produced artificial agents of my research, I am much more fascinated by my physically produced human agents, namely our children. Suha also helped me very much with her encouraging and optimistic spirit to pursue my goal of writing this book.

Siegburg, April 1992   Frank von Martial

Table of Contents

1 Introduction

The ability to coordinate and communicate is part of almost any intelligent behavior and, hence, reasoning about coordination is one of its fundamental components.

Coordination is a way of adapting to the environment. The environment in our approach is populated by agents which intend to execute actions within this environment. The agents coordinate by modifying their intentions. The reason for coordination are the intentions of other agents.

Communication is the medium by which information relevant for coordination is exchanged. The agents communicate about their intentions, which then will be negotiated among the agents. Often agents base their activities on plans. Therefore, the ability to coordinate is tightly coupled with the ability to plan and to communicate.

This work provides a framework (both theoretical and practical) for modelling agents with planning and communicative competence. Based on these foundations we will present a novel approach to coordinate activities. The intended actions of agents are described as plans. Our approach covers the whole spectrum from negative to positive relations between plans. Negative relations may prevent one or several of the plans from being executed as intended. Positive relations are all those relations between plans where some benefit the agents can be derived by combining the plans. The coordination of plans is triggered by the relations which exist between the actions of different plans. With the help of an explicit model of the plan relations a powerful approach for coordination is realized.

The approach pursued in this research differs from the way in which planning in AI is performed. In AI planning, there is given a set of goals, a set of allowable actions in a planning environment. The task is to find a sequence of actions that will bring about a state of affairs in which all of the desired goals will be satisfied. We are interested in *plan coordination*. In plan coordination, there is usually a set of plans given, (i.e., the creation of plans is not a primary task), and the task is to modify this set such that the resulting set of plans can be called "coordinated". Of course, important aspects of such an approach are to define when a set of plans can be called "coordinated" and what operations are possible to transform uncoordinated plans into coordinated plans.

Research done in this work may have impact on several application areas. Potential domains range from very technical, automated domains such as distributed traffic control, manufacturing (scheduling) or cooperating robots to domains where cooperation among humans is of primary interest (computer supported cooperative work, project management).

Overview

This book is divided into nine chapters. Chapter 1 introduces the problems and research issues of this work. The relation with previous research and what is missing is inspected in Chapter 2. The research of this book belongs to the field of *distributed artificial intelligence*, more specifically to the area *multiagent planning*. In Chapter 3 we will develop the basic notations of actions and plans with respect to coordination. In Chapter 4 a classification of the relations between the agents' plans is established, building the foundation to define when a set of individual plans is coordinated. Chapter 5 is concerned with procedures and strategies to resolve the relations in case of conflict and beneficial relations. It is explained how plans can be modified for coordination. Plan coordination is illustrated by several detailed examples. Chapter 6 describes how agents communicate and negotiate. Chapter 7 contains a condensed model of the activity coordination approach presented in the preceding chapters. There are also given examples for coordination problems, which can be tackled within our framework. In Chapter 8 a transfer of our approach to office information systems and the support of human collaborative work are discussed. We will also present an implemented system that supports planning and plan coordination within an office environment. Conclusions are given in Chapter 9.

Object of our research. The primary thesis of this research is a model for coordinating plans that are previously made by autonomous intelligent agents. In other words, we assume the plans are given somehow and we are then interested in coordinating them, e.g. by resolving conflicts. Plan coordination is done via relations resolution and communication. The main contributions of this work include a detailed taxonomy of relations between multiagent plans, strategies for coordination based on these relations, and a communication and negotiation framework for synchronizing plans.

The subfield of multiagent planning, where the planning process is purely *task-driven* (see also the planning taxonomy in Section 2.2.1), is outside the scope of this research. In a task-driven planning multiagent planning system, there is first a goal given, which is then decomposed into subgoals and distributed among several planners (top-down problem solving). In contrast, our research focus is on situations, where the plans of agents are preexisting (*agent-centered* view) and the problem is to reconcile the given plans before they are executed in a common environment.

1.1 Assumptions and Problems

In multiagent worlds the coordination of the diverse activities is one of the most important tasks. In an environment which is populated by intelligent autonomous agents coordination is accomplished through interaction. We examine the interactions which intelligent agents may exhibit when they coordinate their activities at two different levels:

- On the indirect interaction level, the agents interact (indirectly) through the *plans* they intend to execute in the same environment. Agents (intelligent beings) utilize plans to pursue their goals. We show how information in the agents plans, even if they are vague and incomplete, can be used to work towards a coordinated system.

- On the direct interaction level, the agents interact directly by *communicating* with each other from agent to agent. By communication agents announce their intended action or plans, and by communication agents may reach an agreement how to coordinate their plans.

As a direct consequence of these two forms of interactions there are three main concerns of this work:

1. *Planning in Distributed Systems.*
Questions of interest concerning the planning aspect:
What are appropriate requirements for plans in multiagent worlds?
How can plans and their relations (interactions) be modelled in a formally adequate way?
What plan modification operators are necessary for coordination?

2. *Communication and Negotiation among Autonomous Agents.*
The communication framework has to fulfill two functions:
- to transfer plans. The agents communicate about their intended actions ahead of time.
- to reach reconciliation of plans by negotiation. If there exist relations among their plans, the agents will negotiate the consequences of these relations trying to prevent negative interferences and utilize positive interactions.

When coordinating the activities of autonomous agents by negotiation several issues have to be dealt with:

What are the nodes in the communication network and who communicates with whom?

What are the messages exchanged between the communicators?

What are the protocols ('when' and 'how') according to which a negotiation takes place?

3. *Coordinating Plans of Autonomous Agents.*

The first two issues have an important meaning for the coordination of intelligent agents. The clamp which fuses the first two issues is coordination. Thus, the question is how these two aspects can be combined into one coherent coordination and cooperation framework. Until now research in coordination or *distributed artificial intelligence* (DAI) in general has usually focussed on only one of these aspects, planning or communication, but has seldom attempted to combine both of them.

What assumptions concerning agents and their planning activities is this work based on?

Assumptions about agents. Concerning the agents, the assumptions are:

1. Inherent distribution of agents. The world is populated by agents, which are inherently distributed. Most DAI research first considers, how a global problem can be distributed among agents which *then* have to be coordinated. In this work, we are less concerned with the problem of distributing tasks among agents, but rather with the problem of coordinating the activities of these agents *after* the distribution has been performed.

2. The agents are intelligent, autonomous problem solvers. An *autonomous* agent has its own goals, intentions, capabilities and knowledge.

3. The agents may incorporate the actions of other agents as part of their plans (multiagent planning).

4. There is equal distribution of control and authority (non-hierarchical agents).

5. Agents may have different skills.

6. The agents broadcast or exchange their plans before execution in order to allow other agents greater access to their anticipated future behavior.

7. The agents tell the truth concerning their plans.

8. There is no overall planning task which has to be solved in close cooperation. Each agent wants to solve its individual problem, i.e. the agents are not originally constrained to cooperate, or at least they do not – a situation which occurs quite often in real world settings (inherent distribution of planning activities).

9. The agents have a cordial relation and are not hostile against each other (cooperative behavior, benevolent assumption).

Assumptions about plans. Concerning the plans, the assumptions are:

1. The actions of plans require resources.
2. The actions of one plan are not necessarily sequentially, even not partially ordered. In fact, plans may contain concurrent or overlapping actions.
3. There are negative and positive interactions among activities.
4. The plans, which are exchanged among agents, may be partial and not completely developed.
5. The actions of plans may be specified at different levels of abstraction.
6. Plans are executed in the same environment.
7. Plans may contain temporal information.

Some of these assumptions such as the fact that the agents tell the truth concerning their plans facilitate coordination. But most of these assumptions such as that incompleteness of plans and that they contain temporal information pose requirements which are hard to be taken all into account into one coherent framework.

Open problems. When we try to evaluate research dealing with issues above we encounter several typical deficiencies.

Although there has been considerable work on centralized multiagent planning, where a central planner generates a plan for several executing agents, there has been relatively little work involved in connecting the planning process with the process of communication and making commitments about actions and plans.

In multiagent worlds, the interactions between the diverse agents are a prominent interest. Usually, research is concerned only with a portion of the whole spectrum of interactions which may occur between planning agents. Mostly, resources mean the only concept for reasoning about how different activities interact. We need theories about multiagent interactions which go beyond these restricted approaches.

There is a controversy between theoretical (e.g., logic based) and practical (e.g., implemented) approaches to DAI problems. Theoretical models allows to mathematically prove theories what cooperating agents can and cannot do, however, they are usually far away from practical systems. On the other hand, practical approaches often lack sufficient degree of abstraction in that for instance clear definitions of plans and coordination are missing.

In dynamic multiagent domains with asynchronously interacting agents the problem of dealing with vague and incomplete information is always given. However, there is hardly any work providing adequate mechanisms for coping with these problems.

1.2   Solution: A Relation Driven Coordination Process via Negotiation

The two key factors in solving the problem of coordinating plans are: First, to define a taxonomy of relations which may hold between the plans of different agents and, second, to develop a communication framework which is suited for autonomous agents to exchange their plans and to negotiate about how to resolve the relations between their plans.

1.2.1 Scheme for Coordinating Plans of Agents

The scheme of coordinating the individual plans is illustrated in Fig. 1. This figure is a simplification of the actual coordination process, because it neglects the aspects of a dynamic environment (real time aspects), i.e. it does not reflect how coordination, planning and execution activities are interleaved. This aspect will be explained in more detail in Chapters 6 and 7, where we present a model of interleaved coordination and execution embedded in a negotiation framework.

Figure 1 is meant to give a first understanding of how planning, communication and coordination are coupled without considering the aspect of execution. First, the agents develop their plans autonomously. Then, they transfer their individual plans to each other, a dedicated coordination agent or a blackboard which can be read by all agents. In order to reconcile these plans several tasks have to be executed:

– recognize and evaluate the possible relations between the plans,
– work out solutions to deal with these relations,
– initiate and perform negotiations.

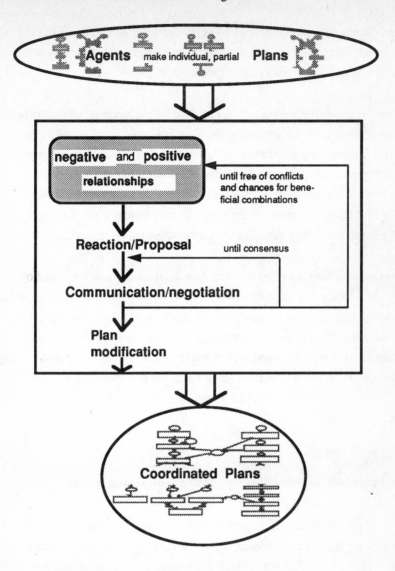

Figure 1: A relation driven coordination process.

Each agent may utilize subagents to perform these tasks. As a result of the coordination process the individual plans are reconciled with respect to their negative and positive relations. This means for each agent to adapt its plan because of the existence of other agents with their plans. The result of coordination can also be seen as a set of plans being integrated into one global plan although the individual plans still exist.

The communication structure is given by a network whose nodes are interpreted as agents, and whose edges are interpreted as communication channels. Agents can be both human and automated and are considered as autonomous problem solvers.

One way to coordinate the activities of agents is to let one agent generate a plan and distribute actions to individual agents according to the plan. However, there are difficulties with this approach. First, the planning agent needs to know all the expertise that each agent has. The collection and maintenance of such a knowledge base causes too much overhead and is quite hard to realize. Second, the planning process takes longer than if each agent works out a plan for itself in parallel. Meanwhile, much of the resources may be idle while waiting for the actions assigned. In our approach, both planning and coordination is performed in a distributed fashion.

The agents first plan their activities and then coordinate their plans. Coordination is achieved by communication. Communication can be performed in two different ways: implicitly by information sharing or by explicitly exchanging messages. In the first case, agents exchange information through data structures which are accessible to all agents. In message passing systems, all the information to be exchanged is contained in the messages being sent or received by the agents. Because the shared information scheme requires common data structures which violates the objective to preserve the agents' autonomy, we will focus on the message passing paradigm.

1.2.2 Coordination as Improvement Instead of Optimization

The process of coordination is done concurrently with re-/planning and execution activities of the agents, i.e. planning and execution are interleaved. Not only the execution of actions of a plan but also the coordination actions such as message passing and relation detection consume time. It might happen that during the negotiation of resolving a conflict one agent needs to execute the action under consideration and, thus, the negotiation is terminated without having reached an agreement. In this case, the other agent might be forced to modify its plan. During the process of coordination the "world time" proceeds, which means that coordination takes place under real time constraints and the autonomous agents are situated.

Because of the asynchronous interactions we can not yield for an optimal set of coordinated plans but rather try to let the agents improve (coordinate) their plans as much as possible. Agents coordinate as best as they can given their current view, rather than waiting for a complete view of the other agents' plans. Thus, in our approach we do not attempt to build an optimal solution which only were possible with complete information and sufficient time for coordination both from a computational and communicative perspective. The ability to deal with partial information is essential in dynamic domains where complete, up-to-date information might not be available to any agent.

1.2.3 Types of Agents

Agents can have several roles in a coordination process. A *planner* is an agent who has established a plan and broadcasts its intention to other agents. An *executor* (affector) is an agent who executes an action. This agent does not negotiate about plans. An agent acts as a *coordinator* of a conversation if it initiates a resolution of a plan relation.

Agents can play one or two or all of these roles in a given coordination process. If the executor and planner of an action is the same agent, this agent is planning for its own activities. But an agent may also be planner and coordinator at the same time. If there is a dedicated agent whose only role is coordinator this agent is called a *mediator*.

If an agent is only coordinator of a conversation it acts as a mediator in the process of reaching an agreement. When this agent receives the intended action or whole plans of the other agents, it checks whether there are actions which make a negotiation necessary. The coordinator, acting as an independent mediator, enters in negotiation with each of the parties, proposing and modifying compromises until a final agreement is reached. Since the authority resides in the agents, they have to give feedback to the coordination agent in order to decide which trade-offs are acceptable.

Negotiation, which is originally a multilateral affair between the agents involved, is via coordination agents transformed into a set of *bilateral* negotiations and the coordination agent's coordination *strategy*. In the "mediated" case, the agents do not interact directly with each other but each agent only communicates with the coordination agent, which acts as a mediator.

It is a complex task to prepare and monitor a negotiation among autonomous agents. Before a coordinator initiates negotiation between the agents involved in a negative or positive action relation it has to work out a proposal for a compromise. It then has to take care that the conversation is successful by reaching an agreement in a reasonable amount of time. For the performance of a negotiation the coordination agent may employ a variety of strategies. Strategies may depend on several aspects, of which the most important is the reason of a negotiation, i.e.

the kind of relation between the actions. The coordination agent selects a proposal based on the following factors: temporal relation between the actions, resource type of conflict (consumable versus non-consumable), relation between duration of action and associated interval, amount of resources needed more than available (a relative value), the preceding proposals (if existing). A proposal contains a suggestion for each agent involved in the conflict.

In general, there are two possibilities for exchanging messages. The agents can broadcast information about their intended actions to each other (multicast conversation). This may incur a large amount of overhead because more information must be exchanged and because agents may duplicate each other's reasoning about coordination. This speaks in favor of having a mediator to whom the agents transfer their plans ahead of time. Having mediators means that only one agent has to spend its resources on reasoning about coordination and can enforce consistent views.

However, even with a mediator, the final decision whether and how to coordinate rests with the *autonomous* agents involved. It would affect the autonomy of the agents if there were a central instance that would force the agents to perform plan modifications which are required for coordination. Thus, the task of a mediator (coordinator) is to detect whether chances for plan synchronizations exist, to explore how the agents should modify their plans to utilize it, and then, to inform the agents about it. The agents themselves will then decide, whether and how to utilize an existing relation. The process of reaching a decision (commitment) is embedded into a negotiation framework.

It is important to note that the coordination concept is not dependent on having a dedicated coordination agent. Whether and how many agents in the system act as coordinators (*coordination responsibilities*) is an issue of the system organization in general (*meta-level organization*). An organization depends on the specific application and the number of agents. There is a great range of different organizations possible ranging from having only one dedicated coordinator to each agent being himself both planner and coordinator. In the latter case, when an agent has received a plan of another agent, s/he[1] starts reasoning whether there is a need for coordination, i.e. an unresolved plan relation exists between the received plan and his plan.

---

[1] Usually, we use masculine adjectives and pronouns to refer to agents, but they should be read as "his", "her" or "its" (for automated agents), as the reader desires.

Depending on the application and the number of agents in the system the number of coordination agents may vary. For instance, agents which are idle may take the role of a coordinator. If it turns out that a coordinator is overloaded, he may request other agents to take some of his load.

1.2.4 Phases of Activity Coordination

Coordination consists of several phases (Fig. 2):

1. *Relation Detection.* The relations (negative or positive) which exist between two individual plans (partial or complete) have to be detected.
2. *Topic Selection.* The next negotiation topic is selected. A topic treats one of the relations which have been detected in phase 1.
3. *Strategy Selection.* In each relation case there may be a variety of ways (strategies) possible how to handle (solve) it. The coordination agent uses heuristics to select the most reasonable strategy.
4. *Negotiation.* Attempt to mediate between the parties. A coordinator does not force the agents to accept a prescribed solution. He tries to achieve a commitment which is accepted by the participants. This commitment is reached by a (controlled) negotiation between the planners. If one strategy cannot be completed successfully, an alternative is tried.
   The coordinator selects an approach and makes a proposal for the agents involved. An agent can accept a proposal, reject it, modify parameters of it or may suggest a different approach to tackle a relation.
5. *Plan Modification.* The agents modify their plans according to the result of the negotiation.

Coordinators keep records of the actions which they are currently managing along with their relations to other actions and the state the respective negotiation has reached. The arrival of messages from ongoing negotiations calls for an update of the action list, a screening of this structure and an activation of one of the above phases, which in turn may eventually result in the dispatch of some new messages.

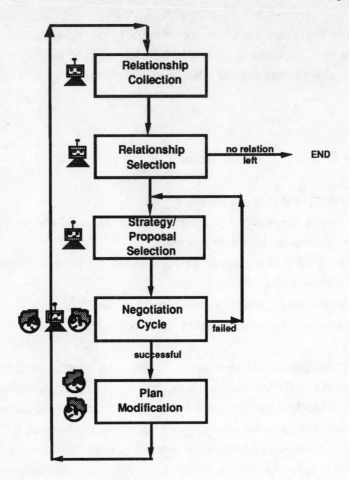

Figure 2: Phases of plan coordination

1.3 The Examples Used in this Book

There are several examples and scenarios, some worked out in detail, which focus on different aspects of the coordination approach. As these examples are scattered throughout this book, a centralized listing seems beneficial:

- *Art and Bert* (4.1 and 7.4): This example covers a variety of plan relations, both negative and positive ones, and shows how the involved plans can be coordinated. In Chapter 4 this example is informally introduced and in Chapter 7 it is described using the formalism developed.

- *Conflict Evaluation Example* (5.1.3.3): This example contains a set of conflicts between several abstract (not further specified) actions and examines the strategies to resolve these conflicts.
- *Pursuit Game* (5.1.2.1): In this domain, there are five agents, one robber and four policemen, whose task it is to capture the robber. This scenario illustrates some features of conflicts.
- *Autonomous Mobile Vehicles* (5.1.2.2): It is indicated how autonomous mobile vehicles can use the conflict relation to avoid collisions.
- *Favor Resolution* (5.2.4): A short example illustrates the favor relation and the corresponding plan modifications.
- *Delivery Scenario* (5.2.5): By giving crisp descriptions of plans and the costs associated with executing plans, we investigate how agents can take advantage of the favor relation.
- *Distributed Project Planning* (8.2): This paragraph motivates project planning as an application by pointing out parallels between our planning concept and project planning.
- *VIPS – Planning Office Procedures* (8.3.1): Illustrates (by giving screen copies of a system implemented by us) how an individual agent (office worker) can use a knowledge based tool for multiagent plan creation.
- *COORS – Coordination of Office Plans* (8.3.2): This example shows screen copies of coordination of plans, which can be constructed using the VIPS system.

The main purpose of these examples is to demonstrate that these diverse application areas all fit into our framework. Also, they are used to illustrate different points of interest.

2 Cooperation and Coordination of Intelligent Agents

2.1 Distributed Artificial Intelligence - An Overview

This section provides a general overview of Distributed Artificial Intelligence, its related fields, its motivations, principles and history. For more complete information about DAI in general, the reader is referred to the surveys by Lesser and Corkhill [1987], Bond and Gasser [1988] and Durfee, Lesser and Corkhill [1989].

Definition. *Distributed Artificial Intelligence* is concerned with solving problems by applying both artificial intelligence techniques and multiple problem solvers [Decker 87]. A minimum definition of a DAI *system* is that it must include at least two agents, that these agents have some degree of information and/or control autonomy, and that some nonempty subset of the agents display sophistication in an artificial intelligence sense (capability of reasoning, planning, etc.) [Rosenschein 86].

What can be distributed?
F. Hayes-Roth lists six primary domains for DAI distributions [Hayes-Roth 80]:
- space
- time
- instrumentality
- resources
- information
- interpretation.

These dimensions are tightly related with the distribution of *control*. It is clear that agents who have at their disposal more resources, information or instrumentality, have more control than others.

Subfields of DAI. DAI can be split into six subareas (see also [Benda 89]):
1. Coordination (synergy, balance between control and communication, etc.),

2. Communication and Negotiation (communication, interactions between agents),

3. Intelligent Agents (autonomy, tolls for building agents, etc.),

4. Distributed Reasoning (distributed planning, shared knowledge and belief),

5. Distributed Interfaces (group interfaces, conferencing, teleoperations, etc.),

6. Technological Basis (distributed operating systems and data bases, etc.).

2.1.1 Distributed Artificial Intelligence and Related Disciplines

How does DAI compare with research fields working on similar problems?

DAI versus Connectionism. The definitions of DAI assume that the individuals do have some intelligence, which is opposed to the connectionist view where simple, unintelligent computing elements combine to form an intelligent whole [Feldman and Ballard 82].

Intelligent Agents. An intelligent agent does not simply react to its environment but instead uses knowledge (possibly heuristic) to make informed decisions about how to act [Durfee 88]. Each agent is capable of sophisticated problem solving and can work independently, but when they cooperate with each other, the combined abilities of the agents go beyond their individual capabilities so that the size and scope of the problems they can solve as a group increases dramatically.

DAI versus Distributed Processing. DAI differs in several aspects from the topic of *distributed processing*. Typically, for instance, most of the processing in such systems is done at a central site and remote processors are limited to basic data collection. Only data and no control is distributed and the processors do not cooperate in a substantive manner.
Distributed processing systems address the problem of coordinating a network of computing agents to carry out a set of disparate and mostly *independent tasks*. There is much less interdependence between tasks than in DAI. This often leads to a concern with issues such as access control and protection, and results in viewing cooperation as a form of compromise between potentially conflicting views and desires at the level of system design and configuration.

James Hendler writes on this issue [Hendler 91]: "The discussion (in distributed processing) centers on how bits of data that make up a computation can be physically moved among machines. ... DAI is however full of terms borrowed from *sociology*: negotiation, interaction, contracts, agreement, organization, cohesion, social order, and collaboration. ... By concentrating on the issues involved in determining how a set of separate agents can give rise to global *intelligent* behavior the DAI researcher is forced to go beyond consideration of the computation itself."

Distributed Problem Solving and **Multiagent Systems** are subfields of DAI and lie at the two extremes of the same spectrum. Actually, most systems and approaches are likely to lie away from the two extreme points of the spectrum. The goal of *Distributed Problem Solving* (DPS) is to create a team of coarse-grained cooperating agents that act together to solve a *single* task, such as monitoring a network of sensors [Decker 87; Lesser and Corkhill 87]. In a *pure* DPS, the problem is divided into tasks, and special task performers (agents) are designed to solve these tasks for that problem only. All interaction (cooperation, coordination if any) strategies are incorporated as an integral part in the design of the system. It is a kind of top-down designed system, since agents are designed to conform to the requirements specified at the top.

In contrast to DPS, in a *pure Multiagent System* (MAS) the agents are autonomous, potentially preexisting, and typically heterogeneous. A MAS does not require a restriction to a single task. Research is concerned with coordinating intelligent behavior among a collection of autonomous intelligent agents how they can coordinate their knowledge, goals, skills, and plans jointly to take action or to solve problems [Bond and Gasser 88]. Although an agent here can also be a special task performer, its has an "open" interface, which is accessible to everyone (using the right standard). The agents may not only be working towards a single goal, but also toward separate individual goals that interact.
A MAS can also be viewed as a bottom-up designed system, since in principle the agents are designed first (agent-centered view), and the solution strategy (top) for a given problem is specified later.

In order to stress the aspect of cooperation in DPS, sometimes the term *Cooperative* Distributed Problem Solving is used. Durfee, Lesser and Corkhill [1989] define *Cooperative DPS* as the study of "how a loosely-coupled network of problem solvers can work together to solve problems that are beyond their individual capabilities. Each problem-solving node in the network is capable of sophisticated problem solving and can work independently, but the problems faced by the nodes cannot be completed without cooperation. Cooperation is necessary because no single node has sufficient expertise, resources, and information to solve a problem. Different nodes might have expertise for solving different parts of an overall problem."

Parallel AI. Another field, which is related to DAI, is *Parallel AI*, which is concerned with developing parallel computer architectures, languages, and algorithms for AI. These efforts are primarily directed toward solving the performance problems of AI systems, and not toward conceptual advances in understanding the nature of reasoning and intelligent behavior among multiple agents. Although Parallel AI is considered as a subdiscipline separate from DAI [Bond and Gasser 88], it is important to note that developments in concurrent languages and architectures may have profound impacts on DAI system architectures, reliability, knowledge representation, and so on.

"Centralized" AI. In most contemporary AI research and practice, the unit of analysis and of development is a computational process with a single locus of control, focus of attention, and knowledge base - a process inherited from von Neumann computer architectures and from psychology [Gasser 91]. The basic mechanisms of reasoning and problem solving generally are bound to a single, monolithic conception of knowledge and action. DAI is, however, interested in approaches to analyzing and developing intelligent "communities" which comprise collections of interacting, coordinated knowledge-based processes.

2.1.2 Historical Perspective

DAI is a term which was "born" in the United States. The first official DAI meeting, called *The Workshop on Distributed AI*, was held 1980 at the MIT in Boston. Since that time a small group of invited researchers met every year, except for one year, for the DAI Workshop in the United States. The *10th International AAAI DAI Workshop* was held in Bandera, Texas, in 1990 with 34 participants.

Reports on the DAI workshops can be found in [Davis 80, 82], [Fehling and Erman 83], [Smith 85], [Gasser 87], [Sridharan 87]. Several publications particularly containing DAI papers (monographs) have appeared until now. The first publication was a special issue on Distributed Problem Solving and DAI of *IEEE Transactions on Systems, Man, and Cybernetics* in January 1981 [SMC-11 81]. This volume contains also several papers from the first DAI Workshop. In 1987 and 1989, two monographs on DAI appeared, which were mainly based on papers of previous DAI workshops, edited by Huhns and Gasser, [Huhns 87], [Gasser and Huhns 89]. There also exists a *Readings in Distributed Artificial Intelligence*, edited by Bond and Gasser [1988]. Surveys of DAI and DPS research have been given by Rosenschein [1986], Decker [1987], and Durfee, Lesser and Corkhill [1989].

DAI is still a young and dynamic discipline with vivid discussions about its identity. A search for definitions has been characteristic of DAI and it seems worth to reproduce some of the earlier definitions, mainly from DAI Workshops, to provide an idea of where we are now:

- R. Davis in 1980: "Distributed Artificial Intelligence (DAI) is concerned with those problems for which a single problem solver, single machine, or single locus of computation seems inappropriate. ... In distributed problem solving there is a single task envisioned for the system. .. The systems are perfectly willing to accommodate one another. There is cooperative behavior between willing entities rather than frameworks for enforcing cooperation as a form of compromise between potentially incompatible entities." [Davis 80].

- This definition has undergone some changes and criticism in the last years. Rosenschein and Genesereth stipulate the possibility of having several tasks for the system. In the real world agents may have conflicting goals, [Genesereth and Rosenschein 83]. They argue that we should not take the willingness of the agents to cooperate ("benevolent assumption") for granted. They have researched the cooperation–spectrum form normal to antagonistic.

- McArthur, Cammarata and colleagues [Thorndyke et al. 81; McArthur et al. 82]: "DAI is concerned with problem-solving situations in which several agents cooperate to achieve a common set of objectives"

- V. Lesser, whom insiders call the "granddaddy of DAI", and D. Corkhill in 1983: "A cooperative problem-solving system is a distributed network of semi-autonomous nodes that are each capable of sophisticated problem solving and that cooperate with other nodes to solve a single problem."

- M. Fehling and L. Erman write in 1982 that for most work on DAI the following definition fits: "A DAI system is a network of individual intelligent systems designed to cooperate in some way." [Fehling and Erman 83].

- They continue with an alternate definition: "A DAI system is composed of a large number of elements each of which is capable of a very limited amount of problem solving, and the intelligence of the overall system (its global coherence) is a result of the pattern of interaction among these "dumb" elements." Connectionist models pursue this latter perspective.

- R.G. Smith argues in 1984 that "DAI is concerned with cooperative solution of problems by a decentralized and loosely coupled collection of knowledge sources, each embodied in a distinct processor node." [Smith 85].

- M. Ginsberg in 1985: "DAI is the study of how a group of individual intelligent agents can combine to solve a difficult global problem." [Ginsberg 87].

- L. Gasser in 1985: "Distributed AI is the branch of AI concerned with the problem of co-ordinating the actions of multiple agents for problem solving and intelligence. " [Gasser 87].
- V. Jagannathan and R. Dodhiawala in 1985: "DAI refers to the subarea of AI which is concerned with the problem of utilizing multiple processors in the solution of AI problems." [Jagannathan and Dodhiawala 87].
- A. Bond and L. Gasser in 1988: "DAI is the subfield of AI concerned with concurrency in AI computations, at many levels." [Bond and Gasser 88].

European Initiatives. Since 1989 there exists also a European DAI convention, called *European Workshop on Modelling Autonomous Agents and Multiagent Worlds (MAAMAW)*, the first of which took place at King's College in Cambridge, UK. The two following workshops took place in Paris and Kaiserslautern. The proceedings of the first two European workshops were edited as books *"Decentralized A.I."* by Y. Demazeau and J.P. Müller [1990 and 1991].

2.1.3 Motivating Distributed AI

Why DAI? Huhns [1987] and Durfee, Lesser and Corkhill [1989] have identified six primary reasons why one would want to study and utilize DAI:

1. *Technological Basis*. Advances in hardware technology for processor construction and inter-processor communication make it possible to connect together large numbers of sophisticated processing units that execute asynchronously. A range of connection structures is possible, from a very tight coupling of processors through shared or distributed memory, to a looser coupling of processors through a local communication network or to a very loose coupling of geographically distributed processors through a communication network. Because of limited communication bandwidth or limited processing power, the processors cannot share all their information, but must be able to work together anyway.

2. *Inherent Distribution*. Many AI applications are inherently distributed. The applications may be spatially distributed, such as interpreting and integrating data from spatially distributed sensors or controlling a set of robots that work together on a factory floor. The applications might be functionally distributed, such as bringing together a number of specialized medical-diagnosis systems on a particularly difficult case or developing a sophisticated architectural expert system

composed of individual experts in specialities such as structural engineering, electrical wiring, and room layout. The applications might be temporally distributed (pipelined), as in a factory, where production lines consist of several work areas, each having an expert system responsible for scheduling orders. A DAI system that manages the distribution of data, expertise, processing power, and other resources has significant advantages over a single, monolithic centralized problem solver. These advantages include: faster problem solving by exploiting parallelism; decreased communication by transmitting only high-level partial solutions to nearby nodes rather than raw data to a central site; more flexibility by having problem solvers with different abilities dynamically team up to solve current problems; and increased reliability by allowing problem solvers to take on the responsibilities of problem solvers that fail.

3. *Design and Implementation Benefits (Modularity).* A DAI system supports the principles of modular design and implementation. The ability to structure a complex problem into relatively self-contained processing modules leads to systems that are easier to build, debug, and maintain and that are more resilient to software and hardware errors than a single, monolithic module. For example, the general field of medical diagnosis is complicated and extensive. To manage the field, medical experts divide it (and themselves) into many specialities. If we wanted to build a general medical diagnosis system, we could exploit the modularity of the field, building knowledge-based systems for each speciality in parallel and with a minimum of interaction between systems. Because they are more focussed, debugging and maintaining these small systems would be much simpler than if we had built a single, colossal system.

4. *Epistemological Reasons* (Cognitive models of cooperation). Cooperation, and more generally coordination, are complex and little understood phenomena. One approach to validating theories about such phenomena is to develop and test computer models that embody those theories. Just as AI systems are used to validate theories of problem solving and intelligence in linguistics, psychology and philosophy, DAI systems can help validate theories in sociology, management, and organizational theory [Fox 81]. DAI can provide insights and understanding about interactions among humans, who organize themselves into various groups, committees, and societies in oder to solve problems. Moreover, the technology developed in these studies could lead to more effective use of computers as tools to improve coordination among people. Developing mechanisms that parallel human methods for coordinating their interactions can improve our understanding of humans, and in particular about how humans iteratively converge on decisions about how to share resources and avoid harmful interactions for their mutual benefit.

Les Gasser views DAI as useful "because it helps us to explore the fundamental aspects of self-hood and intelligent behavior which are the outcome of interaction with others - it is "social intelligence" in the sense that it does not exist apart from social interaction. .. What do agents have to know and how do they have to reason in order to interact in organized ways? We develop a specific computer-implementable model of negotiations." [Gasser 87].

5. *Societal Foundation* (Man Machine Interaction with man as human agent and machine as automated agent). One of the goals of AI is to develop systems that become part of our everyday world. These systems would perform many of the mundane and boring tasks that require human intelligence, thereby freeing up human intelligence so that it can be reserved for more exciting meditations. To be accepted, these AI systems must interact with people on even terms — if people must become AI literate to use these systems, the systems will not be accepted into human society. For AI systems to integrate into the society of intelligent agents, they must have the ability to flexibly and intelligently cooperate and coordinate with each other and with people. DAI represents first steps towards this long-term goal.

6. *Synergy* (New Classes of Problems). There are problems, which are too large for a centralized system. These problems can only be solved by the *cooperation* of several independent systems (*synergy* effect, *emergent functionality*). For instance, multiple expert systems with different, but possibly overlapping expertise, could cooperate to deal with problems that are outside the scope of a single system.

2.1.4 Dimensions of Distributed AI

Basic Questions and Problems of Distributed AI
Bond and Gasser have characterized six basic problems that current DAI system had begun to tackle and which appear in some form in all DAI application domains [Bond and Gasser 88], [Gasser 91]:
1. How to formulate, describe, decompose, and allocate problems and synthesize results among a group of intelligent agents.
2. How to enable agents to communicate and interact: what communication languages or protocols to use, and what and when to communicate.
3. How to ensure that agents act coherently in making decisions or taking action, accommodating the nonlocal effects of local decisions and avoiding harmful interactions.

4. How to enable individual agents to represent and reason about the actions, plans, and knowledge of other agents in order to coordinate with them; how to reason about the state of their coordinated process.

5. How to recognize and reconcile disparate viewpoints and conflicting intentions among a collection of agents trying to coordinate their actions.

6. How to engineer and construct practical DAI systems; how to design technology platforms and development methodologies for DAI.

Classifying Work in DAI

How can research in DAI be classified? What assumptions underlie the work? In [Sridharan 87] eight dimensions to categorize where a particular work, result, or claim fits were listed (Table 1). Each of the dimensions forms a spectrum in itself and is not binary (yes-no) in character.

DIMENSION	SPECTRUM OF VALUES
System Model........	Individual........................Committee......................Society
Grain.....................	Fine...Medium....................Coarse
System Scale.........	Small..Medium.......................Large
Agent Dynamism...	Fixed.......Programmable.......Teachable..........Autodidactic
Agent Autonomy....	Controlled.....................Interdependent.........Independent
Agent Resources....	Restricted...Ample
Agent Interactions.	Simple...Complex
Result Formation..	By Synthesis..By Decomposition

Table 1: Dimensions for Categorizing DAI Systems [Huhns 87]

The dimensions in more detail:

1. *System Model.* Shall the system be viewed as a synthesis of a single intelligent agent from distributed components or as an organization of multiple intelligent agents (committees, societies)?

   Sometimes, we are aiming at a large collection of intelligent agents to solve problems together, leading to a "society" model of computation. At the other extreme, we employ relatively simple computational elements to produce some intelligent behavior. At the medium part of this spectrum, we can discuss a group of expert systems, each with some limited intelligence in its respective domain, attempting to solve a problem with cooperation and possibly some conflicts, thus forming a "committee".

2. *Granularity*. To what extend can the problem (data, task, communication packets, and so on) be decomposed?

3. *System Scale*. How many computing elements are employed, from a serial processor or a few (2-16) processors up to a million elements on a connection machine?

   Because distribution might or might not imply actual parallel processing using computing elements, a quite separate dimension is *scale*, which accounts for the number of computing elements employed.

   Economic necessities probably do not permit *coarse* grain coupled with large scale. *Fine* grain coupled with small scale probably is too weak a combination to be of interest. Really, the two dimensions can vary independently.

4. *Adaptiveness*. Are the elements of the system (part of the organization, structure, interaction patterns) fixed or adaptable? Has the system learning capabilities?

   Some systems are build from *programmed* elements, whereas others lend themselves only to *learning* systems. In between lie systems where part of the organization, structure or interaction patterns are fixed and programmed, but the system has aspects that are *adaptable*. Large scale and learning are heavily correlated, and small scale and programming seem correlated. DAI strives finally for a goal first stated by Corkhill, Lesser and their colleagues: adaptive organization self-design by a collection of problem solvers or intelligent agents.

5. *Control Distribution*. How is the control in the system distributed? To which extent are the elements autonomous?

   Another variable is the degree to which element seems *autonomous* or each element seems fully *controlled* and devoid of volition. The reader might detect a possible correlation between autonomy, coarse grain, and a society model and between fully controlled, fine grain, and an individual model. However, these correlations seem accidental and extraneous. No compelling logical necessity exists for these correlations. It is conceivable to have central control in a large-scale, fine-grained systems.

   [Decker 87]: "Totally free groups (called teams or committees) to master-slave relations. Teams exhibit no control hierarchies and are naturally data driven. ... Some nodes in the hierarchy are given control over to the construction of intermediate solutions or providing global direction to nodes below them in the hierarchy. At this point control is passed not by orders but through negotiation. ... Low-level agents are data driven, high level nodes are goal driven, and any intermediate nodes may be pulled between these two directions."

6. *Resource Availability*. What resources (as communication bandwidth, computation, memory, devices, but also knowledge or expertise) are to which extent for whom available? Resource availability in the system and limits of their utilization form one of the most crucial concerns for the designer. Whether the resources are *ample* or whether they are tightly *limited* affects the design and its effectiveness and can tilt the balance in favor of one design or another.

7. *Interaction Type/Communication*. What type of interaction between the elements of the system are allowed? The range goes from very *simple*, as well as uniform types of interaction to complex interactions.
   Neural nets and connectionist models tend to emphasize simple, as well as uniform, types of interactions. Autonomous agents collected in a contract net have relatively complex interactions.

8. *Problem-solving Strategy* (top down versus bottom up). Does the system work by *decomposing* the problem into components (top down) or by *synthesizing* existing elements? Methodologically, they impose different constraints on the system designer, and thus, the designer can face substantially different sets of design issues.

Not all dimensions are relevant to all systems, and not all systems within this eight-dimensional space may be considered as DAI systems (e.g. a neural network). In particular, some research aims at a general-purpose architecture and language for DAI that would be characterized by a range of possible attribute values for some of the dimensions.

This list may be extended by further dimensions, for instance the degree of *cooperativeness*, ranging from highly cooperative (unselfish) until hostile (total antagonism) [Werner 90; Werner and Reinefeld 90] and the *communication methodology* employed [Decker 87]. A more refined approach to classify research in DAI/Cooperative DPS has been put forward by Decker, Durfee and Lesser [1988].

Table 2 shows (by adding markers) how we would characterize our research along these dimensions.

DIMENSION	SPECTRUM OF VALUES
System Model.......	Individual.....................Committee.....................Society
Grain....................	Fine..............................Medium...............Coarse
System Scale.........	Small..................................Medium......................Large
Agent Dynamism...	Fixed......Programmable.....Teachable..........Autodidactic
Agent Autonomy....	Controlled....................Interdependent.........Independent
Agent Resources....	Restricted..Ample
Agent Interactions.	Simple...Complex
Result Formation..	By Synthesis....................................By Decomposition

Table 2: Classifying our research

2.1.5 Application Domains for DAI Systems

Potential application domains for the coordination framework put forward in this work are populated by intelligent, autonomous agents. The agents can be both human or automated agents. There should be an inherent distribution of agents, activities and resources. Some sort of cooperative problem solving should be required.

Application areas in general, (see also [Durfee et al. 89a]):

- *Distributed Interpretation*. Distributed interpretation applications require the integration and analysis of distributed data to generate a (potentially distributed) semantic model of the data. The most prominent domain is the distributed sensor network, called DVMT [Lesser and Corkhill 83].

- *Distributed Planning and Control*. Distributed planning and control applications involve developing and coordinating the actions of a number of distributed effector agents to perform some desired task. Example application domains include distributed air-traffic control [Thorndyke et al. 81], cooperating robots, remotely piloted vehicles [Steeb et al. 81], distributed process control in manufacturing [Paranuk 85; Hynynen 88], and resource allocation control in a long-haul communication networks [Adler et al. 89]. Usually, data is inherently distributed among agents, in this case because each has its own local planning database, capabilities and view of the world state.

– *Cooperating Expert Systems*. One means of scaling expert systems technology to more complex and encompassing problem domains is to develop cooperative interaction mechanisms that allow multiple experts systems to work together to solve a common problem. Illustrative situations include controlling an autonomous vehicle (with expert systems for system status, mission planning, navigation, situation assessment, and piloting) or negotiation among expert systems of two corporations to decide price and/or delivery time on a major purchase.

– *Computer-Supported Cooperative Work (CSCW)*. Coined by Irene Greif in 1984, the phrase "computer-supported cooperative work" was intended to delineate a new field of research focused on the role of the computer in group work [Greif 88]. Computer technology promises to provide people with more and better information for making decisions. However, unless the computers also assist people by filtering the information and focussing attention on relevant information, the amount of information can become overwhelming [Chang 87; Huhns et al. 85; Malone 88; Malone et al. 88]. By building AI systems that have coordination knowledge we can remove some of the burden from people. Example domains where this is important include intelligent command and control systems and multiuser project coordination [Croft and Lefkowitz 87, 88; Nirenburg and Lesser 86; Sathi et al. 88] and distributed project planning [Sathi 87; Sathi and Fox 89].

The following list adds some specific applications for DAI approaches:
– distributed air traffic control [Findler and Lo 88; Thorndyke et al. 81],
– continuous speech understanding by Hearsay-II [Erman et al. 80],
– well-log zoning and load balancing in distributed computing systems using contract nets [Davis and Smith 83],
– flexible manufacturing system, managing and control of factory environment [Sathi and Fox 89],
– highly interactive man-machine dialogues (Allen, DAI-Workshop 81),
– managing organizations, intelligent management system [Fox 80; Fikes and Henderson 82; Malone 87],
– planning of linguistic actions [Lochbaum et al. 90],
– organization and retrieval of documents by a distributed system of intelligent servers in the MINDS project [Huhns et al. 85],
– distributed vision (M. Hanvey, DAI workshop 1982),
– monitoring and control of large communication systems [Conry et al. 86],

- organizational modelling with Ubik [deJong 90],
- material handling (transportation and storage) by a distributed architecture [Paranuk 85],
- project management [Sathi 87],
- distributed production management (manufacturing) [Hynynen 88],
- person-machine-interaction [Goodson and Schmidt 87].

2.2 Activity Coordination via Multiagent and Distributed Planning

S. Vere writes on multiagent planning: "Another immensely difficult topic is the generation of plans for multiple sentient agents that may have to communicate and negotiate to achieve and preserve mutual and conflicting goals" in [Shapiro and Eckroth 88].

In a multiagent planning approach to cooperation, agents form a multiagent plan that specifies their future actions and interactions [Durfee, Lesser and Corkhill 89]. Coordinating agents by multiagent plans is different from other approaches in that one or more agents possess a plan that indicates exactly what actions and interactions each agent will take. This differs from approaches such as contracting, in which nodes typically make pairwise agreements about how they will coordinate and where there is no complete view of network coordination presented.

Problems addressed. In a multiagent planning approach to cooperation, agents form a multiagent plan that specifies their future actions and interactions. What basic DAI problems (see also Section 2.1) are addressed by multiagent planning?
- *Task allocation*. Multiagent planning is one way of allocating particular tasks to particular agents. Other approaches to allocate tasks embrace market mechanisms [Malone 87, 88; Fox 81], organizational roles and voting.
- *Achieving coordination*. Multiagent planning is a medium to achieve better coordination by aligning behavior of agents towards common goals, with explicit division of labor. Techniques such as centralized planning for multiple agents, plan reconciliation, distributed planning, organizational analysis, and appropriate control transfers are ways of helping to align the activities of agents by assigning tasks.

2.2.1 A Planning Taxonomy

A *multiagent plan* is a plan which has been generated for multiple executing agents [Bond and Gasser 88]. *Multiagent planning* is the process of creating a multiagent plan. An important aspect of multiagent planning is whether planning is done by a single agent or by several agents. In *centralized multiagent planning* there is one agent which generates plans for multiple agents. In *decentralized (distributed) multiagent planning* also the planning activities are divided among the agents. In future, we will refer to the latter form of planning as *distributed planning*. In Sections 2.2.5 and 2.2.6 we will describe some related work in multiagent planning.

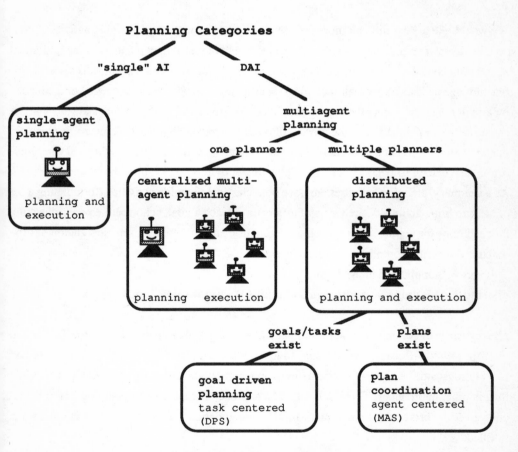

Figure 3: Planning categories

Figure 3 shows an overview of the different kinds of planning. It also covers *single-agent planning* which is only applicable in domains with a single agent, which plans and executes his own actions in a usually static domain, i.e. is based on the "closed world assumption".

We will distinguish between two classes of subproblems of distributed planning: *task-driven planning* and *plan coordination*. In a task-driven planning planning system, there is first a goal or task given, which is then decomposed into subgoals and distributed among several planners (top-down problem solving). These planners have to generate plans to solve their subproblems. In contrast, *plan coordination* is concerned with situations, in which the plans of agents are pre-existing (*agent-centered* view) and the problem is to reconcile the given plans before they are executed in a common environment. In Section 2.2.3 we will give a more detailed differentiation between the problem of planning and the problem of plan coordination.

We would like to be a little bit more precise about what we mean by "planning activities" concerning *distributed* planning. We do not want to speak of distributed planning if the individual agents only contribute goals which then will be planned for by a single agent. It is also not sufficient if agents just deliver their individual plans which then will be synchronized or reconciled by a central agency having the role of an arbiter. Distributed planning includes always that the agents are actively involved in the process of reaching a reconciliation. That means that also negotiation is an inherent component of distributed planning, and hence negotiation and communication also belong to what we mean by "planning activities" concerning distributed planning. As a summary, planning activities embrace both classical planning activities (formulating a set of steps to bring about a desired state of affairs or to reach a goal, action refinements, checking preconditions for actions, etc.) as well as negotiation and communication. Negotiation has the function of binding commitments among agents.

This may be summarized in the slogan:

distributed planning = multiagent planning + communication.

The relevance of communication for multiagent planning is also stressed by Durfee, Lesser and Corkhill [1989]: "Because agents engaged in a multiagent planning process need to share and process substantial amounts of information, more computation and communication is required than in other approaches. This implies that an approach for multiagent planning has to be accompanied by protocols for communication and negotiation." This requirement is not always fulfilled.

In multiagent planning, one or more agents have information about each agent's activities and can discover and prevent the duplication of effort. Another objective is to detect and avoid inconsistencies before they can occur. Interactions between the separate activities of the agents must be identified, and any conflicts should be identified and fixed before the plans are executed. A multiagent plan determines exactly what actions each agent should take and when.

In distributed planning, a single plan is produced by the cooperation of several agents. Each agent produces a subplan, but there may be conflicts among subplans that need to be reconciled.

Mutual plan construction is not well understood. It is confounded by disparities in goals and intentions, as well as disparities in world knowledge. All the problems of multiagent planning exist along with the problem of inconsistent world views due to distribution.

For the activities of several agents to be aligned using planning, interactions in the plans of different agents must be controlled. Plan interactions may involve incompatible states, incompatible order of steps, or overuse of resources. A multiagent plan is built to avoid inconsistent or conflicting actions, and is typically used in agent networks to identify and plan around resource conflicts. Rather than risking incoherent and inconsistent decisions that agents might make using other approaches, multiagent planning insists that agents plan out beforehand exactly how each will act and interact. Multiagent planning is one way of controlling these interactions.

2.2.2 Single-agent and Multiagent Planning

Monolithic, Single-agent Planners. The applicability of single-agent planners is severely restricted because most real worlds involve dynamic processes beyond the control of a single agent.

Traditional single agent planners STRIPS [Fikes and Nilsson 71], NOAH [Sacerdoti 77], NONLIN [Tate 77], SIPE [Wilkins 84] are not applicable in a multiagent settings due to several reasons:

– the world is assumed to be static and only affected by a single agent's actions,
– plans are constructed by one agent;
– tasks are usually carried out by one single agent;
– plans are concerned with prevention of conflicts, not with cooperation;
– single-agent planners cannot reason about actions that the agent can not control;
– there is no concept for concurrent activities;

- there is no cooperation and coordination between several agents;
- communication does not occur.

Another problem which appears primarily in connection with, but is is not restricted to, single-agent planners is that plans are typically designed prior to, and distinct from, their execution. These plans have been constructed for a set of future conditions that are known in advance and are frozen. The implicit assumption is that the conditions for which a plan is being formed, usually called start state, will not change prior to execution. Even when it is assumed that the plans will be executed in single-agent environments, in which the only state changes are a result of the single agent's actions, it may be wrong to expect that the world stays fixed during an indefinitely long planning period. Even if the environment contains no other human or robot agents, nature often intrudes. As a consequence, these planners are only inadequately capable to respond to a changing environment, e.g. by replanning or plan adaption or interleaving planning and execution.

Both in single and in multiagent planning problems, the constraints arising from resource availability are an important factor to determine adequate solutions. This was recognized in the design of SIPE [Wilkins 84]. However, the mechanisms for reasoning about resources and the resolution of resource conflicts differ whether there is a central planner or not.

Applying single-agent evaluation criteria to multiagent planning? The most important issues for evaluating single-agent planners are soundness, completeness, optimality, efficiency and search control [Kartram and Wilkins 89]. A planner is said to be *sound* if all the plans that it produces are correct. A plan produced by a planner is correct if the execution of the plan, starting from the initial state of the world, transforms the world to a goal state. A planner is said to be *complete* if it will produce a correct plan whenever a feasible plan exists. *Optimality* is concerned with some measure of the quality of a produced plan. Most AI researchers refer to a plan that is not redundant as an optimal plan, because no action stated in the plan needs to be undone, i.e. there is no unnecessary action in the plan. Performance (*efficiency*) measures for AI planners include the number of predicate instances to characterize a domain, the number of operators and, last but not least, the time it takes for a planner to formulate a plan. To be complete, a planner must *control search,* although the search space can vary depending on the design of the planner. Search control is one of the least-understood aspects of domain-independent planning, and there has been little progress made in intelligent search control.

Not all of these criteria can be successfully applied to single-agent planners. However, for approaches developed for multiagent planning it is even more difficult, if not impossible, to evaluate them as proposed here for single-agent planners. There are several reasons for that. In order to prove *soundness* and *completeness* a formal logic-based theory for multiagent planning is required. However, such a theory does not exist yet and is probably hard to achieve in an environment where different individuals interact asynchronously. *Optimality* is a criteria which is hard to apply in open and dynamic domains, where the behavior of agents is not under the control of a single instance (Compare also the discussion on "Coordination as improvement instead of optimization" in Section 1.2.2). If *search control* is barely understood for single-agent domains, this goes even more for multiagent domains. The only measure, which can easily applied to multiagent planning is *efficiency*. This has been shown extensively by the evaluation of partial global planning [Durfee 88].

We think when it comes to evaluating multiagent planners there may be other issues more relevant for evaluation (see also [Decker et al. 88]), for example coherence, consistency, responsiveness, and fault tolerance.

Although relations within a single agent plan have been explored in great detail in traditional planning systems (before 1980), they are not applicable in a multi agent setting due to several reasons: first, the world is assumed to be static and only affected by a single agent's actions, tasks are only carried out by a single agent; second, there is no concept for concurrent activities; third, there is no cooperation and coordination between several agents.

2.2.3 Plan Coordination Versus Planning Versus Plan Recognition

The focus of our research is the coordination of distributed planners. How is the problem of plan coordination related to other planning research in AI, namely planning and plan recognition?

AI Planning. Research in AI on (automatic) *planning* is generally concerned with ways of solving problems in the following form:
Given
(i)   a set of goals
(ii)   a set of allowable actions, and

(iii)   a planning environment: a description of the world in which the plan is to be executed,
         an initial state of affairs.

Find a sequence of actions that will bring about a state of affairs in which all of the desired
goals are satisfied.

Problems of this form were the first to be explored in automatic planning. We will therefore refer to them as *classical planning problems*. Classical AI planning can be described in a simplified form as: **planning: 2^{goals} ——>$2^{actions}$**, i.e. for a given goal a plan (= a set of actions) has
to be generated.

Plan Recognition. Closely related to the creation of plans is the recognition of plans [Kautz
and Pednault 88]. A *plan recognition* problem consists of the following factors:

(i)   a set of allowable actions,

(ii)   a set of observed actions, and

(iii)   a plan recognition environment: descriptions of the world in which the observed actions
        were performed.

A solution of the plan recognition problem may include elements of the following:

(i)   a set of expected goals,

(ii)   a library of typical plans,

(iii)   a preference ordering over the space of plans.

The general goal of a plan recognition problem is to find an explanation for the observed actions
in terms of one or more plans that can be attributed to the actor. The plan recognition in a simplified form is expressed as **plan recognition: $2^{actions}$ ——> 2^{goals}**. In general only certain
plans are acceptable explanations. Such a plan relates a typical pattern of actions to a goal that
one may reasonably expect to arise in the current context. The process of inferring a plausible
plan involves the use of heuristic assumptions and libraries of common plans.

Multiagent plan recognition. Plan recognition can also become a *DAI* problem, if either
several recognizers or several actors to be observed are involved. Consequently, we can differentiate between two types of multiagent plan recognition:

1. *Recognition of multiple agents' activities*: The problem is the recognition (interpretation) of
   plans in domains with multiple agents. Retz-Schmidt has developed a centralized process
   for the recognition of plans, intentions, interactions between multiple agents [Retz-Schmidt
   91a, 91b]. Information is extracted from image sequences. She has done experiments to
   observe the behavior and recognize the intentions of agents in a soccer game. An important

feature of her system REPLAY-II is the natural language verbalization of the recognized intentional entities.

2. *Recognition by multiple agents* (distributed plan recognition): The recognition process can be shared among several agents. Hecking has developed a logic of belief for plan recognizers [Hecking 88, 90]. Based on this model he can describe different plan recognizers having different deductions about plans and goals of one or more agents. His model has been applied to an intelligent help system for users having troubles with a UNIX-like operating system.

Plan Coordination. Our concern is the problem of coordinating plans. The input for a plan coordination problem consists of several (partial) plans which have to be coordinated. In a plan coordination problem with distributed autonomous agents the actions belong to several planners and/or executors. Outcome of the coordination may be a synchronized set of actions. A simplified view of the coordination problem: **plan coordination: $2^{2^{actions}} \longrightarrow 2^{2^{actions}}$**.

The *plan coordination* problem is concerned with ways of solving problems with an *input* as follows:
(i)   a set of intended actions (=plans of autonomous agents).
(ii)   a description of the (state of the) world in which the plans are to be executed (the coordination environment.)
(iii)   operations to modify actions.

Output is a set of intended actions (= plans of autonomous agents) which is coordinated. We will develop a definition when a set of actions is coordinated in Chapter 4.
Coordination is similar to *replanning*, because both mean to adapt plans due to circumstances (here: the actions and plans of other agents), which were not known and could not be taken into account during the initial planning process.

In order to coordinate, agents one must be able to perform the following principle operations:
(i)   communicate, i.e. send and receive messages,
(ii)   reason about plan interferences,
(iii)   develop solutions for coordination,
(iv)   modify plans.

2.3 Selected Related Work

Before giving a review of related work, we will outline some of its features.

Agents. What is an agent? We prefer models with sophisticated intelligent, preferably autonomous, agents and no models where by the cooperation of relatively simple computational agents intelligent behavior is produced.

Control distribution. The question of how control is distributed is tightly connected with how autonomous the agents are. The tendency in the work surveyed is to have independent and not centrally controlled agents.

Representation of actions and plans. The representation of actions and plans is an essential part of a domain characterization. We will mention for each work the concept for actions and plans, as far as they are described in the referred publications.
We can differentiate between two general kinds of action representation leading to two different planning paradigms, the *state-based* and the *event-based* planning paradigm. The state-based paradigm has its origin in McCarthy's situation calculus [McCarthy and Hayes 69] and is exemplified in planning systems such as STRIPS [Fikes and Nilsson 71] and NOAH [Sacerdoti 77]. DAI research supporting a state-based planning paradigm can be found in [Georgeff 83, 84; Pednault 87; Zlotkin and Rosenschein 89a, 90a, 90b]. Within an event-based model, the state of the world at any point in time is merely a record of the events that have occurred and their interrelations. Several researchers have emphasized an *event-based* domain description for multiagent planning [Hewitt 77; Lansky 87, 88; Pelavin 88].

Time. Temporal information is crucial in multiagent domains and therefore should be taken care of in action and plan representations. In state-based planing models temporal aspects appear in the form of temporal precedence. In an approach which employs a PERT type representation of actions, e.g. [Dean 86a, 86b; Koo 88], absolute temporal values are given (for instance start and end time). Others use relative temporal expressions, e.g. by employing Allen's interval-based representation [Allen 83, 84], to model time [Lansky 87, 88; Pelavin 88].

Resources. A notion of resources should be incorporated in every multiagent planning system. Often, resource requirements are an inherent part of tasks or plans. For many DAI researchers, resources mean the only concept for reasoning about how different activities interact. Not every approach has a concept for resources. But some explicitly handle resources and the resolution of conflicts between actions or agents competing for the same limited and sharable resources [Conry et al. 86; Dean 86; Kuwabara and Lesser 89; Steeb et al. 81].

Point of synchronization. When are plans synchronized? Plan synchronization can be performed at several points. It can be done during problem decomposition [Corkhill 79]. It can be done by aligning partial plans incrementally [Durfee and Lesser 87], or by reasoning about interactions and dependencies as a part of planning [Rosenschein 82]. It can also be done after plan construction [Georgeff 83].

2.3.1 Centralized Multiagent Planning

In this section we will describe some related work in the field of centralized multiagent planning.

Cammarata, McArthur and Steeb

Cammarata, McArthur and Steeb (1983) have developed a system for centralized multiagent planing. The task of the planner is to detect potential conflicts and solve them. Their domain is *air traffic control*, where one **agent** is associated with each aircraft [Steeb et al. 81]. The main goal for an agent is to construct a flight **plan** (single agent plan) to reach an assigned destination and satisfy the constraint that an appropriate separation from other airplanes is maintained. Goal interactions come in the form of shared conflicts. A *conflict* between two or more agents arises when, according to their current plans, the agents will violate minimum separation requirements at some point in the future. When shared conflicts arise agents must negotiate to resolve them. Through a process of negotiation, the agents choose a coordinator. A great deal of their work has been devoted to discuss a variety of architectures and strategies how to select this coordinator. Each agent sends this coordinator relevant information, and the coordinator uses this information to build a multiagent plan. A **multiagent plan** specifies all the agents' planned actions, including the actions that it, or some other agents, should take to avoid collisions.

The only form of relation concerned are conflicts. Details of plan representation, conflict resolution and negotiation are not given.

Dean

Dean has worked on a specific aspect of multiagent planning, temporal reasoning about events in multiagent domains with respect to potential resource conflicts [Dean 86a]. He extends classical predicate-calculus data base systems to deal with time. **Actions** (tasks/goals) are represented as a time token whose corresponding interval determines the period of time during which the process is performed. An action (task) has associated with it a number of constraints: constraints that specify the current estimate of the duration of the task, and constraints on when the task begins and ends (deadlines). A **plan** is simply a partially ordered set of tasks. A PROLOG like predicate calculus data base system is used for reasoning. A complete, or fully specified, plan is one in which all unreduced steps are primitive. The system reasons about the duration of events and the spans of time over which resources are available.

The planning process is performed by two components: First, a problem-solving component is responsible for making choices concerning which plan to use for carrying out a task and what to do when those choices turn out to be ill advised, and second, a temporal reasoner maintains an accurate picture of the world changing over time. This component is responsible for recording why certain planning choices were made and under what conditions certain actions will achieve or fail to achieve their intended effects. It is able to detect when the reasons for choosing a plan are undermined as a result of unforeseen circumstances. If an interaction is detected, then the reasoner notifies the problem-solver and provides information concerning what parties are involved and what alternatives are available. In [Dean 86b] the tool for keeping track of the intended activities of a group of independent agents (multiagent plans) is applied to the coordination of human (employee) activities. It is no planning system. It does reasoning about resource conflicts focusing on time dependent aspects. Dean uses an extended PERT-chart representation capable of handling partial orders and fuzzy metric information.

Georgeff

Georgeff has pursued a centralized multiagent planning approach where the plans of individual agents are first created, and then transferred to a central planner, which then analyses them to identify potential conflicts between agents competing for limited resources [Georgeff 83].
Georgeff has developed several formalisms for reasoning about concurrency in multiagent domains. He has developed a formal model to combine separate plans of independent agents. The primary concern is to avoid destructive interference caused by simultaneous access to a shared resource.

Synchronization between single-agent plans is identified as the main problem. Multiagent plans are synthesized from simpler single-agent plans and coordination is achieved by applying standard operating systems methods (CSP primitives of Hoare, e.g. insertion of r/w primitives) in plans such that conflicting regions will not both be entered at the same time.

An **action** is a sequence $s_1, s_2,.., s_n$ of sets of states, intuitively those states over which the action takes place. The *domain* of an action is the initial set of states s_1, and the *range* of the action is the final set of states sn. The *moments* of an action are the intermediate set of states $s_2,.., s_{n1}$.
A **planning problem** is a four tuple $P = (S, I, A, G)$, where S is a set of states, I is the designated set of initial states $I \subseteq S$, A a set of primitive actions, G a set of goal states $G \subseteq S$. A **single-agent plan** P is a description of a sequence of actions $a_1, a_2,.., a_n$ from A such that (i) a_1 is applicable to all initial states I (i.e. the domain of a_1 contains I), (ii) for all i, $1 < i < n$ the action a_i is applicable to all states in the range of a_{i-1}, and (iii) a_n achieves the goal G (i.e., the range of is contained in G). A **multiagent plan** for a problem P is a collection of plans for subproblems of P which are synchronized to be applicable to all initial states I and to achieve the goal G.

A multiagent plan is created by combining two plans into a multiagent plan such that conflicts are avoided and as many as possible actions are allowed to proceed in parallel. Plan reconciliation is achieved in three stages by a single global agent. First, two kinds of analysis are performed: an interaction analysis, which means to establish which situations occurring in the single-agent plans are compatible with one another, and, a safety analysis, which is to determine which of the feasible situations could lead to a deadlock. The idea of this analysis is to identify critical regions in the single-agent plans. Finally, unsafe state sequences are coalesced into critical regions, and conventional synchronization mechanisms based on communication acts are applied. The communication acts concern properties of actions, resources, and physical constraints at the time of execution of the plan [Georgeff 83]. Once these critical regions have been determined, standard operating-system methods can be used to enforce synchronization of the actions in the plans so that conflicting critical regions will not both be entered at the same time.

In later papers, Georgeff has pursued this centralized multiagent planning approach further (the composition of single-agent plans to a multiagent plan), using alternative representations for events in multiagent domains [Georgeff 84, 86, 87]. In [Georgeff 86] a representation is developed that can succinctly describe the set of actions that may negate some property. This formalism is a modification and extension of situation calculus to allow for simultaneous events and actions. An event in this theory is modeled by a transition function. This function is a mapping from a situation to a set of situations, instead of a mapping from situation to situation as in the situation calculus.

Georgeff considers only harmful interactions. The problem is to identify critical regions in the plans which is solved by standard operating systems constructs.

Konolige and Nilsson

One of the first AI papers that deals with planning in multiagent domains was presented by Konolige and Nilsson [1980]. Until that time research on systems for generating and executing plans of actions assumed a single planning agent operating in a world that was static except for the effects of the actions of the planning agent itself (see discussion above). The focus of this paper is on modeling multiagent plans. **Actions** (operators) are modelled as standard STRIPS operators [Fikes and Nilsson 71]. **Plans** are represented by goal/subgoal trees composed of planning operators and their preconditions. Agents take into account the possible actions of other agents by assuming that other agents generate and execute plans to achieve their goals.

The idea of a **multiagent plan** is simple and is based on the assumption that each agent has a STRIPS like planning system. The action of another agent generating and executing a plan is modelled by a "spontaneous operator", which is like an ordinary planning operator except that whenever its preconditions are satisfied, the action corresponding to it is presumed automatically executed. Thus, by planning to achieve the preconditions of a spontaneous operator, a planning agent can incorporate such an operator into its plan.

Lansky

Lansky has developed a model of concurrent activities and has built a multiagent planner based on this model [Lansky 87, 88]. Within her framework first-order logic constraints, temporal ordering, and simultaneity can be expressed. First-order-temporal-logic formulas are used to describe domain constraints.

The possible plans that satisfy the domain description are called **world plans**. A world plan is described formally as a structure $W = \langle E, EL, G, =>, \rightarrow, \leftrightarrow, \in \rangle$ consisting of a set of *events* E, *elements* EL, and *groups* G, plus their interrelations, as there are the *temporal ordering* $=>$:(ExE), the *causal relation* $\rightarrow$:(ExE), the *simultaneity relation* $\leftrightarrow$:(ExE), and a transitive *subset relation* between events and the regions in which they are contained, as well as between elements and groups and the surrounding regions in which they are contained $\in$:(Ex(EL$\cup$G)) $\cup$ ((EL$\cup$G)xG). The task of her multiagent planner is to construct a world plan, all of whose executions satisfy a given set of domain constraints and achieve some stated set of goals. The **planning problem** is given by a structural description of the domain, the constraints associated with each element and group, a set of initial conditions (which might be expressed as a set of initial events that have taken place or as a set of atomic state formulas assumed to be initially true), and the set of goal constraints to be achieved. Given the initial world plan characterized by user input data, the planner repeatedly chooses a constraint (either a domain or goal constraint), checks to see whether it is satisfied and, if it is not, either backtracks to an earlier decision point in the planning process or continues on, modifying the world plan so that the constraint is satisfied.

Morgenstern

Morgenstern has investigated under which circumstances is it possible to execute an already existing, multiagent plan and how agents can reason about their actions [Morgenstern 87].

Agents are assumed to be friendly agents, who wish to do what they are asked to do. Agents are constrained to tell the truth, and if an agent wishes to do an act and he can, then he will. There is no planning process. She builds a theory upon a first order logic of knowledge, in which knowledge is represented as a relation on strings, and integrates it with an extensive, set-theoretic model of action.

Actions and *events* are defined as set of intervals, intuitively those in which the action or event takes place. Actions are classes of the form $\{i \mid \phi(i)\}$, where $\phi(i)$ is a wff free only in i. For example $\{i \mid \exists a \text{ Puts-on}(a,B11,B12,i)\}$ describes the act of putting block B11 on block B12. $\{i \mid \exists a,$ bl1, bl2 Red(bl1) and Puts-on(a, bl1, bl2, i)} describes the act of putting a red block on some other block. Events differ from actions in that the performing agent is in some way restricted, e.g. $\{i \mid \exists a,$ bl1, bl2 Child(a) and Puts-on(a, bl1, bl2,i)} describes the event of a child placing one block on another. **States** are ordered by the < relation, indicating precedence in time. The predicate R(Ev, S1, S2) is true if S2 is the result of event's Ev occurrence in S1. Occur(Ev, S1, S2) is true if Ev occurs between S1 and S2. A central knowledge notion is *knowledge* about actions. The predicate *know* takes as arguments an agent, a string representing a sentence, and a situation. For instance $\exists p$ (Know (John, p, S5) and $\neg$Know(Bill, p, S5) means that John knows something that Bill doesn't know. Her theory of the knowledge precondition problem for actions is based on an axiom: if $f(\text{arg}_1,..., \text{arg}_n)$ is an action, f is primitive, and an agent knows standard parameters for each arg_i, then he knows how to perform those actions. In the sequence, she defines when an agents knows how to perform a sequence of actions, how to perform a conditional action, how to perform a while-loop, how to perform concurrent actions etc.

Plans are defined as any structure of events constructed with event operators of sequence, conditionals, while loops, and concurrency. Under what circumstances can an agent successfully execute a plan? The basic concept is that an agent can execute a plan if he knows that he will be able to perform all the actions in the plan for which he is the actor, and he can predict that the other events in the plan will take place at the proper time.

Pelavin

Pelavin has developed a *formal model of action and time* for domains where the planning agent may *concurrently* execute a set of actions in a world where other agents and external forces are simultaneously producing changes [Pelavin 88]. Has developed an interpreted logic, i.e. a logic with a semantic model.

His primary interest lies in planning problems that involve external events and concurrent actions, which in principle may be executed by different agents (centralized multiagent planning). One of the essential features of his logic is that it provides a formal basis for determining when two or more plan instances, concurrent or sequential, can be executed together.

An **action** pi (called "plan instance" by Pelavin) is specified by describing the conditions that will inevitably hold at planning time if pi occurs, and conditions C under which it is inevitable

at planning time that if C holds then pi is executable. For example, consider the action *move-box@I* which corresponds to bringing about the event "move the box against the wall" during interval I by sliding the box along the floor. This action may be specified as
(INEV Ip (IF (OCC *move-box@I*) (∃?i2 (AND (MEETS I ?i2) (HOLDS (against box wall) ?i2))) and (INEV Ip (IF (AND (∃?i0 (AND (MEETS ?i0 I) (HOLDS (near agent box) ?i0))) (HOLDS no-obstruction-in-path I)) (EXECUTABLE move-box@I))).

The first expression says that it is inevitable at planning time Ip that if *move-box@I* occurs then the box will be against the wall immediately after the occurrence of *move-box@I*. The second statement says that under all possible circumstances at planning time, *move-box@I* is executable if the agent is by the box just prior to execution and there is no obstruction that will be in the way while the box is being moved.

Plans can be constructed by composing simple actions together. The issue is to find out under which conditions a composite plan is executable in relation to the conditions under which its components are executable when taken alone. A rough view of executability for composite actions (plan instances) is as follows. The composition of pi1 and pi2 is *executable* with respect to some branch b if (i) they are both executable at b, and they do not interfere with each other at b, or (ii) one of them, say pi1, is executable in b, the attempt of pi1 enables the conditions under which pi2 is executable and they do not interfere with each other at b.

The specification of the **planning problem** contains the standard "ingredients": (i) a goal condition to be solved, (ii) a description of the world in which the plan is to be executed (the planning environment), and (iii) for each member a1 of a set of simple actions, the conditions under which a1 can be executed and the effects produced by a1 (the action specifications). **Result** of the planning process is a plan, which is a composition of simple actions, that can be executed and if executed achieves the goal in any world that meets the description given by the planning environment and the action specification. His planner is able to determine the conditions under which a composition of simple actions can be executed together, and to determine the combined effects of a composition of simple actions.

Pelavin models interactions among simultaneous actions (*constructive relations*: an interaction between two actions that can be executed together but not separately, an interaction involving an external event that enables the agent to perform some action). The *destructive interactions*, referred as interference, consider resource conflicts and actions that are alternative choices, only one of which can be performed at one time.

Rosenschein et al.

Rosenschein and his colleagues have done research both in the field of centralized multiagent planning and distributed planning. First, we will review the activities in centralized multiagent planning.

In [Rosenschein 82] operators borrowed from speech act theory build the basis of a multiagent plan synchronization approach. Speech acts from Cohen and Perrault [1979] are modeled as operators in a planning system. Operators for requesting and informing, such as *request to inform* and *request to request*, can be defined such that compositional adequacy is achieved. For instance, CAUSE-TO-WANT(x,y,act) is used by agent x to cause y to adopt x's goal as its own, but only if y believes he has the capability to satisfy the goal and the ACCEPT predicate is true. The question for a centralized planner is "How can I induce other agents to reach my goal?"

Actions are parameterized. The **planning problem** is specified as a goal, which may both contain state descriptions and instantiated operators. A goal could be "a person using an intelligent agent at Stanford would like file REP.PRESS at MIT to be printed on the Dover printer at CMU" is expressed as D-PRINTED(REP.PRESS.CMU). Working backwards from this goal a plan is then being constructed. The basic idea is similar to STRIPS like planning, where the planner tries to fulfill the preconditions of operators. The resulting **plans** are represented as AND/OR trees.

Katz and Rosenschein [1989] took the STRIPS representation of actions, and directed acyclic graphs (DAGs) as plan representations to allow parallel execution. **Agents** are regarded as homogeneous processing units. An **action** (operation) is represented by three sets: a precondition set, a delete set and an add set. The **problem** is whether a given set of actions can be executed in parallel.

They do not tackle the inference problem between parallel actions explicitly. An algorithm for the generation of plans is formally developed. The system contains a supervisor for planning and distribution of operations and several agents for execution.

Stuart

Stuart has implemented a synchronizing program for multiple agent plans [Stuart 85]. This program (centralized planner) gets as input *one* multiagent plan, which contains potential conflicts (event failures). The output is a plan in which synchronizing operations are inserted to sequentialize critical operations. The paper addresses the problem of ensuring that a plan does not deadlock, or allow any event to fail.

An **agent** is an acceptor for strings. The formal model for an agent is similar to a non-deterministic finite automaton. **Actions** are modeled as having a begin and an end. An action is is composed into discrete transformations of the world, which are called events. An action is a set of possible finite sequences of events. Events have a similar form as in STRIPS. The **state** of the environment in which an action executes consists of a world state, and a set of actions currently being executed. If an agent executes an action, one of the possible sequences of events for that action is selected non-deterministically and added to the environment state. Given a set of actions A, memory states M of an agent and a set of signals S, a **plan** is recursively defined by: (i) For any $a \in A$: a is a plan for executing a single action, (ii) For any $m \in M$, $s \in S$: (set m), (send s) and (guard m s) are synchronizing primitives; (iii) If p_1 and p_2 are two plans, then $p_1;p_2$ is the plan to execute them in sequence, p1||p2 is to execute them in parallel, $p_1|p_2$ is to execute one or the other by nondeterministic selection and p_1* executes p_1 an arbitrary number of times. The **planning problem** is to take information about the environment, and find an agent which has some desired effect on the world, such as the ultimate achieving of a goal world state, no matter what choices the environment makes. The plan resulting from synchronization is similar to a program written in the parallel programming language CSP [Hoare 78]. In a later paper, Stuart uses branching time temporal logic to describe the possible and safe executions of plans [Stuart 87].

Wilensky

In Wilensky's systems PAM and PANDORA several agents are modeled which can have both cooperative and uncooperative relations [Wilensky 83]. **Actions** and **plans** are represented (implemented) in a frame based language with varying types and numbers of slots. The vocabulary for action representations is based on Schank's conceptual dependency theory [Schank 75]. The systems plan only for one agent but consider the goals and plans of the other agents to modify their own plans. The goals and plans of the other agents are predetermined and do not change during the planning process. Wilensky has dealt with a range of goal relations which are all considered from the viewpoint of one single agent. Only this agent can change its plan. He concentrates on conflicts among the goals of a single-agent planner, i.e. situations in which one person possesses several goals simultaneously. Thus, coordination does not play a role in his investigations. Also, interactions are only considered from a single planner's point of view, which plans only his own activities.

2.3.2 Distributed Planning

We will describe some selected research in decentralized multiagent planning.

Conry, Lesser et al. (multistage negotiation)

Conry, Meyer and Lesser [1986] have developed a negotiation protocol for cooperatively resolving resource allocation conflicts (see also [Conry, Meyer and Pope 89]). It is a distributed planning problem in the sense that there is no dedicated agent which has a complete and accurate view of the network. A problem exists if goals of the agents are not attainable. This may be the case when there are several goals competing for the same limited resources. Their negotiation approach, called *multistage negotiation*, provides a mechanism for reaching a consensus among nodes with conflicting goals.

The *application domain* is the monitoring and control of a complex communication system. This system consists of a network of sites, each containing a variety of communication equipment, interconnected by links. These sites are partitioned into several geographic subregions with a single site in each subregion designated a control facility (**agent**). Each control facility (agent) has the responsibility for communication system monitoring and control within its own subregion and corresponds to a single node (agent) in the distributed problem solving network. Agents are not motivated purely by self interest. They are interested in cooperating to achieve some goals pertinent to system performance.
In this context, planning is used to find alternative plans for user circuits (point-to-point connection) which have been interrupted as a result of some failure or outage. *Resources* are the links between sites. A **plan** is a list of alternating sites and links. The *goal* of a plan is to connect the first site in this list with the last one in this list. In case of a failure of a link (sort of a

resource conflict), there may be an alternative plan (route in the network) to reach a goal, namely to connect two sites. The satisfaction of possibly all goals is a *distributed planning problem*, because there is no single agent knowing all the plans.

Problem solving is done by producing restoral plans for each circuit. When an agent generates a plan to fix a connection problem, he has to differentiate between two kinds of goals. *Primary goals* are those instantiated locally by an agent in response to an observed outage of a circuit for which the agent has primary responsibility (because the circuit terminates in the agent's subregion. An agent's *secondary goals* are those goals which have been instantiated as a result of a contract with some other agent. The achievement of secondary goals requires the commitment of the agents to whose responsibility the goal belongs.

There are two kinds of *communication* relevant for planning: *Requests* for confirmation of other agent's tentative commitments, and *responses* concerning the impact of its own proposed commitments on others. The protocol (*multistage negotiation*) starts with an initial plan generation and consists of several cycles of sending requests for secondary goals, local examination, generating alternative plans and sending responses.

Kuwabara and Lesser [1989] have extended the work of Conry, Meyer and Lesser [1986] and have developed a protocol to resolve resource allocation cooperatively in a distributed network. There exist *global goals*, initiated by agents. For each global goals there exist a variety of *global plans* which can achieve it (OR junction). A global plan has several *subgoals* (AND junction), which have alternative *plan fragments* for their realization (OR junction). The goal-plan structure can be illustrated as an AND-OR tree. For the solution of a subgoal there are resources required. A conflict arises when several agents request the same resource for their subgoals. There are alternatives for conflict resolution (= the search space), because for each goal g_i there exist a variety of alternative plans $g_{i1},..., g_{in}$.

Plans are characterized by the resources they require. Temporal information is not existent, i.e. it is implicitly assumed that plans are executed simultaneously. There is a one stage refinement of plans possible, i.e. from global plans to alternative sets of plan fragments.

The *application domain* is to find a path in a communication network from one place to another. A resource corresponds to a communication link.

There are three negotiation phases: *Asynchronous search phase* (phase 1), where each agent tries to find conflict solution for his own goals. If an agent cannot find a solution, he moves in the *coordinated search phase* (phase 2), where the agent forces other agents to examine possibilities that have not been previously checked. If no solution can be found, an agent switches to the *overconstrained resolution phase* (phase 3), where the agents determine goals to be solved and negotiate which global plan to use to satisfy the goals. Each agent makes the same decision on the minimum set of goals to be de-committed in order to resolve the overconstrained situation.

Conflicts are solved by either selecting or alternative plans or, if this does not work, by discarding goals. This is a much more abstract view of conflict resolution than is pursued in our work. In our approach there is more information (e.g. temporal) available which may guide conflict resolution.

Corkhill

Corkhill's distributed implementation of NOAH has been the first effort to plan and to synchronize plans distributively [Corkhill 79]. NOAH [Sacerdoti 77] has no explicit representation for the actions of other agents and it has been extended by Corkhill to model different agents. High-level goals are allocated to individual agents. Such a division between goals is appropriate because conjunctive goals are nearly independent in such hierarchical planning methods. Based on a hierarchical planning process, plans are synchronized level by level, i.e. agents communicate shared variables between goals and resolve conflicts at each level before refining plans to lower levels. Thus, plan synchronization is done during plan construction by building smoothly interacting plans hierarchically.

Actions and **plans** in NOAH [Sacerdoti 77]: A procedural net (**plan**) is a graph structure whose nodes represent actions at varying levels of detail, organized into a hierarchy of partially ordered time sequences. An **action** at a particular level of detail is represented by a single node in the procedural net. The nodes are linked to form hierarchical descriptions of operations, and to form plans of action. Each node in the procedural net may refer to a set of child nodes that represent more detailed subactions. When executed in order, the child nodes will achieve the effects of their parents. The parent-child relationships allow the system to represent and reason about actions in a hierarchical fashion.

Sometimes it is misunderstood that NOAH allows for concurrent and multiagent plans. In fact, NOAH simply allows for the representation of unordered actions during the intermediate stages of planning. This is not the same as representing concurrency: the final output of NOAH is always an ordered sequence of actions. Moreover, NOAH has no explicit representation for the actions of other agents (although this could conceivably be built in, as Corkhill has demonstrated). Since in any case, NOAH cannot handle concurrency, general multiagent planning is clearly impossible here.

Corkhill's model suggests a simple message-passing communication process, which allows for sending and acknowledging requests only. It neglects the problem how agents can resolve interactions.

Coordination is done from level to level (synchronous planning). However, in worlds populated by autonomous and possibly heterogeneous agents, more flexibility is desirable in that agents, although having developed their plans at *different* level of detail (asynchronous planning), may want to coordinate their activities.

Durfee and Lesser (partial global planning)

Durfee and Lesser have done extensive work in the field of multiagent planning. In their work on *partial global planning*, they proposed a framework for coordination that allows the agents to tentatively plan coordinated interactions and to modify their plans in response to unanticipated situations [Durfee 88; Durfee and Lesser 87, 89]. Each node represents its own local view of network activity in a so-called partial global plan. A variety of ways of how nodes coordinate is provided; individual nodes are free to form local goals and plans based on their local knowledge and priorities, and the nodes' coordination responsibilities and their criteria for choosing what plans to communicate can be changed to modify how and whether nodes decide to coordinate.

Partial global planning builds on a multiagent testbed, called the *Distributed Vehicle Monitoring Testbed* (DVMT) [Lesser and Corkhill 83]. In the DVMT acoustic sensors are dispersed in a two-dimensional area, where each sensor has a limited range. Vehicle monitoring is the task of generating a dynamic, area-wide map of vehicles moving through the monitored area. Distributed vehicle monitoring typically has a number of processing nodes, with associated acoustic sensors. Each processing node can communicate with other nearby nodes. As a vehicle moves through the monitoring area, it generates characteristic acoustic signals.

An **agent** (node) is a blackboard based problem solver [Erman et. al 80] with knowledge sources and levels of abstraction appropriate for vehicle monitoring. A knowledge source performs the basic tasks of extending and refining hypotheses, where a hypothesis represents a partial interpretation of some signal data. A *hypothesis* is characterized by one or more time-regions (where the vehicle was at discrete sensed times), an expected belief-range (the confidence in the accuracy of the hypothesis), a blackboard-level (depending on the amount of processing that has been done on the data), a list of event classes (classifying the frequency of vehicle type), and a list of sat-hyps (a list of hypotheses that satisfy the expectations).

Three types of plans are differentiated in *partial global planning*: local plans, node-plans and partial global plans. A **local plan** is the representation of a plan maintained by an agent — they call agents "nodes" — that is pursuing the plan. It contains information about the plan's objective, the order of major plan steps, how long each step is expected to take, and detailed actions that have been taken or will be taken. A **node-plan** is a representation of a plan that nodes communicate about. It contains basically the same information as a local plan except that the details about short-term actions are omitted. A **partial global plan** (PGP) is the representation of how several agents are working toward a larger goal. A PGP contains information about the larger goal, the major plan steps that are occurring concurrently, and how the partial solutions formed by the agents should be integrated together. A PGP is *global* in the sense that it may, but does not necessarily, encompass the local goals of several agents, and is *partial* in that only part of the network might participate in it.

An **action** is a potential application of domain problem-solving knowledge on specific hypothesis to achieve certain goals. The attributes of an action are stored in a list containing: a *knowledge-source-type* (a list of possible KSs that could be invoked); a *knowledge-source-instantiation* (the specific KSI to be instantiated); a *duration* (expected duration of the action); and a *result* (indicates a hypothesis or partial solution generated by the action). When the action is taken, a list of hypotheses that satisfy the expectations is inserted into the sat-hyps slot, so that past actions will point to the hypotheses that they generated.

How is coordination performed? Durfee has explored a variety of heuristics, strategies and organizations for coordination. Basically, coordination is viewed as a planning task. Agents need to plan complementary actions and anticipate their interactions. Each agent has a partial global planner (PGPlanner), which builds a node-plan from each local plan. Guided by a meta-level organization, agents exchange PGPs and node-plans so that one or more of them develop more encompassing PGPs. When combining PGPs into a single, larger PGP, an agent merges the smaller PGP's activities to represent the concurrent activities of participating agents, and can reorder the activities to improve coordination. An agent invokes its partial global planner (PGPlanner) to find current plans and activities for the set of nodes that it is responsible for coordinating. When a PGPlanner is invoked, it begins by processing node-plans (local plans) and PGP messages. The PGPlanner is responsible for finding PGPs for some subset of agents in the network. The PGPlanner's task is among others to remove or reorder activities of agents to avoid redundancies, to specify when and to whom agents should send their partial solutions to other agents such that they can be integrated into an overall solution, to determine how agents should transfer activities to make better use of their computational resources and expertise.

Within this framework, Durfee has explored many aspects of distributed problem solving with variations in strategies of local planning and styles of negotiation.

The planner is a DVMT-specific problem solving approach suited to blackboard-based interpretation systems. Decker and Lesser are working on an extension of PGP, called Generalized PGP, to overcome this [Decker et al. 88].

We support Durfee's and Lesser's suggestion that plans are broadcasted or exchanged in order to allow agents greater access to the anticipated future behavior of others. In contrast to our work, plans in the DVMT consist of *computational* actions of nodes with fixed spatial positions, in our approach the agents can freely move around and may affect the environment with their actions. In the DVMT, agents cooperate to solve a single problem, namely, the tracking of vehicles moving through an area monitored by acoustic sensors. This leads to a *task centered model* in contrast to our *agent centered* model.

Grosz, Lochbaum and Sidner

Grosz and her colleagues have done research in, what they call, "collaborative planning" [Grosz 90; Grosz and Sidner 88; Lochbaum, Grosz and Sidner 90]. They stress a strong coupling of natural language processing and multiagent planning. They investigate how agents can cooperate during the planning process. There is no single agent in control of the system. Agents make cooperative plans that include actions by each of them. A **plan** (individual plan) is defined as a configuration of beliefs and intentions about actions and their executability rather than a data structure encoding a sequence of actions. It also contains a means of expressing simultaneous actions (both agents act at the same time) and conjoined actions (actions of two agents taken together achieve a desired result). **Multiagent plans** (SharedPlans) are defined in terms of act-types and relations among them. An **action** is an instantiation of an act-type. An act-type is a triple, consisting of the act-type's *parameter list*, the *agent* who performs the activity, and the *time interval* over which the action occurs. Act-type relations include generation, enablement, sequences of acts and simultaneous acts. SharedPlans are constructed incrementally. The idea is that agents have partial plans, which are expressed as having a set of beliefs and intentions about actions. Thus, the construction of a sharedPlan is seen as developing a state of mutual belief of the agents.

Koo

Koo has investigated the synchronization of plan based activities [Koo 88; Koo and Wiederhold 88]. Synchronization is achieved in a distributed manner by communication of the agents. Planning is based on a PERT chart type of plan. A **plan** is a network of states, where a state is a set of predicates that describe the world at a certain time and an arc is the action that changes the values of certain predicates in a state. Koo gives an alternative definition that a **plan** is a network of actions where a node represents an action and an arc represents a precedence relation between two actions. The two definitions are dual to each other in that one can always be derived from the other. A plan has the following attributes: an initial state, a final state and a duration. Operators (**actions**) are represented in a STRIPS like style, i.e. consisting of name, preconditions and postconditions, and a duration. *States* are represented as having predecessors, successors, earliest start, latest start and status.

Koo considers only a small aspect of interactions, which are possible between the plans of autonomous agents. The only type of interaction, that he is concerned with, are precedence constraints, i.e. an agent has to consider whether it is possible for him to insert a new action, being requested by another agent, into his existing plan. Automatic detection of conflicts and beneficial (implicitly existing) relations between plans are no issues in his thesis.

Rosenschein et al.

In several approaches Rosenschein and his colleagues have used a game theoretic model for modeling the interaction of agents [Genesereth et al. 84; Rosenschein 86; Rosenschein and Genesereth 85]. A payoff matrix describes at what expense two players can make their moves. They have a very simplistic and restricted notion of actions and plans. Moves (a notion coming from game theory) may be interpreted as **actions**. There is no further specification of actions. **Plans** consist of, usually only one, pairs of sequential actions with alternating agents. Their notion of actions and plans, being very restrictive on the the one hand, is, on the other hand, computationally very attractive in that it allows for the production of theoretical results.

In [Genesereth et al. 84] it is investigated how high-level, autonomous, independently-motivated agents ought to interact with each other so as to achieve their goals. They explicitly discard the benevolent agent assumption and consider only situations in which communication between the agents is impossible, which differs from our assumptions. But sufficient sensory information is available using plan recognition techniques. They illustrate that the need for communication in any interaction can be reduced if there is a model of the decision process of the other agent.

In a later paper, they focus on the aspect of communication to resolve conflicts among agents [Rosenschein and Genesereth 85]. Interaction is more important than coordination. The agents must be able to negotiate, compromise and promise. Communication is used to resolve conflicts. There are players (= agents) and a set of possible moves for each player. A payoff matrix construct is used to model the outcome for agents.

Zlotkin and Rosenschein have published a couple of papers where agents negotiate about the reconciliation of plans [Zlotkin and Rosenschein 89a, 89b, 90a, 90b, 90c]. Again game theoretic techniques play a decisive role, here for the analysis of multiagent negotiation. Plans have the standard AI form: A single-agent **plan** to move the world from state s to state f is a list $[o_1,..., o_n]$ of operations such that $f= o_n(o_{n-1}(...o_1(s)...))$ [Zlotkin and Rosenschein 89b, 90b]. A **joint plan** (multiagent plan) to move the world from state s to state f is a pair of single-agent plans (P_A, P_B) and a schedule. A schedule is a partial oder over the union of actions in the two-agent plans. It is a partial order and hence allows for simultaneous actions by different agents.

2.4 Communication and Negotiation

There exist a variety of conversation and negotiation oriented approaches to coordinate distributed problem solvers.

Communication has several functions with respect to multiagent planning:
– During the planning process: Multiagent planning requires that agents share and process a substantial amount of information. The distributed construction of a multiagent plan requires a high degree of interaction between the participating agent (remember our slogan "distributed planning= multiagent planning + communication"). These interactions between agents may be guided by protocols for communication.

– Execution: Once a multiagent plan has been constructed, the synchronization between the actions have to be monitored. This can be achieved by sending messages between the agents or by having a central instance monitoring the execution.

We will not consider the latter case further, because it has only secondary importance for multi-agent planning. The problem of communication and negotiation during planning is the most crucial one and the following listing of communication approaches provides snapshots in this direction.

The **contract net** [Davis and Smith 80, 83; Smith 80; Smith and Davis 81] models transfer of control in a distributed system with the metaphor of *negotiation among autonomous intelligent beings*. The net consists of a set of nodes that negotiate with one another through a set of messages. Nodes represent the distributed computing resources to be managed. There are two types of nodes: managers and bidders. The *manager* identifies a task to be done, advertises it and assigns it to other nodes for execution. The *Bidders* are nodes that offer to perform a task. A bidder whose bid has been accepted by the manager becomes a *contractor*. When a proposal is accepted, it becomes a binding contract to both agents. The proposal may be rejected, if it does not comply with the assigned agent's plan or other internal constraints. The assigning agent may propose it to another agent or rearrange its plan.

Nodes communicate by means of different classes of *messages*. A manager issues a *task announcement* describing the task to be done and the criteria for bids. Bidders send *bids* to announce their willingness and ability to perform a task. The *award* message from the manager to the successful bidder establishes that bidder as the contractor for the task. The contractor send an *acknowledgement* of the award, either accepting or rejecting it (extended version of 'contract net'). The contractor send *reports* to the manager announcing status (interim report) or termination of a task (final report). The manager may send a termination to a contractor to interrupt its performance of a contract prematurely. Idle nodes may broadcast their availability with a *node availability announcement* (extended version).

Two forms of cooperation are considered: 1. Nodes assist each other by sharing the computational load for the execution of subtasks of the overall problem. Smith and Davis argue that negotiation is a natural way of distributing tasks among problem-solving agents. 2. Nodes assist each other by sharing partial results which are based on somewhat different perspectives on the overall problem.

A characteristic that makes the contract net inadequate for distributed planning is that agents are assumed to dedicate themselves to a committed task until it is completely executed. This assumption excludes the possibility of interacting tasks among agents' plans, which is considered as a major issue in distributed planning.

The contract net model differs from our model in that negotiation is used as a means to decompose problems and allocate tasks and not to resolve interactions between plans.

Negotiation has been the main focus of **Sycara** in her work on DAI [Sycara 85, 88, 89a, 89b]. She focuses on non-cooperative multiagent interactions. How to find a compromise if there is a dispute between the agents? A planner (mediator) has as input the conflicting goals (in my case: plans) of multiple agents and as output a compromise acceptable by the agents. Her system also uses a program as mediator, which enters in negotiation with each of the two parties, proposing and modifying compromises and utilities until a final agreement is reached (application: resolving labor disputes). For planning she integrates case-based reasoning and preference analysis techniques.

Negotiation as a means to resolve conflicts was the main focus of other researchers in this field. Adler and his colleagues at GTE Laboratories presented a classification of conflicts in resource-level conflicts and goal-level conflicts [Adler et al. 89]. Domain is telephone network traffic control. They use a blackboard architecture [Hayes-Roth 85].

Sathi and Fox [1989] have dealt with negotiation for adjusting resource allocations ("reallocation") to reflect new requirements. Negotiation is required to solve the reallocation problem. During negotiation agents iteratively exchange offers for buying and selling resources until a compromise is reached. Their methodology builds upon a market-like mechanism to regulate resource allocations. In our case, resource conflicts are handled by explicitly considering the temporal constraints of resource requirements.

There is another class of communication oriented approaches to distributed problem solving, which is based on **object-oriented concurrent programming** techniques [Hewitt 80; Kornfeld and Hewitt 81; Maruichi 89; Tokoro and Ishikawa 84]. Agents in these models or systems are mainly seen as extended objects in the object-oriented programming sense with sophisticated message-passing and message interpretation capabilities. Sometimes the term "*agent*-oriented" programming is used.

2.5 Critique of Existing Multiagent Planning Approaches

We want to point out some open problems and weaknesses of current research in multiagent planning, and use them as a motivation for our own research.

The approaches concerning *pure communication* approaches (Section 2.4) do not provide any means to handle interactions among agents' plans. The protocols provide little information for agents to synchronize their plans. Also, the relationship between internal planning and communication have not been addressed.

A comparison between our approach and other coordination and multiagent planning systems can be made from at least four standpoints: (1) The crispness of the action and plan model (the representation of actions and plans), (2) the variety of relations being considered, (3) the flexibility in planning, and (4) the way in which planning and negotiation are integrated. These points will be reflected in the following listing.

– *Centralized* multiagent planning approaches do not consider aspects of communication and negotiation as part of the planning process. Although there has been done some work on centralized multiagent planning, there has been relatively little work involved in connecting the planning process with the process of communication and making commitments about actions and plans. (**4**)
  In our approach, planning and communication are merged into one model.
– Often, resources mean the only concept for reasoning about how different activities *interact*. When there is a harmful interaction between actions of different plans, then there is something that can be considered a resource for which the actions are contending. Coherence and coordination are often only defined via the regulation of resources. Multiagent planning has focussed and usually restricted itself on the issue of detecting and resolving conflicts among different agents plans. (**2**)
  Although the requirements for resources and resolving conflicts pose an important concept of interaction, it is not the only one. In our work, we have found and investigated further concepts of plan interactions. We not only consider remedies to handle conflicts but also

deal with situations in which beneficial effects (e.g., synergy) can be achieved by reconciling plans.

- Many approaches do not give (except, a few more formally oriented) exact definitions of plans. Most approaches miss exact descriptions how plans may be modified in order to be reconciled with other plans. **(1)**

  Our approach, which is based on an exact definition of plans, considers also crisp definitions of plan modifications.

- Theoretical models of cooperation allow to mathematically prove theories of what cooperating agents can and cannot do, and about how assumptions about their domains and characteristics affect their capabilities. However, formal models are usually far away from practical systems and provide only little help to bridge the gap between theories and implemented systems.

  The descriptions given in our approach can straightforwardly be used as the basis for an implementation. This statement will be underpined by providing a variety of detailed scenarios and by pointing to an existing implementation.

- No approach to multiagent planning is based on an *explicit* taxonomy of relations which may hold between the actions of single-agent plans. **(2)**

  There is no explicit notion of, what we call, multiagent plan relations. These relations play a prominent role in our coordination framework as they are the core (the driving force) of our coordination approach.

- Still, multiagent planning systems are poorly suited to dynamically changing domains, where agents cannot wait for complete information about potential interactions before they begin acting. **(3)**

  The problem of dealing with vague and incomplete information is taken care in our approach by (i) allowing agents to transfer only parts of their plans and, (ii) handling actions and interactions at different levels of abstraction.

3 Actions and Plans in Multiagent Domains

In this chapter, we will develop a formal framework for plans in distributed environments. Let us briefly review the requirements for a framework that supports plans and their coordination in multiagent domains:

- We need a notion of what is happening while an action is occurring. Purely sequential interactions among actions is not sufficient. We need to express concurrent (overlapping, parallel) actions.
- Actions have to be modelled together with their temporal relations.
- There has to be a concept for multiple agents, because both the planning process is distributed and the execution of a plan is shared among several agents.
- The plans, which are exchanged among agents, may be vague and not completely developed, which means that planning and plans should be allowed at several levels of abstractions.
- Communication among planners is essential and hence should be taken explicitly into account.

The framework we will put forward will meet these requirements to some extent. A special difficulty for this coordination framework was the integration of these widespread requirements, such as temporal relations and refinement, planning and communication, positive and negative interactions between different plans

Although there has been considerable work on planning, there has been relatively little work on the complications involved in connecting the planning process with the process of communication and making commitments about actions and plans.

3.1 Basic Notions

A **variable** denoting elements of the domain is any sequence of lowercase alphanumeric characters in which the first character is lowercase alphabetic. Variables beginning with an uppercase letter in outline font, e.g. A, will be used to denote sets of elements. We shall use x,

x_1, x_2, y, z and $a, a_1, a_2, ..., i, i_1, i_2, ..., g, g_1, g_2, ..., p, p_1, p_2, ..., r, r_1, r_2, ..., t, t_1, t_2, ...$
to denote variables. Additional type conventions will be introduced later.

Functions are denoted by strings in which the first is a lowercase character.

Predicates are denoted by strings in which the first is an uppercase character.

A set of types or sorts may be assigned to each function symbol and variable. The set of types
is given by:

SORTS = {OBJECTS, RESOURCES, AGENTS, ACTIONS, TIME-POINTS, INTER-
VALS, DURATIONS, PLANS, SET, ACTION-SET, RES-SET, AGENT-SET, PLAN-SET}
with

OBJECTS is the class of physical objects in the universe of discourse.

RESOURCES $\subseteq$ OBJECTS denotes the finite set of resources in the universe of discourse.

AGENTS $\subseteq$ OBJECTS denotes the finite set of agents in the universe of discourse.

ACTIONS is the class of actions in the universe of discourse.

TIME-POINTS is the class of points of time in the universe of discourse. It is a fully
    ordered set of values from $\mathbb{R}$ taken to correspond to time.

INTERVALS is the class of temporal intervals in the universe of discourse.

DURATIONS is the class of temporal units in the universe of discourse. DURATIONS is a
    linearly ordered set of numbers corresponding to the real numbers.

SET is a set of objects which are introduced via lists (tuples).

Subsorts of SET will be defined as tuples (lists) of elements also.

We will give an example how lists can be formalized for ACTION-SET. The other subsets of
LISTS can be defined analogously.

If a is an action, then

cons(a, nil): ACTION-SET

If x is an ACTION-SET, then

cons(a, x) : ACTION-SET.

car(cons(a, x)) = a

cdr(cons(a, x)) = x

RES-SET $\subseteq$ SET are the sets of all sets of resources

ACTION-SET $\subseteq$ SET sets of actions

PLANS is the class of plans in the universe of discourse.

PLAN-SET $\subseteq$ SET are the lists of plans

Operations on sets like $\in$ are defined for lists and will be used analogously as for sets. Example: $\in (x, y)$ iff $x = car(y)$ or $\in (x, cdr(y))$.

We will use a naming convention for variables to denote special types. A **variable** denoting a type of object may either consist only of the first character or of a sequence starting with a character and followed by a sequence of digits. If the first character of a variable is one of the following it will denote a special type of object in the universe of discourse:

a for actions, ACTIONS

i for intervals, INTERVALS

g for agents, AGENTS

p for plans, PLANS

r for resources, RESOURCES

t for points of time, TIME-POINTS

Using these typing conventions for variables we can abbreviate the standard notation of well sorted formulas. For instance,

$$\forall x: \text{ACTIONS } \exists y:\text{AGENTS } y = executor(x)$$

can now be written as

$$\forall a \; \exists g \; g = executor(a).$$

A variable beginning with an uppercase letter in outline font denotes a **set** of the corresponding sort. For instance, $\mathbb{I}_1$ or $\mathbb{I}1$ might be a set of intervals and $\mathbb{G}$ a set of agents.

Event Based versus State Based World Model

One can differentiate between two approaches for representing events (actions) and their effects: a *state*-based representation and a *event*-based representation of the world.

Our model is based on an *event-based representation* of plans with an explicit concept for expressing time [Lansky 87, 88]. This representation of actions and plans allows reasoning about plan interferences, which are an integral element in dynamic, multiagent worlds. In an event-based approach, the world is represented in terms of a set of interrelated events[1] (actions). The *state of the world* at any point in time is mainly a record of the events (actions) that have occurred and their interrelations.

In a *state-based representation*, the world is viewed as a series of states that are changed by events or actions. Events are modeled solely in terms of their state-changing function. The *situation calculus* [McCarthy and Hayes 69] has given rise to the state-based planning paradigm, exemplified by such systems as STRIPS [Fikes and Nilsson 71] and NOAH [Sacerdoti 77]. In the situation calculus an event is represented by a function that takes a situation, which is an instantaneous snapshot of the world, and yields the situation that would result from applying the events to its argument. Events can be combined to form sequences. The result of applying the sequence $e_1, e_2, .., e_n$ to situation s is recursively defined as the result of applying $e_2, .., e_n$ to the situation that results from applying e_1 to s.

One limitation of the situation calculus is that is does not model simultaneous events and, consequently, only sequential interactions are allowed in planners based on this paradigm. This refers to an *enablement interaction* where an earlier action brings about a later one's preconditions and a *harmful interaction* where an earlier action ruins a later one's preconditions. These interactions are captured by the precondition-add-delete lists provided for each action in a state based system. These lists, however, do not describe parallel interaction between actions, which definitely occur in multiagent worlds. Without a model supporting parallelism, it is not clear what the potential types of parallel interactions are.

Planners which are based on the state-based paradigm can be characterized by: given a set of sentences describing conditions that are initially true and a set of sentences describing goal conditions to be achieved, a sequence of actions must be found that when applied to any situation where the initial conditions hold yields a situation where the goal conditions hold. In such a framework, the description of the world in which planning is done, only describes the initial situation, i.e., the situation that holds just prior to plan execution. As a result, this representa-

---

[1] In our model, we only use actions. An *action* is a special kind of event, namely, one that is performed by an agent.

tion is only adequate for planning problems where all changes in the world result from the planning agent's actions.

The conditions that are true in the initial situation will remain true until the agent performs an action that negates it. Consequently, the future is uniquely determined by the initial situation and the sequence of actions that the planning agent chooses to perform from this situation.

This type of planning environment does not provide for planning problems where the world may be affected by external events that occur while the agent is executing a plan.

For coordinating the plans of multiple agents it is necessary to deal with interactions of actions which may happen in parallel. This interactions will be modelled by *directly* relating actions with each other (event-based) instead of *first* evaluating the effect of actions on the world state and *then* checking what this means for the other actions.

In the next section, the *local* executability of actions will be defined. This is the only notion which deals with the effect of a *single* agent's actions on this single agent's plan, and thus the state-based paradigm would be sufficient, may be even more elegant, if only this case would be considered. But, for consistency reasons, we have to use an event-based notation also.

Executability of Actions

An action is locally executable if it is executable as far as only the agent's individual plans are concerned, i.e. without an agent knowing the plans (intentions) of other agents. But, first we need some other definitions.

Definition (undoing actions):
Let a be an action and A be a finite set of actions $\{a_1, a_2..., a_n\}$.
Undo: ACTION x ACTION-SET ——> {T,F}
Undo(a, A) means that the effect of an action a is not valid any more if an action from A has happened afterwards.

Preparing actions will play an important role for defining executability. A set of preparing actions for an action a is a minimal set of actions which enables action a to be executed.

Definition (preparing actions):
The predicate **Pre**(a, Al) states that the actions in Al are *preparing actions* for the action a.

A consequence of Pre$(a, A1)$ is that a cannot be executed, if the actions in $A1$ have not been carried out first. For an action a there may exist several sets of preparing actions, but it is sufficient if only one of them has been executed.

Whereas the predicate Pre defines preparing actions, it is also useful to have a predicate denoting the opposite case, namely, which actions must not have happened before another one. Therefore the following definition:

Definition (preventing actions):
Anti-pre(a, A) states that with respect to the variable bindings, A is the set of actions, which must not have happened before a ("anti-preparing"). This means, that if an action from A has happened before a, and has not been undone, i.e. the effect is still valid, a can not be executed.

Action a, which is part of agent $g's$ plan, is (locally) executable iff
(i) there exists a set of preparing actions which all have been executed and none of them has been undone,
    and, conversely,
(ii) all actions which may not have happened before a, i.e. with Anti-pre(a, A), have not happened before a or have been undone afterwards.

The following definition captures *local executability* with respect to the effect of the plan of agent g.

Definition (local executability):
Executable$(a, g) \Leftrightarrow$:
$\exists A1$ with Pre$(a, A1)$ and $\forall a_1 \in A1$: Occurred$(a_1) \land$ if exists $A2$ with
Undo$(a_1, A2)$ then $\forall a_2 \in A2 \neg$Occurred$(a_2) \lor$ Prior(a_2, a_1)
$\land$
$\forall A3$ with Anti-pre$(a, A3)$: $a_3 \in A3 \land$ Occurred(a_3)
$\Rightarrow \exists A4$ Undo$(a_3, A4) \exists a_4 \in A4$ with Prior(a_3, a_4)

Prior(a_1, a_2) is a temporal predicate, meaning that the execution of a_1 is finished before a_2 begins. It will be defined in Section 3.3.

3.2 Actions

Now we shall introduce actions and parameters of actions. Actions are the components of *plans*, which will be defined in the last section of this chapter.

Resources are the objects that are needed (consumed or released after usage) to accomplish problem-solving work. Typical resources that are allocatable in DAI systems include machines, processing time and money. Resource allocation and distribution is clearly an essential issue in distributed systems and we shall define resource conflicts in Chapter 4, and the resolution of conflicts is an issue in Chapter 5.

We will introduce some terms to deal with resources.

Definition (resources required by an action):
res: ACTIONS ———> $2^{RESOURCES}$
res(a) denotes the set of resources for an action a.

Definition (amount of resource):
amount$(r, a) \in \mathbb{R}^+$ is a natural number to denote the amount of resource r used by a.

An action is not necessarily executed by the same agent who has planned this action, i.e. an agent may create a plan for other agents. Hence, we will differentiate between the planner and executor of an action. Later, with respect to negotiation about plan coordination, we will also need a *coordinator* (coordinating agent) for a specific action.

Definition (planning agent, partial function):
planner: ACTIONS ———> AGENTS
planner(a) denotes the agent who has established (a plan for) a.

Definition(executing agent, partial function):

executor: ACTIONS ——> AGENTS

executor(a) denotes the agent who is to execute a.

Time in Multiagent Planning. Temporal information is an essential part of plans: when will a plan be executed? When are the actions of a plan to take place and how long will the execution of the actions take? (time in *planning*).

In a distributed planning environment, time is essential because it is important for agents to bind themselves in a timely manner. If agents make commitments about the execution of their plans with other agents, temporal constraints have to be included. An agent who promised to perform a certain action without giving a date virtually did not promise anything, since it can be postponed indefinitely (time in *commitments*).

Moreover, temporal information will play an important role for coordination, because it helps to relate plans of different agents to each other and to find solutions for plan reconciliations (time for *coordination*).

As primitive temporal elements we use time points and durations. A time interval will be represented as a pair of time points which are its end points.

The duration of an action expresses how long a planner expects an action to last.

Definition (duration of an action):

dur: ACTIONS ——> DURATIONS

dur(a) denotes the duration (amount of time) of action a.

Definition (start point of an action):

start: ACTIONS ——> TIME-POINTS

start(a) denotes the (earliest) start time of an action.

Definition (end point of an action):

end: ACTIONS ——> TIME-POINTS

end(a) denotes the latest finishing time of an action.

Axiom:

Start and end time of an action are points of time with $\forall a \; \text{end}(a) > \text{start}(a)$.

We will now define intervals as an ordered pair of points with the first point earlier than the second.

Definition (intervals):

$\text{INTERVALS} = \{[t_1, t_2) \mid t_1 < t_2, \; t_1, t_2 : \text{TIME-POINTS}\}$.

The next term denotes the time of an occurrence associated with an action. The time of an action is an interval during which this action may happen. An action interval may last longer than the duration which was specified for it. This means that an agent does not know beforehand the exact start and end time for an action.

Definition(time of an action):

time: $\text{ACTIONS} \longrightarrow \text{INTERVALS}$

$\text{time}(a) = [\text{start}(a), \text{end}(a))]$

3.3 Temporal Relations

Temporal relations between actions are essential both for defining *multiagent plan relations* (Chapter 4) and for developing coordination strategies (Chapter 5).

There are two forms of temporal knowledge to which the underlying primitives must attend:
- *Absolute* temporal knowledge is explicitly linked with a particular period of time along some date line. The predicates dur, start and end model absolute temporal data.
- *Relative* temporal knowledge relates temporal objects without referencing any specific periods of time.

Relative temporal relations between two actions will be based on the parameter function *time*. This chapter is devoted to model relative temporal knowledge by specifying the temporal relation between two intervals. For this purpose, we will use the binary predicates of James Allen [Allen 83, 84].

In Allen's formalism, a global notion of time is developed that is independent from the agent's actions. Temporal intervals are introduced to refer to chunks of time in a global time line. For any action, one can describe the temporal interval over which the change associated with the action takes place. Thus, there is a notion of what is happening while an action is occurring. We need such a notion in a world which is affected by several agents.

3.3.1 Interval Relationships

In all, there are thirteen, mutual exclusive, primitive interval relationships. All other interval relationships can be defined as a disjunction of these thirteen primitives. In Fig. 4 there are seven relationships. Together with their inverse relationships - equality does not have an inverse relation - there are thirteen relations. The domain of the predicates defined in this chapter is INTERVALS x INTERVALS and the range of the predicates is {T, F}.

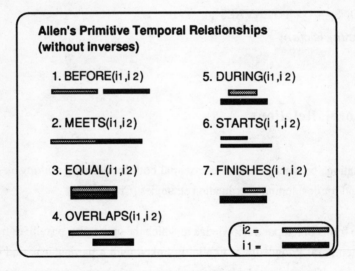

Figure 4: Primitive temporal relationships

The predicate Meets(i_1, i_2) is true iff the interval denoted by i_1 immediately precedes the interval denoted by i_2, with no gaps in between.

Definition:

Meets: INTERVALS x INTERVALS ——> {T, F}

$\forall i_1, i_2$ **Meets**$(i_1, i_2) :\Leftrightarrow$ end(i_1) = start(i_2)

In the following, we will develop a minimal definition of the thirteen temporal relations using only the meets relation.

Definition (inverse of meets):

$\forall i_1, i_2$ **Is-met-by**$(i_1, i_2) :\Leftrightarrow$ Meets(i_2, i_1)

Time interval i_1 is before i_2, and they do not overlap.

Definition:

$\forall i_1, i_2$ **Before**$(i_1, i_2) :\Leftrightarrow \exists i_3$ Meets$(i_1, i_3) \wedge$ Meets(i_3, i_2)

Definition (the inverse of before):

$\forall i_1, i_2$ **After**$(i_1, i_2) :\Leftrightarrow$ Before(i_2, i_1)

Definition (i_1 and i_2 are the same interval):

$\forall i_1, i_2$ **Equal**$(i_1, i_2) :\Leftrightarrow \exists i_3 \, i_4$ Meets$(i_3, i_1) \wedge$ Meets(i_3, i_2)
$$\wedge \text{Meets}(i_1, i_4) \wedge \text{Meets}(i_2, i_4)$$

Overlaps(i_1,i_2) is true iff i_1 starts before i_2, and they overlap.

Definition:

$\forall i_1, i_2$ **Overlaps**$(i_1, i_2) :\Leftrightarrow \exists i_3 \, i_4 \, i_5 \, i_6 \, i_7$
$$\text{Meets}(i_3, i_1) \wedge \text{Meets}(i_3, i_4)$$
$$\wedge \text{Meets}(i_1, i_6) \wedge \text{Meets}(i_6, i_7)$$
$$\wedge \text{Meets}(i_4, i_2) \wedge \text{Meets}(i_2, i_7)$$
$$\wedge \text{Meets}(i_4, i_5) \wedge \text{Meets}(i_5, i_6)$$

Definition (the inverse of overlaps):

$\forall i_1, i_2$ **Is-overlapped-by**$(i_1, i_2) :\Leftrightarrow$ Overlaps(i_2, i_1)

During(i_1, i_2) is true iff time interval i_1 is fully contained within i_2.

Definition:

$\forall i_1, i_2$ **During**$(i_1, i_2) :\Leftrightarrow \exists i_3\, i_4\, i_5\, i_6$

$$\text{Meets}(i_3, i_4) \wedge \text{Meets}(i_4, i_1)$$
$$\wedge \text{Meets}(i_1, i_5) \wedge \text{Meets}(i_5, i_6)$$
$$\wedge \text{Meets}(i_3, i_2) \wedge \text{Meets}(i_2, i_6)$$

Definition   (inverse of during):

$\forall i_1, i_2$ **Contains**$(i_1, i_2) :\Leftrightarrow$ During(i_2, i_1)

Starts(i_1, i_2) is true iff i_1 has the same beginning as i_2, but ends before i_2 ends.

Definition:

$\forall i_1, i_2$ **Starts**$(i_1, i_2) :\Leftrightarrow \exists i_3\, i_4\, i_5$

$$\text{Meets}(i_3, i_4) \wedge \text{Meets}(i_3, i_2)$$
$$\wedge \text{Meets}(i_1, i_4) \wedge \text{Meets}(i_4, i_5)$$
$$\wedge \text{Meets}(i_2, i_5)$$

Definition (inverse of starts):

$\forall i_1, i_2$ **Is-started-by**$(i_1, i_2) :\Leftrightarrow$ Starts(i_2, i_1)

Finishes(i_1, i_2) is true iff i_1 shares the same end as i_2, but begins after i_2 begins.

Definition:

$\forall\ i_1, i_2$ **Finishes**$(i_1, i_2) :\Leftrightarrow \exists i_3\, i_4\, i_5$

$$\text{Meets}(i_3, i_4) \wedge \text{Meets}(i_3, i_2)$$
$$\wedge \text{Meets}(i_4, i_1) \wedge \text{Meets}(i_1, i_5)$$
$$\wedge \text{Meets}(i_2, i_5)$$

Definition (inverse of finishes):

Is-finished-by$(i_1, i_2) :\Leftrightarrow$ Finishes(i_2, i_1)

3.3.2 Complex Temporal Relationships

It is convenient to have a more temporal predicates, which in fact can be defined as a disjunction of primitive relations.

The predicate In summarizes the relationships in which an interval i_1 is wholly contained in another interval i_2.

Definition:

$\forall i_1, i_2$ **In**$(i_1, i_2) :\Leftrightarrow$ During$(i_1, i_2) \lor$ Starts$(i_1, i_2) \lor$ Finishes(i_1, i_2)

Definition (i_1 and i_2 end at the same (point of) time):

$\forall i_1, i_2$ **Ends=**$(i_1, i_2) :\Leftrightarrow \exists i_3$ Meets$(i_1, i_3) \land$ Meets(i_2, i_3)

Definition (i_1 and i_2 begin at the same time):

$\forall i_1, i_2$ **Begin=**$(i_1, i_2) :\Leftrightarrow \exists i_3$ Meets$(i_3, i_1) \land$ Meets(i_3, i_2)

Definition (i_1 is before i_2.):

$\forall i_1, i_2$ **Prior**$(i_1, i_2) :\Leftrightarrow$ Meets$(i_1, i_2) \lor$ Before(i_1, i_2)

Definition (Two intervals are disjoint iff they have not any point of time in common.):

Disjoint$(i_1, i_2) :\Leftrightarrow$ Prior$(i_1, i_2) \lor$ Prior(i_2, i_1)

Lemma:

$\cap (i_1, i_2) \neq \emptyset$ iff Disjoint(i_1, i_2)

Definition (The interval i covers a set of intervals I.):

Cover: $2^{\text{INTERVALS}}$ x INTERVALS ——> {T, F}.

Cover$(I, i) :\Leftrightarrow \forall ix \in I$ (In$(ix, i) \wedge \exists iy \in I$ Begin=(i, iy)

$$\wedge \exists iz \in I \text{ Ends}=(i, iz))$$

Convention: Interval relations will sometimes be directly applied to actions. In this case, the relation is between the time of the actions, e.g. Before(a_1, a_2) is an abbreviation of Before(time(a_1), time(a_2)).

3.4 Plans

The agents' activities are based on plans. Although we are not concerned with planning per se, we need a notion of planning, i.e. questions of interest are: What is a plan, how can agents develop their plans and what domain knowledge is assumed for planning? This information is not only necessary for understanding the agents' planning process but also plays an important role for the coordination process, because coordination entails re-planning and plan modification.

3.4.1 Plan Structure

A plan consists of a set of actions and a relation between these actions.

Definition (plan):

A **plan** is a pair $p = (A, SUB)$, $SUB \subseteq A \times A$.

SUB reflects the current state of a plan in terms of what refinements have been made so far. SUB contains ordered pairs of actions, where the second action is an element of a set of actions which has been used to refine the first action. A pair of actions $(a_1, a_2) \in SUB$ can be read as "the action denoted by a_2 is a subaction of a_1 within the plan p". Subrelations develop dynamically during plan generation and coordination.

An action may be refined by a number of finer grained actions which describe an action in more detail. The process of creating subrelations is called *plan refinement*. Sub(a_1, a_2, p) means that

a_2 has been generated by the expansion (refinement) of a_1. We will introduce a predicate Sub to denote the subrelations.

Definition (subrelations):
 Sub$(a_1, a_2, p) :\Leftrightarrow p = (A, SUB) \wedge a_1, a_2 \in A \wedge (a_1, a_2) \in SUB$

The structure of a plan can be visualized as a directed graph with root node p. The root's successor nodes are the most abstract actions in the plan. The leaf nodes represent the most operational actions.

We will sometimes use a somewhat sloppy notation "$a \in p$" to denote that a belongs to the action set A of p: Let $p = (A, SUB)$. $a \in p :\Leftrightarrow a \in A$. In a similar way, we will use other set operations for plans.

Axiom: All actions in a plan have the same planning agent.
$\forall a_1, a_2 \in p$: planner$(a_1) =$ planner(a_2)

The Cover relation is used to describe the time interval of a plan.

Definition (interval of a plan):
time: PLANS ——> INTERVALS
time$(p) = i_1$ with **Cover**$(\{i | i = time(a), a \in p\}, i_1)$

The following recursive definition expresses that an action a_2 is either a direct subaction of an action a_1 or a succeeding descendant of a_2, i.e. there exists a series of refinements of a_2 where one contains a_1.

Definition:
Sub+$(a_1, a_2, p) :\Leftrightarrow$ Sub$(a_1, a_2, p) \vee \exists a_3$ (Sub$(a_3, a_2, p) \wedge$ Sub+(a_1, a_3, p)).

The relation Sub*(a, A, p) is true iff A is the set of all subactions of an action a at lower levels within a plan p. A is the set of all subactions (recursively applied) of a.

Definition (all subactions):

$\text{Sub*}(a, A, p) :\Leftrightarrow \forall a_1 \text{ Sub+}(a, a_1, p) \Leftrightarrow a_1 \in A.$

The inverse relationship of Sub, namely "a_2 is a superaction of a_1 within the plan p", is defined as follows:

Definition (inverse of sub):

$\text{Super}(a_1, a_2, p) :\Leftrightarrow \text{Sub}(a_2, a_1, p).$

The predicates super and sub describe relations between actions of a single plan in a *vertical* direction. A subaction gives a more detailed description of its superaction, i.e. on a lower level of abstraction.

For a given plan (= state of planning) a *leaf* action is an action without any subaction.

Definition:

$\text{Leaf}(a, p) :\Leftrightarrow \forall a_1 \neg \text{ Sub}(a, a_1, p).$

Leaf actions are the currently "most operational" actions of a plan. The super actions of leaf actions have only statistical functions in that they reflect the plan development (refinement) process.

The concept of plan refinement is analogous to the concept of hierarchical planning. Plan refinement and sub relations constitute a hierarchy of action representations in which the highest level is a simplification, or abstraction, of the plan and the lowest level is a detailed, operational plan.

In contrast to traditional AI planners there is not necessarily a sequential or partial order between the actions of p. In our approach the relations between actions are defined as temporal constraints. Temporal constraints are expressed using the interval relations as defined in Section 3.3.

3.4.2 Domain Predicates

In environments where autonomous agents dynamically create and execute plans, plan information may be vague and not up-to-date. This means, in terms of plans, that the agents may have developed their plans at different levels of abstraction (detail). Even within each plan, actions may have different degrees of detail. For a coordination process which has to anticipate potentially beneficial or harmful plan interactions, it is necessary to explore how the agents might develop their plans. We have tackled this issue by allowing the agents to broadcast their plans at any time (asynchronously) and at different levels of abstraction. As a consequence, the coordination mechanism has to be supplied with domain knowledge about plans and their refinements.

An agent which wants to detect interactions in advance needs to expand plans. In order to do this the reasoner must have knowledge about actions and their possible refinements in the application domain.

Definition (An action a is an atomic action.):
Atom(a) iff a is at the finest level that is appropriate for the domain. An atomic action can not be refined any more.

Both the predicate Atom and the predicate Leaf express some atomic feature, but the predicate Atom is a domain specific predicate, whereas the predicate Leaf is a predicate local to each plan. An action which is atomic and part of a plan is always a leaf action, as it cannot be refined any more, i.e.

Lemma: $\forall p \; \forall a \in p \; \text{Atom}(a) \Rightarrow \text{Leaf}(a, p)$.

For every action a which is not atomic there exists a set of possible refinements, each of which is a nonempty and finite set of actions $\{a_1,.., a_n\}$, i.e.

$$\forall a \; (\exists A \; \text{Refinement}(a, A) \; \Leftrightarrow \; \neg \text{Atom}(a)).$$

Refinement(a, A) is a *domain specific* predicate. Refinement(a, A) means that a can be refined by the more detailed set of actions A. For a given action a, there may exist a variety of possible refinements Refinement(a, A_1), Refinement(a, A_2), Refinement(a, A_3), etc.

3.4.3 Plan Refinement

It is interesting to see how the domain predicates Atom and Refinement can be applied to plans. An action of an individual plan is refinable to a set of more detailed actions iff the action is a leaf action, i.e. has not yet been refined or a refinement has been withdrawn, and if there exists a refinement relating the action under consideration with these more detailed actions, i.e. for a given action a, a set of actions A_1 and a plan p,

Definition (refinement within plan):
   Refinable$(a, A_1, p) :\Leftrightarrow a \in p \land \text{Leaf}(a, p) \land \text{Refinement}(a, A_1)$.

The execution of a refinement of a plan with a refinable action a is performed by the operator refine(a, A_1).

Let PLANS be the set of all plans ranging over the action set of a given domain, a an action of this action set and it holds Refinement(a, A_1).

Definition (refinement operator):
refine(a, A_1) is a partial mapping from P into P with
refine(a, A_1): PLANS $\longrightarrow$ PLANS and for a given plan $p = (A, SUB)$
refine$(a, A_1)(p) = (A \cup A_1, SUB \cup \{(a,a') \mid a' \in A_1\})$.

Example: With $p = (\{a_1, a_2, a_3\}, \emptyset)$
             refine$(a_1, \{a_4, a_5\})(p) = (\{a_1, a_2, a_3, a_4, a_5\}, \{(a_1, a_4), (a_1, a_5)\})$.

A **current refinement** of an action a within a plan p consists either of all leaf subactions below a or only a, if a is leaf action, and is defined as

Definition (leaf actions below a):

$\text{rm}(a, p) := \{a_1 \mid \text{Sub+}(a, a_1, p) \wedge \text{Leaf}(a_1, p)\} \cup \{a_1 \mid a_1 = a \wedge \text{Leaf}(a_1, p)\}$.

In terms of a plan's tree structure (which has been generated by applying refine operations), this means that $\text{rm}(a, p)$ contains all leafnodes of the subtree below a.

Successive applications of the refinement operator are expressed by relating an original plan and the resulting plan. Let p and p' be two plans, then

Definition (refinement history):

$\text{Refines}(p, p') :\Leftrightarrow \exists\, a_1,...,\, a_n,\, A_1,...,\, A_n,\, p_1...p_{n+1}. p_1 = p,\, p_{n+1} = p' :$
$\qquad \forall\, i = 1,...,n\ p_{i+1} = \text{refine}(a_i, A_i)(p_i)$.

The predicate Refines is reflexive, i.e. $\text{Refines}(p, p)$ is true. In this case, the index n used in the definition is 0.

It is obvious that if this predicate is true, then for all i the refined actions are leaf actions and the applied refinements are defined for the domain, i.e. $\text{Leaf}(a_i, p_i)$ and $\text{Refinement}(a_i, p_i)$, respectively.

Definition (collect the most operational actions in a plan):

leaves: PLANS —> 2^{ACTIONS}

Let $p = (A, SUB)$, then $\text{leaves}(p) = \{a \in A \mid \text{Leaf}(a, p)\}$.

We need to express plan refinements because the (planning) agents may have developed their plans up to different levels of details. That means, the agents' planning processes are *not* synchronized by forcing them to develop their plans up to the same level or describing their plans always at the atomic level. This is an aspect of respecting the autonomy of the agents within the system. As a result, the plans which are received may contain actions at different levels of abstraction. And in order to detect relationships between different plans, which is part of the coordination process, it may become necessary to refine actions.

Refinements and Temporal Constraints

It is reasonable to "enrich" the refinement operator by temporal constraints. In order to do so, Allen's interval relations are useful. This paragraph briefly discusses how plan refinement and temporal information can be blended with each other.

When an action is refined, the temporal relations between the sub-actions may be specified, too. The refinement relations between the actions, i.e.

$\forall$ a if $\neg$Atom(a) then $\exists A_1,..., A_n, A_i \subseteq A, i{\geq}1$ with Refinement$(a, A_1, C_1) \wedge$ Refinement$(a, A_1, C_2) \wedge ...\wedge$ Refinement(a, A_n, C_n). The C_i are sets of interval relations using Allen's terminology.

refine': ACTIONS x ACTION-SET x PLANS x "temporal constraints" —> PLANS

e.g. $p = \{a_1,...,a_3\}$ with leaf$(a_1) = $ T, refine$(a_1, \{a_4, a_5\}, C)$ leads to $p = \{a_1, a_2, a_3\}$ with Sub(a_1, a_4, p) and Sub(a_1, a_5).

Of course, refinement with temporal constraints should also be reflected in the notion of plans, in the sense that temporal relations have to become part of the plan definitions. We will not elaborate on that.

Example: An agent might have the plan to prepare a meal. There are several possibilities to refine (execute) the abstract action buy-vegetables one of which is refine(buy-vegetables, {go-to-market-place, get-carrots-from-dealer1, get-cauliflower-from-dealer2}, {Prior(go-to-market-place, get-carrots-from-dealer1), Prior(go-to-market-place, get-cauliflower-from-dealer2), Equal(get-carrots-from-dealer1, get-cauliflower-from-dealer2)}, plan-for-preparing-meal).

Question: How is temporal data on interval and duration propagated at plan refinement? For every action a there exists a set of possible refinements, each of which is a set of actions $\{a_1,..., a_n\}$. When an action a is refined to $\{a_1,.., a_n\}$, the temporal information is propagated as follows:

$$\forall\, i \in \{1,..,n\}\ \text{time}(a_i) = \text{time}(a).$$

This is the default value which may be modified again. The values are bounds for the subactions' intervals: the startpoint is greater or equal to i_1 and the endpoint is less or equal to i_2.

The following computes the overall duration from the durations of the subactions.

$$\text{dur}(a)= \sum_{i=1}^{n}\text{dur}(a_i).$$

Furthermore, there is a set of constraints which describe the temporal relations, e.g. $\{$Before(a_2, a_3), Meets$(a_4, a_6)\}$. Actions, for which no constraint is specified may be executed concurrently.

Two actions a_1 and a_2 can be executed concurrently (they are *concurrent*), if there are no restrictions concerning the order of their execution.

Resource requirements may not be defined for all abstract actions. An action a is *abstract* iff $\neg$Atom(a). But they are definitely known for atomic actions. The following constraint describes the resource requirements of a refined action:

Axiom: Resources for a refined action $a \in p$, $\text{res}(a) = \bigcup_{\{ai \mid \text{Sub}(a, ai, p)\}} \text{res}(a_i)$.

3.4.4 Coordination Input

What information about their intended actions (plans) do agents convey to each other?
The agents are not forced to synchronize their planning processes by developing their plans up to the same level or describing their plans always at the atomic level. Therefore, we need to express plan refinement because the planning agents may have developed their plans up to different levels of detail. This is an aspect of respecting the autonomy of the agents within the system. The agents might not want to plan their activities in extensive detail in advance. Often, the details will be planned shortly before execution. As a result, the plans which are received may contain actions at different levels of abstraction. And in order to detect relationships between different plans, which is part of the coordination process, it may become necessary to refine actions.

We assume that when agents broadcast their intentions, they transmit only the leaf actions of their plans. This assumption is reasonable because the agents may have eliminated or do not want to reveal (privacy reasons) the history of their plan development. The history of plan development is reflected in a plan's substructure and is suppressed if only the leaf actions are conveyed.

Example: An agent has a plan p as shown in Fig. 5. But the individual plan, which is conveyed to the other agent(s), consists only of the most operational actions, i.e. $p = (A, SUB)$ with $A = \{a_3, a_5, a_6, a_7, a_8, a_9, a_{11}, a_{12}, a_{13}, a_{14}\}$ and $SUB = \varnothing$.

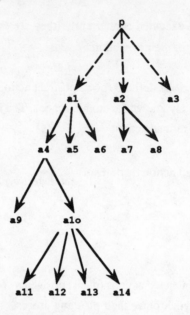

Figure 5: A hierarchically structured plan

We will call a plan which has been created by one autonomous agent an **individual plan.** The common feature of the actions in an individual plan p is that they have the same planning agent planner(p), i.e. $\forall a_1, a_2 \in p$: planner(a_1) = planner(a_2).

3.4.5 No Explicit Notion of Goals

The reader may miss a definition of goals for planning. We have omitted this in our work for the following reasons:

- *No state-based representation.* Usually, i.e. in standard AI planning, a goal is a description of the world state, which should be achieved if the plan has been executed. This interpretation of a goal is more adequate in a planning approach which is based on the state based world model and not so useful for the event based approach which we pursue.

- *Coordination versus Planning*. For the coordination of plans goals can be more easily "skipped" than for planning, because planning can be seen as a mapping from goals to actions whereas coordination is rather a mapping from plans to a "coordinated" set of plans (see also discussion in Section 2.2.3).

- *Abstract actions as goals*. Abstract actions describe very generally what an agent wants to achieve, e.g. to build a house. In this sense, abstract actions can be interpreted as goals, which can be accomplished by refining them to the atomic level and then executing them. Subactions of abstract actions resemble subgoals. Thus, in fact, abstract actions represent an indirect concept for goals.

- *The agents' privacy*. Although it might be helpful for coordination if the agents know of each other's goals, this opposes the agents privacy and autonomy. Each agent knows of course his own goals and has these goals in mind when negotiating about plan synchronization, but he might not exhibit his goals to the other agents.

- *No "traditional" plan structure*. Our concept of a plan deviates from the concept of plans in traditional AI contexts, where a plan contains all the actions which are necessary to achieve the goals of that plan. We rather comprehend a plan as a collection of actions, which will be executed during a certain time period, i.e. a temporal unit is the binding factor for the actions of our plans and not the goals behind them. Thus, a plan in our sense may contain a variety of actions which may actually be part of several "traditional" planners with several goals.

Summary. In this chapter, we have developed a model of actions and plans in multiagent domains and have indicated how individual planning can be done. The concept for plans and actions presented here is not intended to be the basis for a pure planning process, but rather for the *coordination* of diverse plans (see discussion in Section 2.2.3).

Essential features of our model include the ability to deal with concurrent actions, temporal constraints, multiple agents, and plans with varying accuracy. Our concept of plans deviates in some points from the "usual" AI understanding of plans in that we use an event-based notion of actions and we dodge an explicit notion of goals.

The notions of actions and plans are used in the next chapter to identify interactions between different agents' plans and the modifications with respect to coordinating them.

4 Multiagent Plan Relations

In this chapter, a classification of the possible relations between the plans of agents is established. These relations play an important role for reconciling the plans before execution, and can be used to discover situations with negative interferences between plans or situations which involve chances for beneficial combinations, i.e. where agents can cooperate.

After an extensive example, these relations will be formally introduced and then synthesized to a specification of *coordinated plans*.

The taxonomy of plan relations will comprise both harmful (negative) and favorable (positive) relations. A system which hopes to perform a meaningful coordination of individually created plans has to cover the whole range of interactions that can occur among intelligent agents; the detection of negative relations is crucial to prevent conflicts and the detection of positive relations may help to utilize the favorable potential which can exist among different plans.

Although relations within a single agent plan have been explored in great detail in traditional planning systems (before 1980), they are not applicable in a multiagent setting due to several reasons: first, the world is assumed to be static and only affected by a single agent's actions, and tasks are only carried out by a single agent; second, there is no concept for concurrent activities; third, there is no cooperation and coordination between several agents.

4.1 Example

The following example illustrates some of the relations and their roles for the coordination of plans. This example will be formalized in Section 7.4 using the formal framework of the previous chapter.

For the present purpose, plans are visualized as directed graphs with two types of nodes, which are designated to denote multiagent plans:

- Rectangles model actions. A role can be attached to a rectangle which stands for a class of actors who can carry out the modeled activity. A rectangle can describe an action at different levels of abstraction. A high level action can be expanded into a subnet which describes the modeled action in more detail (action refinement). At the highest level of abstraction an ac-

tion can denote a goal. Temporal constraints for executing an action can appear as inscriptions.
- Circles model resources, conditions and synchronizing states.
- Arcs describe precedence (concerning an action's startpoint) and causal relations between objects and actions.

In our example there are the two agents Art and Bert. Both have created their individual plans and want to execute them on September 25, 1988. These individual plans are communicated. Art's plan contains the following actions (Fig. 6):
- Pick up: Actor is Art. Pick up Mr. Smith (guest) from the main station (and give him a lift to the office). Time: 8:30 a.m., September 25.
- Produce video: Actor is Art. Make a demonstration video (using the only video camera in the office) of a program running on Symbolics LM7. Time: Morning, September 25.
- Make phone call: Actor is Art. Make a phone call to Mr. Blund. Time: Between 10:00 a.m. and 11:00 a.m, Sept. 25.
- Answer mail: Actor is Art. Answer the received mail which is in the mail box. Time: Any time on Sept. 25 after having finished the video film.
- Get stamps: Actor is Art. Buy some commemorative stamps at the post office. Time: During lunch break, Sept. 25.
- Give comment: Actor is Bert. Make comments on Art's demonstration video. Time: Sept 25 and Sept. 26. Thus, Art's plan is a multiagent plan.
- Copy papers: Actor is Art. Make a copy of some papers in the library. Time: Afternoon of Sept. 25 or morning Sept. 26 after answering the mail.

This is Bert's plan (Fig. 6 b):
- Pick up: Actor is Bert. Pick up Mr. Smith (guest) from the main station. Time: At 8:30 a.m..
- Give demo: Actor is Bert. Give a demonstration to Mr. Smith on Symbolics LM7. Time: 9:00 - 10:30 a.m.
- Discuss: Actor is Bert. Discuss with Mr. Smith the software which has just been demonstrated. Time: Until lunch.
- Bring package: Actor is Bert. Bring a package to the post office. Time: during lunch break, Sept. 25.
- Read book: Actor is Bert. Read a book. Time: Afternoon, Sept. 25.

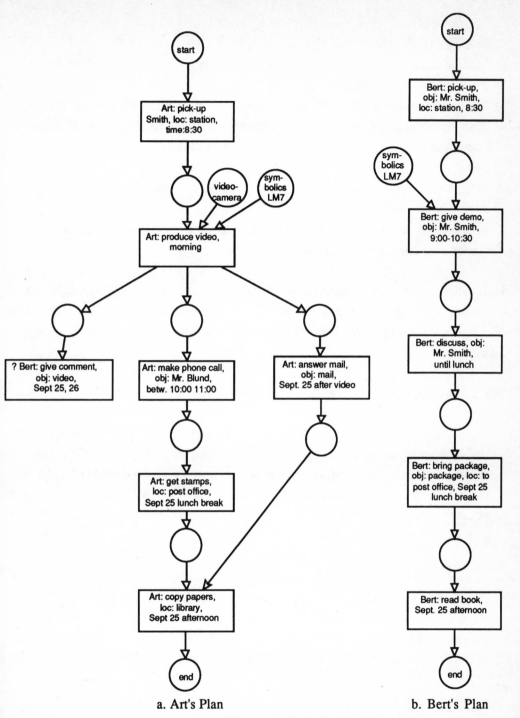

a. Art's Plan

b. Bert's Plan

Figure 6: The individual plans

These are the relations between the two plans (Fig. 7):

— Relation-a (equality): Between Art's "pick up" and Bert's "pick up": the same result is produced by the same action.

— Relation-b (non consumable resource conflict): Between Art's "produce video" and Bert's
   "give demo" there is a resource conflict because of a request for the same nonconsumable
   resource at the same time period. The same resource, namely the Symbolics LM7, is required.

— Relation-c (favor): Between Art's "get stamps" and Bert's "bring package": A beneficial effect can be achieved.

— Relation-d (actor request): Between Art's "give comment" and Bert('s plan): Art requires
   another actor (Bert) for the execution of this action.

Positive relations in this case are relation-a, relation-c and relation-d. A negative relation is relation-b (see Fig. 7). It is the agents' task to detect the various relations described above. After
detection they will propose resolutions for negative interactions or to take advantage of positive
interactions.

What are the measures that will be taken to deal with the relations?

- Relation-a: As both workers want to do the same action to achieve the same result, i.e. have
   the same goals, one person can erase this action from his plan because it is redundant.
   Which agent erases the action can be dependent on when the agents wants to do this action,
   at what time the result of the action is needed, or which agent has the most workload and
   wants to be relieved of some of his work. The agents negotiate on the basis of these factors
   and agree that Art will do the action and Bert is relieved from it.

- Relation-b: Both plans require the same resource at the same time period. During compile
   time there is no decision made which agent has priority over the resource. As it is a non
   consumable resource, a critical region construct is inserted to resolve the conflict during
   plan execution. In this situation other measures are possible, e.g. looking for another
   equivalent resource or asking an agent to modify his plan.

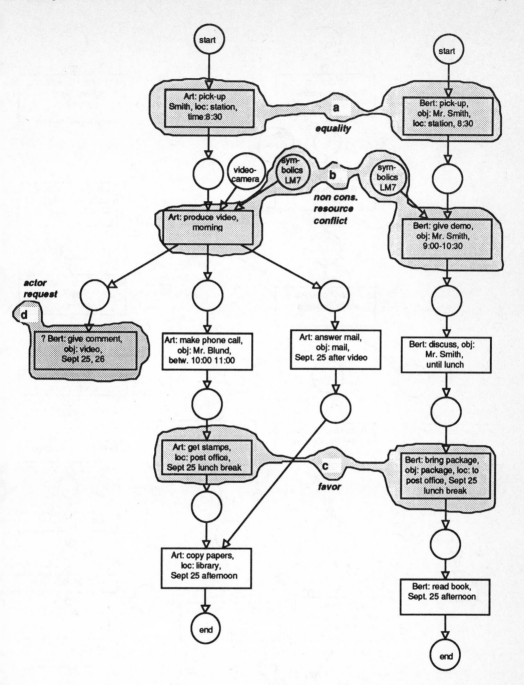

Figure 7: The relations between the individual plans

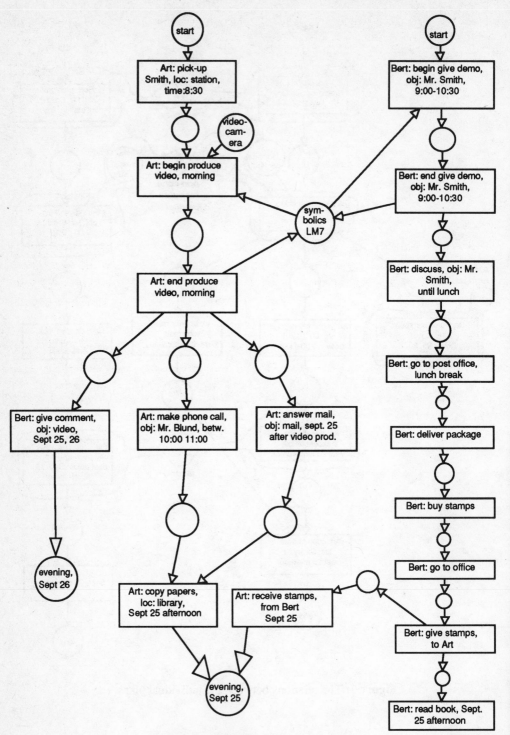

Figure 8: Resulting reconciled plans

- Relation-c: In this case a beneficial effect can be achieved for Art or Bert as both have a job to do at the post office at the same time. Thus, it is sufficient for only one person to go to the post office. The agents recognize this. To handle a package is physically more expensive than to get stamps. In this case, Art proposes plan modifications which are for his benefit. Finally, Bert's action "bring package" is replaced by the following sequence of more detailed activities:
  - "go to the post office"
  - "deliver package". He delivers the package at the proper counter.
  - "buy stamps". He buys stamps for Art.
  - "go to office". He goes back to his office.
  - "give stamps". He gives the stamps to Art.

  On the other hand, Art has to modify his plan only slightly. Instead of going to the post office and buying the stamps he only has to "receive stamps" from Bert. Art and Bert utilize the beneficial potential between their intentions and agree to the proposed plan modifications.

- Relation-d: Active cooperation is directly requested. It is necessary that Bert agrees to do the action during the time at which Art would like it to be carried out. Art asks Bert whether this is agreeable for him. Bert agrees and thus makes a commitment to support Art's plan.

The global plan resulting from the coordination process is illustrated in Fig. 8.

4.2 Negative Relations

Negative plan relations are all those relations between plans, which may prevent one or both of the plans from being executed as intended. They may involve an incompatible step order or incompatible resource usage. The detection of negative relations is crucial for successful plan execution. Negative relations can be classified by whether their origin is a resource (physical) or an incompatible situation (logical).

A taxonomy of the relations among different agents' plans covering both negative and positive relations is shown in Fig. 9.

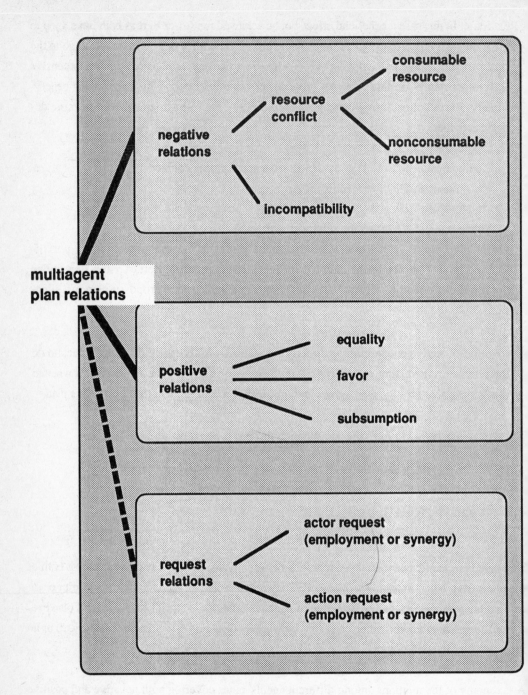

Figure 9: Taxonomy of plan relations

Resource Induced Conflicts

Coherence and coordination in a DAI system are endangered when agents intend to allocate scarce resources. Plans are in a resource driven negative relation if they require more from the same resource than is available at the required time. A resource can be any object which is needed to perform a plan. The prerequisites for a resource to be involved in a conflict are that it is limited and sharable. Resource conflicts between multiagent plans can occur only if a restricted resource is needed by several agents at the same time. Thus, it is important to reason about the time requirement for a resource to ascertain whether there is a potential resource conflict. For instance, access to a nonconsumable resource means no conflict, if the time periods for utilizing this resource do not overlap.

The resource requirements of an action are expressed in terms of res and amount, which were introduced in Section 3.2. Here, only the basic definitions will be given. Concrete examples of conflicts and their resolution can be found in Section 5.1.

Definition (resource availability):

available$(r, i) \in \mathbb{R}^+$ denotes the amount of resource r available during the interval i.

Two classes of resources are recognized: consumable and nonconsumable resources. Requirements for consumable resources are likely to cause a conflict when the amount of the resource, needed by the agents, exceeds the amount available for the agents. Of course the time period requirements have to be considered.

Definition (consumable resource):

Consumable(r) is true iff the resource r is consumable. A resource is consumable if its availability decreases after it has been used in a plan.

The usability of a nonconsumable resource for an agent is limited by its capacity. A nonconsumable resource is likely to cause a conflict if it is required beyond its availability over a fixed period of time.

Definition:

Nonconsumable(r) is true iff the availability of resource r does not change after it has been used in a plan.

Definition (resource deficit):

$Deficit(r, i, A) :\Leftrightarrow (\sum_{\{a \in A | time(a) \cap i \neq \emptyset\}} amount(r,a) > available(r, i))$

A resource conflict between two actions a_1 and a_2 competing for the same nonconsumable resource r is defined as follows.

Definition (nonconsumable resource conflict between two actions):

$Ncrc(a_1, a_2) :\Leftrightarrow time(a_1) \cap time(a_2) \neq \emptyset$

$\qquad \wedge \exists r\, Nonconsumable(r)\, (r \in res(a_1) \wedge r \in res(a_2)$

$\qquad \wedge \neg\, Deficit(r, time(a_1), \{a_1\})$; i.e. each individual action does not

$\qquad \wedge \neg\, Deficit(r, time(a_2), \{a_2\})$; exceed the amount of available resources

$\qquad \wedge Deficit(r, time(a_1) \cap time(a_2), \{a_1, a_2\}))$

Possible versus Sure (inevitable) Plan Relations

We will differentiate between two kinds of plan relations:

1. *Sure relations* between different plans are existent at the current degree of plan refinement or for all possible refinements. A resource *conflict* is sure if no refinement is necessary to detect a conflict. A resource for an abstract action may not be known until this action has been refined and the resource requirements are clear. A *favor* relation is sure if the favor action can be inserted in a plan without having determined a refinement before.

2. A relation is *possible* if its detection is only possible via plan refinement. For instance, a conflict might become possible if an action of a pan is refinable in such a way that a special resource is required, i.e. there is one pair of refinements for the two plans (out of a variety of possibilities) in which the plans contain conflicting actions. However, the action might also be refined in another way with a different resource requirement not leading to a resource conflict.

Based on the conflict definition for two *actions* we want to know if a conflict relation holds for two plans p_1 and p_2.

Definition (potential nonconsumable resource conflict between plans):

pot-Ncrc$(p_1, p_2) :\Leftrightarrow$

$\exists p_1', p_2':$ Refines$(p_1, p_1') \land$ Refines$(p_2, p_2') \land$

$\exists a_1 \in$ leaves$(p_1') \land \exists a_2 \in$ leaves$(p_2') \land$

Ncrc(a_1, a_2)

A conflict is sure if for all refinements there exist two conflicting actions within the plans. This also includes that there are two actions in p_1 and p_2, respectively, which are atomic and for which Ncrc holds.

Definition (sure nonconsumable resource conflict between plans):

sure-Ncrc$(p_1, p_2) :\Leftrightarrow$

$\forall p_1', p_2':$ Refines$(p_1, p_1') \land$ Refines$(p_2, p_2') \land$

$\exists a_1 \in$ leaves$(p_1') \land \exists a_2 \in$ leaves$(p_2') \land$

Ncrc(a_1, a_2)

We will now define conflicts of actions competing for *consumable* resources.

Definition (consumable resource conflict between actions):

Crc$(a_1, a_2) :\Leftrightarrow \exists r$ Consumable(r)

$\land r \in$ res$(a_1) \land r \in$ res(a_2)

$\land \neg$Deficit$(r, \text{time}(a_1), \{a_1\})$

$\land \neg$Deficit$(r, \text{time}(a_2), \{a_2\})$

$\land$ Cover$(\{a_1, a_2\}, i)$

$\land$ Deficit$(r, i, \{a_1, a_2\})$

Definition (sure consumable resource conflict between plans):

sure-Crc$(p_1, p_2) :\Leftrightarrow \forall p_1', p_2':$

Refines$(p_1, p_1') \land$ Refines$(p_2, p_2') \land$

$\exists a_1 \in$ leaves$(p_1') \land \exists a_2 \in$ leaves$(p_2') \land$

Crc(a_1, a_2)

Definition (potential consumable resource conflict between plans):

$\textbf{pot-Crc}(p_1, p_2) :\Leftrightarrow \exists p_1', p_2':$

$\text{Refines}(p_1, p_1') \wedge \text{Refines}(p_2, p_2') \wedge$

$\exists a_1 \in \text{leaves}(p_1') \wedge \exists a_2 \in \text{leaves}(p_2') \wedge$

$\text{Crc}(a_1, a_2)$

Incompatibility

There may be other reasons for conflicts between two actions besides resources. Two actions might require exclusive states to exist; in this case, the actions involved are called incompatible. The detection of mutually exclusive states or incompatible actions can not rely on general detection strategies. Domain specific heuristics are required and the detection of incompatible activities must be based on prespecified axioms which state which actions should not occur simultaneously. For instance there may be laws which rule out that two agents become head of the same institute and other specifications of this kind.

Definition (incompatible actions):

$\textbf{Incomp}(a_1, a_2)$ iff both actions can not be executed together.

This definition will be extended to plans as follows:

Definition (potential incompatibility between plans):

$\textbf{pot-Incomp}(p_1, p_2) :\Leftrightarrow \exists p_1', p_2':$

$\text{Refines}(p_1, p_1') \wedge \text{Refines}(p_2, p_2') \wedge$

$\exists a_1 \in \text{leaves}(p_1') \wedge \exists a_2 \in \text{leaves}(p_2') \wedge$

$\text{Incomp}(a_1, a_2)$

Definition (sure incompatibility between plans):

$\textbf{sure-Incomp}(p_1, p_2) :\Leftrightarrow \forall p_1', p_2':$

$\text{Refines}(p_1, p_1') \wedge \text{Refines}(p_2, p_2') \wedge$

$\exists a_1 \in \text{leaves}(p_1') \wedge \exists a_2 \in \text{leaves}(p_2') \wedge$

$\text{Incomp}(a_1, a_2)$

4.3 Positive Relations

An aspect which has been greatly neglected is the potential benefit of *positive relations* between plans of different agents. Positive relations are all those relations between two plans from which some benefit can be derived if they are combined. They allow for the production of a more efficient overall plan. There could be an action in one agent's plan which supports another agent's subgoal or an action might even accomplish this goal. In these cases the plans, of the involved agents, can be changed to employ this beneficial relation. In contrast to the detection and prevention of negative interactions the detection and utilization of positive interactions among plans may not be necessary, but can contribute greatly to the efficiency and output of the overall system behavior. The utilization of positive interactions can be seen as optimizing the plans with respect to their combined cost and efficiency. Strategies for the utilization of beneficial relations depend on the degree of benevolence of the agents towards each other. If the agents are adversaries utilization is hard to achieve.

In case of the positive relations, the beneficial relation is contained implicitly in the plans and a beneficial effect can be achieved by combining two plans. For instance, by chance, a single plan can simultaneously fulfill the goals of several plans or it may do so after some minor adjustment. We will distinguish between three types of (nonrequested) beneficial relations: equality, subsumption and favor.

4.3.1 Equality

Equality of actions is only meaningful for plan coordination if the actions under consideration can also be executed by another agent, i.e. the executor of an action can be exchanged.
An example, which shows what we have in mind is the following: If two agents both happen to have the plan of going from Cologne to Paris and if in both cases the goals dominating these plans are to be in Paris to propose a marriage to Cecile, an equality in the sense that one agent can do the same action *instead* of the other agent, namely to propose a marriage, should not be recognized. On the other hand, if the dominating goals are to deliver a couple of packages, and if the two planners have a cordial relation, a more efficient plan may be worked out using the

equality relation between the two plans. To recognize the desired kind of equality, the following definition seems reasonable:

Definition:
Exchangeable-agent(a) iff the executing agent of action a can be substituted by another agent.

Instead of just having one notion such as Exchangeable-agent, it is possible to incorporate a more fine grained concept of agents and their ability, skill, will and "substitutability" to execute an action. In order to do this we need predicates about the agents themselves, as opposed to our general predicates about actions. But we will not elaborate this.

If two agents happen to have planned the same action in their individual plans only one agent has to carry out the action.

Definition (equality between actions/across plan boundaries):
Equal$(a_1, a_2) :\Leftrightarrow$ Exchangeable-agent$(a_1) \wedge a_1 = a_2$

The actions' *executor*, *planner* and *time* may be different.

Definition (sure equality between plans):
sure-Equal$(p_1, p_2) :\Leftrightarrow \forall p_1', p_2':$
Refines$(p_1, p_1') \wedge$ Refines$(p_2, p_2') \wedge$
$\exists a_1 \in$ leaves$(p_1') \wedge \exists a_2 \in$ leaves$(p_2') \wedge$
Equal(a_1, a_2)

Definition (potential equality between plans):
pot-Equal$(p_1, p_2) :\Leftrightarrow \exists p_1', p_2':$
Refines$(p_1, p_1') \wedge$ Refines$(p_2, p_2') \wedge$
$\exists a_1 \in$ leaves$(p_1') \wedge \exists a_2 \in$ leaves$(p_2') \wedge$
Equal(a_1, a_2)

When we recall that abstract actions can also be interpreted as goals which will be achieved by more finegrained actions, equality on a higher than atom level is equality of goals rather than of actions. In this case, the planners have similar or even the same goals.

4.3.2 Subsumption

The actions of an individual plan implies the accomplishment of another individual plan's action. Or one action can be seen as an instance of a more abstract higher level action. If one action is subsumed by another action, just the subsuming action has to be executed.

An action a_2 is subsumed by another action a_1 if a_2 can become part of a_1's refinement, i.e. there exists a refinement of a_1 such that a_2 is an element of this refinement.

Definition (subsumption, action a_1 subsumes action a_2.):
Subsume$(a_1, a_2) :\Leftrightarrow \exists p_2$ (Refines($\{a_1\}, \emptyset), p_2) \wedge a_2 \in$ leaves(p_2))

Definition (sure subsumption between plans):
sure-Subsume$(p_1, p_2) :\Leftrightarrow \forall p_1', p_2'$:
Refines$(p_1, p_1') \wedge$ Refines$(p_2, p_2') \wedge$
$\exists a_1 \in$ leaves$(p_1') \wedge \exists a_2 \in$ leaves$(p_2') \wedge$
Subsume(a_1, a_2)

Definition (potential subsumption between plans):
pot-Subsume$(p_1, p_2) :\Leftrightarrow \exists p_1', p_2'$:
Refines$(p_1, p_1') \wedge$ Refines$(p_2, p_2') \wedge$
$\exists a_1 \in$ leaves$(p_1') \wedge \exists a_2 \in$ leaves$(p_2') \wedge$
Subsume(a_1, a_2)

4.3.3 Favor

The favor relation covers an interesting, and usually neglected aspect of distributed problem solving and planning. The favor relation does *not* mean that an agent is requested to construct a plan to fulfill another agent's goal or that some task is delegated. The favor relation also does not mean that an agent *happens* to fulfill the goal of another agent. It also differs from approaches to coordinate activities by announcing tasks, posting bids for the announced tasks and then contracting out the execution of tasks [Davis and Smith 83; Smith 80; Smith and Davis 81]. The favor relation can be used as a trigger to coordinate activities in situations which differ from the ones just mentioned. It is useful in situations in which existing preformed plans have to be adjusted, presumably only slightly, to contribute to each other's plans.

A favor relation between two different agents' plans includes that one agent's plan can contribute helpfully to the other agent's plan. The utilization of a favor relation should only require minor modifications of the two plans involved, i.e. a favor should fit within the framework of the existing plans of the agents.

Plans are preformed by autonomous agents and the favor act must either fit within the structure of existing plans or the plans are refinable in such a way that a favor action is possible. Instead of constructing a completely new plan with the goal of doing someone else a favor, an existing plan is modified to include a favor action.

A *favor action* is an action which is done as a favor.

Definition (favor action):
Fv-action(a) denotes that a is suited as a favor action. a is an action that can be executed by both agents involved in a favorable relation. A favor action is an action on which an agent does not insist to execute it by himself or is even pleased if it were executed by another.

Discussion. For special domains it may be desirable to have a more fine grained concept to express whether an action qualifies as favor action or not. For instance, there might be a predicate *Executable-by(a,g)* for a favor action a, which says, that an action is only suitable as a favor action if this action can be executed by the supporting agent. This may bring up the need to model agents with *intentions*, *roles* and *capabilities*, e.g. a potentially *giving* agent might execute a favor action only if he is both able (capabilities) and willing to do it and if he is in the position (role) to execute it. On the other hand, the *receiving* agent may only be willing to accept the favor if the giving agent meets some requirements. We will not explore these aspects here in more detail.

In a different approach, where one single intelligent agent constructs a plan to be carried out by a group of agents, it is more important that a centralized agent knows about availabilities and capabilities of the agents, [Morgenstern 86, 87; Rosenschein 82; Stuart 85]. There is other research where reasoning about agents' beliefs and intentions is more relevant, e.g. in [Cohen and Levesque 87; Moore 88], than in our work, where agents are rather interested in reasoning about the possible effects of external plans on local plans.

We are now ready to define the favor relation. The domain is characterized by a finite set of actions A, the possible plans P over A, the agents G, and the predicates Atom, Refinement, Fv-action and Pre.

Consider a situation with two agents from G with individual plans $p_1, p_2 \in P$. The favor relation, expressing that "a favor of agent(p_1) for agent(p_2) is possible", is defined as follows:

Definition (favor relation):

Favor$(p_1, p_2):\Leftrightarrow \exists p_1', p_2':$

Refines$(p_1, p_1') \wedge$ Refines$(p_2, p_2') \wedge$

$\exists a \in$ leaves(p_2') Fv-action$(a) \wedge$

    (i) $(\exists A1 \subseteq$ leaves$(p_1') \wedge$ Pre$(a, A1))$

  $\vee$ (ii) $(\exists A2\ A2 \cap$ leaves$(p_1') = \emptyset \wedge \forall a_1 \in A2\ \exists A3 \subseteq$ leaves(p_1') Pre$(a_1, A3)$

               $\wedge\ \exists A4 \subseteq A2 \cup$leaves$(p_1') \wedge$ Pre$(a, A4)\ )$

In English: A favor of agent(p_1) for agent(p_2) is possible iff the plans can be refined to p_1' and p_2', respectively, such that p_2' contains an action a which is suited as favor action and after executing a part of his plan ($A1$ case (i) or $A4$ case (ii)), agent(p_1) will be in a state to execute an action, namely a, which agent(p_2) probably needs to do, and would be pleased if he could be relieved of it.

According to the definition there are two alternatives for adding a favor action ("doing a favor"), if need be after refinement:

(i) directly: a can be added to p_1', because a preparing action set exists, or

(ii) indirectly: an additional set of actions $A2$ can be added to p_1', and this set together with the leaf actions of p_1' contains a preparing action set for the favor action a.

The above-mentioned definition differentiates between two cases of deriving a favor relation. It is useful to make the difference between these cases explicit because they embody two "degrees" of a favor, namely whether additional actions have to be included or not. Actually, case (i) can be obtained by setting $A2 = \emptyset$ in the second case, which leads to a simplified definition of the favor relation:

Definition (favor relation, compact form):

Favor$(p_1, p_2):\Leftrightarrow \exists p_1', p_2':$

Refines$(p_1, p_1') \wedge$ Refines$(p_2, p_2') \wedge \exists a \in$ leaves(p_2') Fv-action$(a) \wedge$

$(\exists A2 \; A2 \cap$ leaves$(p_1') = \emptyset \wedge \forall a_1 \in A2 \; \exists A3 \subseteq$ leaves(p_1') Pre$(a_1, A3)$

$\wedge \; \exists A4 \subseteq A2 \cup$ leaves$(p_1') \wedge$ Pre$(a, A4)$)

Chapter 5 contains elaborated examples for the exploitation of the favor relation and Chapter 8 shows an implemented example.

4.4 Request Relations

The relations considered so far are always relations between actions. In this paragraph, we express relations between agents, or, more precisely, between an agent who plans an action and an agent who executes an action.

Although one may see *request relations* as mere communicative acts which should be treated as usual *message types*[1], we have decided to put the request relations as part of the multiagent plan relations rather than part of the communication framework. Request relations express the desire of an agent to let another agent participate in his plan, and this entails that the participating agent might have to change his plan, i.e. a request affects another agent's plan and thus belongs to the multiagent plan relation taxonomy. As in the case of negative and positive relations, request relations require a negotiation between the involved agents in order to reach a commitment.

In the case of a request driven positive relation the planner asks for support concerning the execution of its plan. We differentiate between the request for the execution of activities without a specified actor and for an action with a dedicated actor.

---

[1] Message types will be handled in detail in Chapter 6.

Actor Request. An *actor request* is due to the fact that a plan can be executed by several actors. An agent asks for the assistance or participation of another dedicated agent in its plan, i.e. the support of another agent is explicitly mentioned in the agent's plan (multiagent planning).

Definition (actor request: agent g_1 wants g_2 to execute action a):

$\mathbf{Rreq}(a, g_1, g_2) :\Leftrightarrow$

$\qquad g_1 \neq g_2$

$\qquad \wedge g_1 = \mathrm{planner}(a)$; g_1 is the planning ("requesting") agent

$\qquad \wedge g_2 = \mathrm{executor}(a)$

Action Request. The agent wants an action to be executed by another unspecified agent.

Definition (action request):

$\mathbf{Nreq}(a, g) :\Leftrightarrow$

$\qquad \mathrm{planner}(a) = g$

$\qquad \wedge \mathrm{executor}(a) = "?"$; "?" means "is requested"

4.5 Coordinated Plans

When will plans be called "coordinated"? We are now ready to give a formal answer to this question.

The aim of plan coordination is to work towards plans that do not conflict (harmful interactions) and among which chances for beneficial activities are not neglected (beneficial interactions). We will introduce some notions to characterize negative and positive relations between plans.

Definition (Two actions a_1 and a_2 with $\mathrm{planner}(a_1) \neq \mathrm{planner}(a_2)$ have a *negative relation*.):

$\mathbf{Negative}(a_1, a_2) :\Leftrightarrow \mathrm{Crc}(a_1, a_2) \vee \mathrm{Ncrc}(a_1, a_2) \vee \mathrm{Incomp}(a_1, a_2)$

This definition will be extended to two plans p_1 and p_2 with $\mathrm{planner}(p_1) \neq \mathrm{planner}(p_2)$:

Definition (negative relation between plans):

Negative(p_1, p_2) :$\Leftrightarrow$ $\exists p_1', p_2'$:

Refines$(p_1, p_1') \wedge$ Refines$(p_2, p_2') \wedge \exists a_1 \in p_1'$, $a_2 \in p_2'$ Negative(a_1, a_2)

Definition (Two actions a_1 and a_2 with planner$(p_1) \neq$ planner(p_2) have a *positive relation.*):

Positive(a_1, a_2) :$\Leftrightarrow$

Equal$(a_1, a_2) \vee$ Subsume$(a_1, a_2) \vee$ Favor$((\{a_1\}, \emptyset), (\{a_2\}, \emptyset))$

For two plans p_1 and p_2 with planner$(p_1) \neq$ planner(p_2).

Definition:

Positive(p_1, p_2) :$\Leftrightarrow$ $\exists p_1', p_2'$:

Refines$(p_1, p_1') \wedge$ Refines$(p_2, p_2') \wedge \exists a_1 \in p_1$, $a_2 \in p_2$ Positive(a_1, a_2)

Two plans p_1 and p_2 with planner$(p_1) \neq$ planner(p_2) are *unrelated* (interference free) iff neither negative nor positive relations exist between them.

Definition (interference free plans):

Unrelated(p_1, p_2) :$\Leftrightarrow$ $\neg$Negative$(p_1, p_2) \wedge \neg$Positive(p_1, p_2)

Definition (A set of individual plans is jointly executable if there are no negative relations between any pairs of plans.):

Let $P = \{p_1,..., p_n\}$ be a set of plans with a pairwise different set of planning agents. All p_i are individually correct (executable, i.e. if only a single plan were executed. see definition in 3.6.). Then

Executable(P) :$\Leftrightarrow$ $\forall p_i, p_j \in P$, $i \neq j$: $\neg$Negative(p_i, p_j).

If a set of plans P is not executable, i.e. $\neg$Executable(P), this does not necessarily mean that *all* plans in P are not executable. All plans together are not executable, i.e. there is at least one action in one plan which cannot be executed if the agents try to execute their plans.

We also need a notion for the fact that a set of plans cannot be improved any more by exploiting a positive relation.

Definition (A set of individual plans is *in concord* with each other (not improvable) if there are no positive relations among them.):

Let $P = \{p_1,..., p_n\}$ be a set of plans with a pairwise different set of planning agents.

In-concord$(P) :\Leftrightarrow \forall p_i, p_j \in P, i \neq j:\ \neg Positive(p_i, p_j)$.

A set of plans is coordinated if all plans are executable, i.e. conflicts are prevented, and the favorable potential between the plans is completely utilized. The latter means, that if there are positive relations between plans, they are resolved (exploited).

Definition (A set of plans is coordinated.):

Let $P = \{p_1,..., p_n\}$ be a set of plans with a pairwise different set of planning agents.

Coordinated$(P) :\Leftrightarrow$ Executable$(P) \wedge$ In-concord(P).

The *relation detection problem* is to detect positive and negative relations between the plans. The plan coordination problem has as input a set of uncoordinated plans. A *solution* is a modified set of plans which is coordinated.

In the following chapter we will explore how plans can be coordinated.

5 Handling Plan Relations

How can plans be coordinated? By taking care of plan relations. Multiagent plan relations imply a modification of the agents' plans. In case of conflicts, relations are handled by resolving the conflict, and in case of favor, the relation is handled by utilizing the beneficial potential.

This chapter deals with the handling of plan relations. We will present
- operations for relation resolution and usage, i.e. for plan coordination,
- strategies (heuristics) for applying these coordination operations, and
- examples for coordination in several domains.

Aspects of *communication* for plan coordination will be the issue of Chapter 6.

The first part of this chapter considers negative plan relations and the second part treats the resolution of positive relations, namely the *favor relation*. Finally, an overview of the plan modification operators is given.

5.1 Resolving Conflicts

Regulating the use of sparse resources is an important item when striving for coherence and co-ordination in a DAI system.

The following questions emerge when dealing with the resolution of resource conflicts:
1. What are possible resolutions of conflicts?
2. In which "conflict situation" is which solution appropriate? Usually, there are several alternatives for conflict resolution.
3. In which order will conflicts be solved, if there exist several conflicts between plans?

Only the *sure* type of conflicts (see Section 4.2), i.e. inevitably menacing conflicts, will be considered. A *potential* conflict (pot-Ncrc, pot-Crc) may also be prevented by selecting a different refinement.

We propose strategies for conflict resolution (questions two and three) which exploit *temporal knowledge* about actions: the temporal relations between conflicting actions, absolute temporal information, and information about the type and amount of resource requirements.

5.1.1 Plan Modifications

A sure nonconsumable resource conflict between two actions a_1 and a_2, Ncrc(a_1, a_2) concerning a resource r, can be resolved by making one of the conflict definition's antecedents invalid. However, there is the exception that a conflict is not solved if one or both of the agents increase the amount of resources required such that Deficit$(r, \text{time}(a), \{a\})$, $a \in \{a_1, a_2\}$. Furthermore, we assume that it is not under the conflicting agents' control to increase the amount of available resources, which means that the value of Available$(r, \text{time}(a_1) \cap \text{time}(a_2))$ is fixed.

We differentiate between two kinds of approaches for conflict resolution: *temporal* solutions and *resource* solutions. The alternatives to eliminate menacing conflicts are shown in Fig. 10.

In case of a consumable resource conflict, only resource solutions are applicable. For instance, whereas in a *non*consumable resource conflict an agent may postpone his action until another agent has released the desired resource, it does not make any sense to wait for a *consumable* resource, because this is per definition not existent after an agent has used it.

Temporal conflict resolution. In a *temporal* solution one or both of the intervals associated with the conflicting actions are modified such that $\text{time}(a_1) \cap \text{time}(a_2) = \emptyset$.
A temporal conflict solution can be achieved by either shifting the intervals of the conflicting actions (spread actions) or by shrinking one or both of the intervals (reduce intervals).

If the operator *spread* is applied to actions a_1 and a_2, a_1 will start d_1 time units earlier than intended and a_2 will start d_2 time units later than intended. A *spread* of two actions a_1 and a_2 is performed by shifting a_1 and a_2 in opposite directions. The shift operation will be defined now.

Let $\mathbb{P}$ be the set of all plans ranging over the action set of a given domain, $p = (A, SUB)$, a an action of the actions set, $a \in A$, d a real number. Depending on the intended direction of the shift, d is either negative or positive.

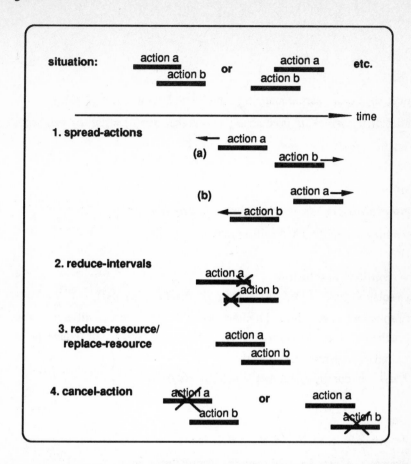

Figure 10: Conflict resolution operations and their effects on temporal relations

Definition:

shift-interval$(a, d): \mathbb{P} \longrightarrow \mathbb{P}$

shift-interval(a, d) is a partial mapping from $\mathbb{P}$ into $\mathbb{P}$ with

shift-interval$(a, d)(p) = p'$, p' is equal to p except that start$(a):=$start$(a)+d$ and end$(a):=$end$(a)+d$.

Definition:

spread(a_1, d_1, a_2, d_2) with $a_1 \in p_1$ and $a_2 \in p_2$

$\Leftrightarrow$ shift-interval$(a_1, d_1)(p_1)$ and shift-interval$(a_2, d_2)(p_2)$

Reduce-intervals is performed by cutting the intervals from both ends. Let $p= (A, SUB)$, a an action in A, d_1, d_2 positive real numbers.

Definition:

shift-point(a, d_1, d_2): $\mathbb{P} \longrightarrow \mathbb{P}$

shift-point(a, d_1, d_2) is a partial mapping from $\mathbb{P}$ into $\mathbb{P}$ with

shift-point$(a, d_1, d_2)(p)= p'$, p' is equal to p except that start$(a):=$ start$(a) + d_1$ and

end$(a):=$ end$(a) - d_2$.

Definition:

reduce-intervals$(a_1, d_1, d_2, a_2, d_3, d_4)$ with $a_1 \in p_1$ and $a_2 \in p_2$

$\Leftrightarrow$ shift-point$(a_1, d_1, d_2)(p_1)$ and shift-point$(a_2, d_3, d_4)(p_2)$

Resource conflict resolution.

A *resource* solution yields $\neg$Deficit$(r,$ time$(a_1) \cap$ time$(a_2), \{a_1, a_2\})$.

A resource solution can be achieved if either one of the agents uses a different resource (replace resource) such that $\neg(r \in$ res$(a_1) \wedge r \in$ res$(a_2))$, or if one or both agents reduce the amount of resource required (reduce resource) such that

(amount(r, a_1) + amount$(r, a_2)) \leq$ Available$(r,$ time$(a_1) \cap$ time$(a_2))$.

Definition:

reduce-resource(r, a, n): $\mathbb{P} \longrightarrow \mathbb{P}$

reduce-resource(r, a, n) is a partial mapping from $\mathbb{P}$ into $\mathbb{P}$ with

reduce-resource$(r, a, n)(p) = p'$, p' is equal to p except that amount$(r, a) :=$ amount$(r, a) - n$.

Definition:

replace-resource(a, r, r_1, n): $\mathbb{P} \longrightarrow \mathbb{P}$

replace-resource(a, r, r_1, n) is a partial mapping from $\mathbb{P}$ into $\mathbb{P}$ with

replace-resource$(a, r, r_1, n)(p)= p'$, p' is equal to p except that amount$(r, a_1) := 0$ and

amount$(r_1, a_1) := n$.

A straightforward and inelegant way of removing the cause of a conflict, which is not investigated further, is to cancel one or all conflicting actions.

Definition:

cancel-action*(a, p)*: $\mathbb{P} \longrightarrow \mathbb{P}$

cancel-action*(a, p)* is a partial mapping from $\mathbb{P}$ into $\mathbb{P}$ with

cancel-action*(a, p)(p) = p′, p′ = p\{a}*.

5.1.2 Examples

We will give two examples (scenarios) for conflicts in multiagent domains.

5.1.2.1 "Robber and Cops"

We will use a similar problem as has been originally presented as *pursuit game* by [Benda et al. 86] and has also been used with minor modifications by [Gasser et al. 89] and [Stephens and Merx 89].

In this domain, there are five agents, one *robber* and four *cops*, which are placed in a rectangular grid spanning *x-max* horizontal by *y-max* vertical units. The agents may move up, down, left or right. The goal of the game is for the cops to capture the robber by occupying the four capture positions surrounding the robber's current location. The capture positions, always measured relative to the robber's location, are shown in Fig. 11 and are referred to as up, down, left, and right (abbreviated *u, d, l,* and *r,* respectively).

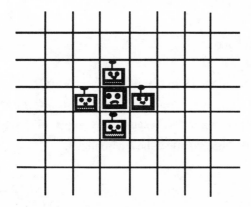

Figure 11: A robber-agent captured by four cop-agents (with antennas)

During a move in this game, each of the five agents may remain at its current position or move one unit in either a horizontal or vertical direction. Cops and robber do not move at the same time, i.e. either the robber moves or the cops move simultaneously. Given these restrictions, the movement of the robber is limited to its current location or any of the unoccupied capture positions surrounding it. The robber's moves are random along these choices.

The goal for a cop is to reach a capturing position. The individual plans are very simple. They consist of only one *action*, namely the next move, which is determined by the following rule:

> If the distance to reach the robber is greater than 1, i.e. the cop is not in a capturing position, move such that the distance is shortened by one.

Of course, there are more complex and more efficient rules feasible. It is not our aim to give an effective way to capture the robber, but to illustrate our terminology. In our approach, the agents' internal behavior is not of concern, but rather their interactions.

In a given situation each cop has an individual *plan* to move to a next location and he conveys his plan (intention) to the other cops. By transmitting these individual plans each agent is aware of the intention of the others and the negotiation procedure is started; The negotiation process is driven by the agents will to prevent conflicting plans. Two agents plans are in a *conflict* if they intend to occupy the same location after their next move. A conflict is resolved, by one of the agent modifying his plan by either moving to an alternative position (*replace-resource*), i.e. an alternative-resource exists if there is a position which will be free and which, in the best case, shortens the distance to the robber or does not increase it.

The domain will now be defined.

Agents. The agents are partitioned into two disjoint sets $G = G1 \cup G2$, a set of planning *and* executing agents $G1 = \{cop1, cop2, cop3, cop4\}$ and set of *executing* agent $G2 = \{robber\}$. The robber agent does not belong to $G1$, because he is no planning agent and he does not publish his plans. His activities (moves) affect the environment.

The cops get to know of the robber's actions via *execution* messages[1]. Although it is not realistic to assume that the robber broadcasts his actions, and thereby showing his current position, the robber's execution messages can be interpreted as the agents' eyes which recognize where the robber has moved. Or, the robber's moves have been transmitted by spies. Thus, it will make no difference if the execution of an action is sensed by sight or whether the execution is transmitted by an *execution* message.

Actions. We assume that there is an unlimited grid, i.e. there are no border positions. Thus, we simplify the description of actions by not having to consider all the exceptional cases of agents at border positions, where one of the position values has reached a maximum value. The actions are the moves from one position in the grid, denoted as (x_1, x_2), to the next, denoted as (y_1, y_2). The set of actions is thus

$A = \{\text{move}((x_1, x_2), (y_1, y_2)) \mid x_1, x_2, y_1, y_2 \text{ are integers},$

$(y_1 = x_1 \wedge (y_2 = y_2\text{-}1 \vee y_2 = y_2\text{+}1)\,) \vee (y_2 = x_2 \wedge (y_1 = x_1\text{-}1 \vee y_1 = x_1\text{+}1)\,)\,)\}$

If an agent does not change his position, this can be denoted as

$\text{move}((x_1, x_2), (x_1, x_2))$.

Resources. The resources are the locations in the grid, i.e.

$R = \{(x, y) \mid x, y \text{ are integers}\}$.

The resources are nonconsumable, i.e. for all $r \in \mathbb{R}$ Nonconsumable(r).

There is one copy of each resource, i.e. for all times and all r available$(r, i) = 1$.

The set of resources required by an action $\text{move}((x_1, x_2), (y_1, y_2))$ is the goal position, i.e. $\text{res}(\text{move}(x_1, x_2), (y_1, y_2)) = \{(y_1, y_2)\}$. An action requires one copy of a resource, i.e. for all resources r and actions a: amount$(r, a) = 1$.

Refinements. The plans considered here consist only of primitive actions. However, a concept for abstract actions could be easily introduced by considering actions which require more than one move. In this case a possible refinement of an abstract action consists of a set of possible moves. We will give an example assuming that there are no obstacles and a refinement seeks a shortest path. The following predicates describe the two possible refinements of the abstract action $move((4, 6), (2, 5))$:

---

[1] Message types will be explained in Chapter 6.

Refinement(move(((3, 6), (2, 5)), {move(((3, 6), (2, 6)), move(((2, 6), (2, 5)))},

{Before(move(((3, 6), (2, 6)), move(((2, 6), (2, 5))))})

Refinement(move(((3, 6), (2, 5)), {move(((3, 6), (3, 5)), move(((3, 5), (2, 5)))},

{Before(move(((3, 6), (3, 5)), move(((3, 5), (2, 5))))})

Preparing actions (local executability). For all actions $move((x_1, x_2), (y_1, y_2))$ with $time(move((x_1, x_2), (y_1, y_2))) = t$. There are several alternative sets of preparing actions:

Pre(move(($x_1, x_2), (y_1, y_2)$), {move(x_1, x_1), (x_1, x_2))})

Pre(move(($x_1, x_2), (y_1, y_2)$), {move((x_1-1, x_2), (x_1, x_2))})

Pre(move(($x_1, x_2), (y_1, y_2)$), {move((x_1+1, x_2), (x_1, x_2))})

Pre(move(($x_1, x_2), (y_1, y_2)$), {move((x_1, x_2-1), (x_1, x_2))})

Pre(move(($x_1, x_2), (y_1, y_2)$), {move((x_1, x_2+1), (x_1, x_2))})

In order to move to a position an agent must have just moved to a neighbor position and the goal position must not have just been occupied by the robber.

Another precondition for the executability of move(($x_1, x_2), (y_1, y_2)$):
Anti-pre(move(($x_1, x_2), (y_1, y_2)$), move(($x, y), (y_1, y_2)$)) with parameter values:
executor(move(($x, y), (y_1, y_2)$)) = robber and time(move(($x, y), (y_1, y_2)$)) = t-1, i.e. in terms of "Allen" Meets(move(($x, y), (y_1, y_2)$), move(($x_1, x_2), (y_1, y_2)$)).

The coordination process. The coordination process is driven by the conflicts which exist among the agents' plans which intend to occupy the same location in the next move. Conflicts are given as defined by Ncrc in Section 4.2. Conflict resolutions might be tried in the following order: First, replace the resource for one agent (Section 5.1.1), i.e. move to another location, which is equally close. Then, conflicting actions might be spread (Section 5.1.1), which means for one agent to postpone the action and wait until the other agent has left the goal position. An alternative for postponing an action is to cancel an action and to establish a new plan after the next "execution round" has been performed.

The global goal, namely to capture the robber, is not specified in advance, i.e. there is no global planning goal. Nevertheless, the cops may capture the robber if this is possible for a given start situation.

The agents do not convey complete plans. Although an agent might create a complete plan ("standard plan") how to reach the robber (which consists of all moves) the agent does not communicate about it. The individual plans which are exchanged consist of only one action, namely the plan's first action.

The environment is not only affected by one agent's actions. As the environment is changed by the robber's moves the planning agents (cops) can not make too detailed plans in advance and then execute them. Having a rough plan in mind, the agents execute only one action of their plans and then consider the change of the environment and their colleagues intentions to modify their abstract plans or make a new plan. This approach is sometimes called *interleaving planning and execution.* As the agents communicate with each other we might extend this term leading to *interleaving planning, negotiation and execution.*

5.1.2.2 Autonomous Mobile Vehicles

The problem tackled now is the coordination of the movements of several vehicles in a dynamic world. This domain has already been explored by others [Burmeister and Sundermeyer 90, Fraichard and Demazeau 90, Steeb et al. 81, Wood 83]. The recent work of Durfee and Montgomery [1990] already provides experimental results in this domain.

Here, we will give only a rough introduction of the domain to point out the applicability of the conflict model. A detailed example of this domain will follow in Chapter 7. The coordination of autonomous vehicles appears for instance in connection with transport and monitoring tasks. Each vehicle has its own plan, namely to drive a certain path.

The agents in this domain are autonomous mobile vehicles. A vehicle is subject to various kinematic constraints which restrict the type of trajectory it can execute. There are constraints on the speed or the shape of the trajectory and so on. The goal of the vehicle is to reach a specific location. In order to reach its goal, a vehicle has a plan, consisting of a trajectory and the velocity. We assume that, while moving towards its goal, a vehicle is capable to perceive its local environment through various means of perception (camera, radar,..). These means of perception correspond to the reception of messages in our model.

The following aspects have to be dealt with:
-   Generation and execution of a plan in a dynamic and uncertain universe.

– Reasoning about future intentions of the independent vehicles.

– Plan adaption via negotiation (communication).

We will outline the utility of our coordination approach with respect to the problem of avoiding collisions.

Conflicts in the traffic domain. In order to avoid collisions, which is the main coordination problem of this domain, we can use the model of *conflicts* and their resolution. The *plans* in this domain are the paths the vehicles intend to drive. The *resources* in this domain are the locations (sections) which are occupied by the vehicles. The lanes of the roads which are divided into subsections (*nonconsumable resources*). A section in a lane can only be used by one vehicle at a given time. The speed of the cars can be used to compute the time when a vehicle is at a certain section (*temporal information*). This means, in terms of plan relations, we know when two agents (vehicle) need the same resource of type "location".

Conflicts in this domain exist if

– two vehicles intend to use the same lane at the same time in opposite direction on a narrow road. Narrow roads may consist of only one lane.

– two vehicles use the same lane in the same direction. But the second vehicle moves quicker than the first vehicle such that it will reach (run against) the other vehicle.

– two vehicles drive on different lanes which cross each other at an intersection.

Collision avoidance in the traffic domain as conflict resolution. Conflicts can be resolved as described in the last chapter. Collisions can be avoided by:

– *spread intervals*: In order to prevent that vehicles enter the same section at the same time, vehicles may adjust their speed or even stop, which corresponds to *shift intervals* (Section 5.1.1). The speed adjustment will be performed by the conflicting vehicles in opposite direction, i.e. one vehicle may slow down (decelerate) or keep the velocity, whereas the other vehicle will speed up (accelerate) or hold the speed.

– *reduce-intervals*: If the location (section) of a vehicle is specified only very roughly, e.g. "drive from a to b on road c", there may be some freedom how long a vehicle is in a certain subsection of a section (road as a rough section). By influencing the interval (duration) how long a vehicle remains in a region (, i.e. requires a resource), conflicts can also be prevented (*reduce-intervals*).

- *replace-resource*: Collisions may be avoided by selecting a different route or lane (pull out, cut in) for one or both conflicting vehicles. In this case the vehicles occupy different regions which corresponds to *replace-resource*.

In Section 7.5.1, after the complete coordination model has been defined, we will give concrete examples for plan coordination within this domain.

The problem of avoiding collisions occurs also in domains with autonomous transport robots which have to deliver material to a number of stations (CIM). Also the favor relation makes sense in this domain. Whereas the *conflict* relation is suited to prevent robots from colliding, the *favor* relation may help to achieve a balanced loading of transport robots or saving energy (see also Section 5.2.5).

Scenarios. The following diagrams display some aspects of conflicts in a traffic domain. Potential conflict resolution strategies are added in brackets.

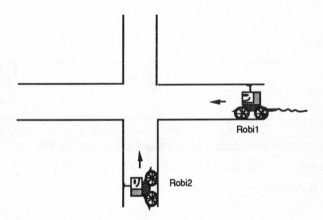

Figure 12:   Two vehicles intend to cross the intersection at the same time. They can solve this conflict if they adapt their speed such that the times when they cross, i.e. use resource r_1, do not intersect (*spread intervals*).

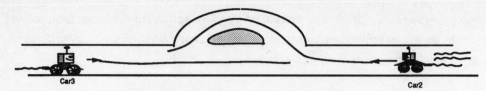

Figure 13:   Two vehicles drive on a narrow road in opposite directions. They can prevent the collision if one vehicle takes the by-route before they meet (*replace-resource*).

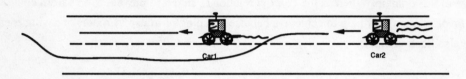

Figure 14:   Car2 is driving faster than Car1 and it will hit Car1 if it does not decelerate (*shift interval*) or overtake (*replace-resource*).

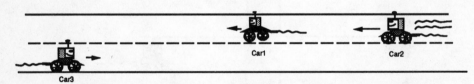

Figure 15:   If Car2 tries immediately to overtake Car1, a conflict with Car1 will be pre-vented, but it will come to a conflict with Car3. A solution is first to decelerate (*shift interval*) and then to overtake (*replace resource*).

5.1.3 Conflict Resolution Heuristics

Resolving conflicts in distributed domains is to a great extent a *heuristic* matter. This section contains strategies for applying conflict resolution operations.

The planning and communication behavior of the agents is highly dynamic and uncertain, and an updated and consistent global view of the state of the network problem solving is difficult, if not impossible, to obtain. Therefore, attempting optimal control at every moment is infeasible from both a computational and communicative perspective. There is no absolutely best strategy, and hence no optimum solution, to solve the problems involved with these issues.

Temporal and resource information, which is specified in the plans, can be evaluated to guide conflict resolution. Finally, conflicts must be handled based on extensive *domain knowledge*.

Given a set of plans and a set of conflicts among these plans (a "distributed planners' conflict set"), four issues have to be considered:

1. What is the *order* in which conflicts are resolved?

   The order in which the conflicts are solved may influence the overall result. A conflict which has been settled already is privileged against the yet unsolved ones. The solution of one conflict might make the solution of another conflict impossible. If a conflict is settled, another conflict might vanish or a new one might arise. In Section 5.1.3.1 guidelines to determine the order in which conflicts are solved will be presented.

2. Which *solution* is preferable for a given conflict?

   As pointed out there are various alternatives for resolving a conflict. Section 5.1.3.2 will offer decision criteria to select among conflicting resolution alternatives.

3. How can a mediator *(coordinator)* promote an agreement among conflicting parties?

   We will give examples how an *impartial* coordination agent selects proposals for conflict resolution for each party individually. (see Section 5.1.3.4)

4. If there is no centralized instance (coordination agent) to govern conflict resolution: How can conflicting agents reach an *agreement* on how to settle a conflict? How can a solution be achieved in an environment involving distributed autonomous planners?

   This involves issues of communication and interaction; what communication languages and protocols to use, what and when to communicate. This aspect is the topic of Chapters 6 and 7.

Another issue is to determine which agent is responsible to resolve a given conflict, i.e. who gets the role of the coordinator? This interesting question has been already explored by other researchers [Cammarata, McArthur and Steeb 83; Steeb et al. 1981].

5.1.3.1 Determining the Conflict Resolution Order

The purpose of a heuristic for ordering conflict resolution is to ensure that as many conflicts are solved as possible.

Consider the set of all conflicts between two different plans p_1 and p_2 and let a_1 and a_2 be conflicting actions of p_1 and p_2, respectively, and $i_1 = \text{time}(a_1)$, $i_2 = \text{time}(a_2)$.

There are several guidelines reasonable to determine the order of conflict solution:

• **Absolute conflict duration.** The duration of a conflict between two actions a_1 and a_2 is the length of their common time interval, i.e.

Definition: duration = length (intersection(i_1, i_2)).

Figure 16: Absolute conflict duration

Conflicts may be handled in descending length of their common interval. A conflict can be considered more serious the longer it is. It may facilitate solving *all* conflicts if longer conflicts are cleared first. It is easier to settle shorter conflicts (by shifting time intervals) than longer ones, and, if the smaller conflicts are solved first (and the positions of their actions fixed), it may turn out to be hard to solve the remaining longer conflicts, whereas there is more flexibility in solving smaller conflicts.

• **Relative conflict duration.** The relative conflict duration (Fig. 17) is defined as

Definition: redu = $\dfrac{\text{length(intersection}(i_1, i_2))}{\text{length}(i_1) + \text{length}(i_2)}$.

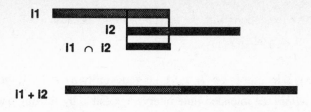

Figure 17: Relative conflict duration (quotient)

The greater the quotient redu the more effort is necessary to solve the conflict in terms of moving the actions (advance or postpone). If the solution of these conflicts is postponed too much it may be difficult or even impossible to find the "temporal space" which is necessary for their solution because the space is already too constrained by previously solved smaller conflicts.

If we use the redu criterion to evaluate the severity of conflicts and we parameterize the temporal relations for two intervals i_1 and i_2, we receive the following order (from severe to unsevere):

redu("Equal(i_1, i_2)") < redu("In(i_1, i_2)") < redu("Overlaps(i_1, i_2)") < redu("Meets(i_1, i_2)") = redu("Before(i_1, i_2)")

reason: redu("Meets(i_1, i_2)") = redu("Before(i_1, i_2)") = 0,

redu("Equal(i_1, i_2)") = 0.5

If $i_1 < i_2$: redu("In(i_1, i_2)") $= \dfrac{\text{length}(i_1)}{\text{length}(i_2) + \text{length}(i_1)} < 0.5$

redu("Overlaps(i_1, i_2)") $= \dfrac{\text{length}(i_1 \cap i_2)}{\text{length}(i_2) + \text{length}(i_1)}$

$< \dfrac{\text{length}(i_1)}{(\text{length}(i_1) + \text{length}(i_2))} = $ redu("In(i_1, i_2)")

• **Inner movability of actions.** The inner movability of actions is defined as

Definition: movability$(a_1, a_2) = \dfrac{\text{length}(\text{union}(i_1, i_2))}{\text{dur}(a_1) + \text{dur}(a_2)}$

where length (union (i_1, i_2)) = length(i_1) + length(i_2) - length(intersection(i_1, i_2))).

Sometimes the time interval associated with an action may exceed the duration of the action by far. This means that the conflicted resource is reserved much longer than actually needed. The idea is to first solve the actions with the least movability because a solution of the other can be based on their time redundancy.

If dur(a_1)+dur(a_2) $\leq$ length(union (i_1, i_2))), i.e. movability(a_1, a_2) $\geq$ 1, then there is a solution for the conflict *within* the intended time intervals possible by shifting one action's start point and the other action's end point.

• **Earliest startpoint**. Actions with the earliest starting point (Fig. 18) of their covering interval are the urgent ones concerning the time which is left until their intended execution. This speaks in favor of handling these conflicts earlier. This aspect is particularly interesting with respect to real time processing.

Definition: startpoint= min (start(i_1), start(i_2)).

Figure 18: Startpoint of a conflict

• **Excessive resource amount**. This aspect considers the resource involved in a conflict, i.e. the degree to which the resource requirements exceed the amount of available resource (Fig. 19). The strategy is to solve conflicts with "bigger" resource problems first. The criterion is defined as

Definition: excessive-resource-amount $= \dfrac{amount(r, a_1) + amount(r, a_2)}{available(r, intersection(i_1, i_2))}$.

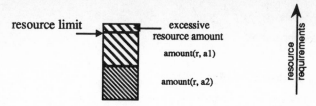

Figure 19: Resource requirements versus resource availability

5.1.3.2 Choosing Among Conflict Resolution Alternatives

In this section, a heuristic is proposed for the decision which conflict resolution to apply. Although this heuristic is conceived to be *domain independent*, the order in which the resolution criteria are applied might be adjusted for special application domains. Temporal relations between the conflicting actions play the dominant role for selecting a conflict resolution for two conflicting actions a_1 and a_2. Here, i_1 and i_2 are the associated action intervals. The first alternative which is true is selected (see also Table 3).

Temporal Relationship	Relative Conflict Duration (redu)	Preferred Solutions (Approach)
1. BEFORE(i_1,i_2)	not existent	not necessary
2. MEETS(i_1,i_2)	not existent	not necessary
3. EQUAL(i_1,i_2)	maximal	1. reduce-resource 2. reduce-intervals 3. spread
4. OVERLAPS(i_1,i_2)	low	1. spread 2. reduce-resource 3. reduce-intervals
5. IN(i_1,i_2)	high	1. reduce-resource 2. spread 3. reduce-intervals

  ▬▬▬▬ i_1 = time(a_1)
  ▬▬▬▬ i_2 = interval(a_2)

Table 3: Temporal relationships and conflict resolution

- **Before**(i_1, i_2) or **Meets**(i_1, i_2):

There isn't any non-consumable resource conflict.

- **Overlaps**(i_1, i_2) (see flow-chart, Fig. 20):

If time overlap is small, try *spread*-actions.

If excessive resource amount is small, try *reduce-resource*.

If time overlap is moderate, try *spread-actions*.

If movability(a_1, a_2) is great, try *reduce-intervals*.

If excessive resource amount is moderate, try *reduce-resource*.

Try *replace-resource*.

Try *spread-actions*.

If movability(a_1, a_2) is sufficient, try *reduce-intervals*.

Try *reduce-resource*.

Try *cancel-actions*.

- **Equal**(i_1, i_2):

If excessive resource amount is moderate, try a *reduce-resource*.

If movability(a_1, a_2) is sufficient, try *reduce-intervals*.

Try *spread-actions*.

If movability(a_1, a_2) is sufficient, try *reduce-intervals*.

Try *replace-resource*.

Try *reduce-resource*.

Try *cancel-actions*.

- **In**(i_1, i_2):

If excessive resource amount is moderate, try a *reduce-resource*.

If time overlap is small, try a *spread-actions*.

If movability(a_1, a_2) is great, try *reduce-intervals*.

Try *spread-actions*.

Try *replace-resource*.

Try *reduce-resource*.

Try *cancel-actions*.

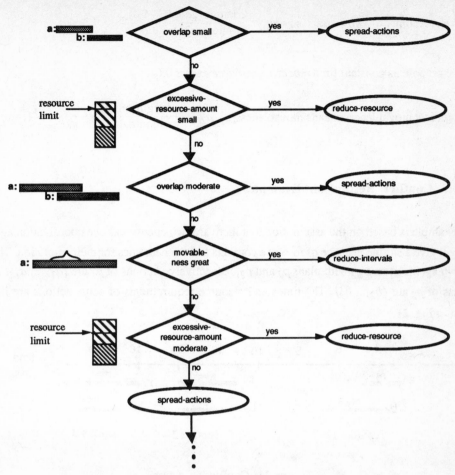

Figure 20: Determine a solution for a given conflict with overlapping actions
(Overlaps(a_1, a_2))

Quantification. The imprecise expressions such as small and medium of the rules above will be given precise values now.

– A time overlap can be considered *small*, if $\dfrac{\text{length(intersection}(i_1, i_2))}{\text{length(union}(i_1, i_2))} \leq 0.2$.

– The excessive resource amount is *small*, if

$$\frac{\text{available}(s,(\text{union}(i_1, i_2)))}{\text{amount-required}(a_1,s)+\text{amount-required}(a_2,s)} > 0.9.$$

– We propose as constant for a *moderate* time overlap 0.4.

–   The movability of two actions is *great*, if $\dfrac{\text{length(union}(i_1, i_2))}{\text{duration}(a_1)+\text{duration}(a_2)} \geq 1.5$.

–   We propose as constant for a *moderate resource excess* 0.6

–   *Sufficient* movableness means movableness$(a_1, a_2) = \dfrac{\text{length(union}(i_1, i_2))}{\text{duration}(a_1)+\text{duration}(a_2)} > 1$.

5.1.3.3 Conflict Resolution Example

The example is based on the assumption that there are two agents and one coordination agent. We will give a simple instance of resource conflicts and the heuristics for their resolution. There are two agents g_1 and g_2 with plans p_1 and p_2, respectively. Actions of p_1 are $\{a_1, ..., a_{14}\}$ and actions of p_2 are $\{b_2,...,b_9\}$. The times and resource requirements of some actions are illustrated in Fig. 21.

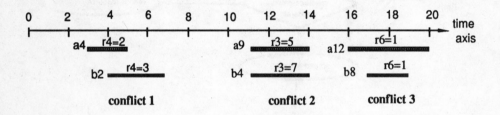

Figure 21: Conflicting actions

The conflicts which exist between these plans are:
Conflict-1: Ncrc(a_4, b_2) and, hence, pot-Ncrc(p_1, p_2). Actions a_4 and b_2 compete for resource r_4.
res$(a_4) = \{r_2, r_4\}$, res$(b_2) = \{r_1, r_4\}$, i.e. res$(a_4) \cap$ res$(b_2) = \{r_4\}$
time$(a_4) = [3, 5)$, time$(b_2) = [4, 7)$, i.e. Overlaps(a_4, b_2)
dur$(a_4) = 2$, dur$(b_2) = 3$
available $(r_4,$ union(time(a_4), time$(b_1))) = 3$
amount$(a_4, r_4) = 2$, amount$(b_2, r_4) = 3$,
amount(a_4, r_4) + amount$(b_2, r_4) >$ available$(r_4,$ union(time(a_4), time$(b_1)))$.

Conflict-2: Ncrc(a_9, b_4). a_9 and b_4 compete for r_3.

time(a_9) = time(b_4) = [11, 14), i.e. Equal(time(a_9), time(b_4))

res(a_9) $\cap$ res(b_4) = {r_3}, amount(a_9, r_3)=5, amount(b_4, r_3)=7

dur(a_9) = 2, dur(b_4) = 1, available(r_3, [11, 14)) = 11

Σamount = 12 > available(r_3, [11, 14)) = 11.

Conflict-3: Ncrc(a_{12}, b_8). a_{12} and b_8 compete for r_6.

time(a_{12}) = [16, 20), time(b_8) = [17, 19), i.e. In(b_8, a12)

dur(a_{12}) = 4, dur(b_8) = 2, res(a_{12}) $\cap$ res(b_8) = {r_6}

amount(a_{12}, r_6) = 1, amount(b_8, r_6) = 1, available(r_6, [16, 10)) = 1.

Conflict Evaluation

The goal is to determine the *order* in which conflicts will be solved. We will use the criteria which were introduced in 5.1.3.1.

– *duration.* duration(conflict-1) = 1, duration(conflict-2) = 3, duration(conflict-3) = 2. The duration evaluation implies a conflict order 2,3,1

– *relative conflict duration.* redu(conflict-1) = $\frac{1}{4}$ = 0.25, redu(conflict-2) = $\frac{3}{6}$ = 0.5, redu(conflict-3) = $\frac{2}{6}$ = 0.33, which means a conflict resolution order 2,3,1

– *earliest startpoint.* startpoint(conflict-1) = 3, startpoint(conflict-2) = 11, startpoint(conflict-3) = 16, which suggests a conflict resolution order 1,2,3

– *inner movability.* movability(conflict-1) = $\frac{4}{5}$ = 0.8, movability(conflict-2) = $\frac{3}{3}$ = 1, movability(conflict-3) = $\frac{4}{6}$ = 0.66, suggesting conflict order 3,1,2

Final decision. We will introduce a weighted sum to decide which conflict to solve next:

value(conflict) = dur(conflict) + redu(conflict) + 0.5*movability(conflict).

value(conflict-1) = 7, value(conflict-2) = 3 .5, value(conflict-3) = 4.5.

Hence, the conflict resolution order is conflict-2, conflict-3, conflict-1.

Individual conflict resolution

(1) Strategy selection for conflict-2: Equal(a_9, b_4) and excessive-resource-amount(a_9, b_4, r_3)
$= \frac{11}{5+7} > 0.6$ is *moderate* (see 5.1.3.2),

therefore, try *reduce-resource*. Proposal for g_1: amount$(a_9, r_3)=4$, proposal for g_2: amount$(b_4, r_3) = 6$. In p_1 the proposal violates other constraints, but p_2 "accepts" and the conflict is solved.

(2) Strategy for conflict-3: In(b_8, a_{12}) and excessive-resource-amount = 0.5, time-overlap $= \frac{2}{4}$
= 0.5, movability = 0.66,
therefore try *spread-actions* with proposal for $g1$: "later"$(a_{12}, 3)$, for g_2: "earlier"$(b_8, 3)$.
Assumed results are for g_1: modify later$(a_{12}, 1)$, for g_2: modify earlier$(b_8, 2)$ and the conflict is solved.

(3) Strategy for conflict-1: Overlaps(a_4, b_2), time-overlap$= \frac{1}{4} = 0.25$ (not small), excessive resource amount$= \frac{3}{5} = 0.6$ (not small). The time-overlap is moderate.

Therefore, try *spread-actions* with proposal for g_1: earlier$(a_4, 1)$, for g_2: later$(b_2, 1)$. Assumed
responses: Both in p_1 and in p_2 the proposals can not be executed because other restrictions
are violated. After trying several alternatives for resolution (as suggested in 5.1.3.2) which
fail, the result is as follows: g_2 reduces b_2's interval such that time$(b_2) = (5, 7)$, and a_4 doesn't
have to be changed. Fig. 22 shows the actions after the conflicts have been solved.

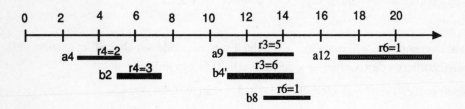

Figure 22: Actions after conflict resolution

5.1.3.4 Proposing Conflict Resolutions

How can an impartial coordination agent proceed in order to promote an agreement between conflicting parties? We want to focus on the aspect of what a coordination agent proposes for each individual agent in a given conflict case and an intended solution. In the case of *cancel-action* one may decide randomly (unless there are reasonable domain dependent criteria) which agent should cancel a conflicting action. The other conflict resolutions involve quantitative decisions concerning the amount of resource reduction for each agent (*reduce-resource*) or the duration how long an action should start earlier or be postponed (*spread-actions*).

Coordinating (mediating) *spread*

Let g_1 be the agent of a_1 and time$(a_1) = i_1$ and, let g_2 be the agent of a_2 and time$(a_2) = i_2$.

In case of Overlaps(i_1, i_2) or Starts(i_1, i_2):

1. Propose for g_1: advance a_1, i.e.

shift-point$(a_1, -$ length(intersec$(i_1, i_2)) + $ pos(length (start$(a_1) - $ start$(a_2)), 0)$, where pos$(x) = x$ if $x \geq 0$ else 0.

Propose for g_2: postpone a_2, i.e.

shift-point$(a_2, 0,$ length(intersec$(i_1, i_2)) + $ pos(length (end$(a_2) - $ end$(a_1))))$.

 If g_1 or g_2 accept, the conflict is solved.

If g_1 and g_2 modify the proposal, such that

length(modify(*time1*)) + length(modify(*time2*)) $\geq$ length(intersec(i_1, i_2)), the conflict is solved. If there is only a small amount of overlap left, try once again as in 1.

2. Propose to postpone for g_1 and to advance for g_2 and proceed as in 1.

3. If 1. and 2. fail, *spread* has failed.

In case of Finishes(i_1, i_2): propose first advance a_2, postpone a_1.

In case of During(i_1, i_2): If end(a_1) nearer to end(a_2) than start(a_1) to start(a_2): advance a_1 and postpone a_2. else: vice versa.

Coordinating *reduce-resource*

Let res be the conflicted resource.

Propose for g_1: reduce-resource(*res, a_1, amount1*) with

amount1 = amount(*res, a_1*) + amount(*res, a_2*) - available(*res*, union(i_1, i_2)).

Propose for g_2: reduce-resource(*res, a_2, amount2*) with

amount2 = amount(*res, a_1*) + amount(*res, a_2*) - available(*res*, union(i_1, i_2)).

If g_1 or g_2 accept, the conflict is solved.

If g_1 and g_2 modify the proposal, such that

modified amount1 + modified amount2 ≤ available(*res*, union(i_1, i_2)),

the conflict is solved. If there is only a small amount of excess left, try once again with new proposals for amount.

As both agents are asked to reduce the whole amount, a solution is already reached if only one agent accepts this proposal. This may speed up the agreement. If the agents modify the proposed resource shortage, we have to check whether the modified amounts fulfill the resource constraints. If there is only a very small amount of excessive requirements, a reduction is tried once more.

In Chapter 6, we will see how such negotiations fit into our communication framework.

5.2 Using the Favor Relation

As we assume that the agents' plans are known before execution it is useful to take as much advantage as possible of beneficial relations between the different preformed plans by having them coordinated. Exploiting positive relations is not only beneficial for the profiting individual but may also be useful for the whole system. The relation, which we focus on in this section, is the *favor relation*. Based on the model of the the favor relation as defined in Chapter 4 we describe a method for checking whether the favor relation holds for two independently generated plans and how it can be utilized. Quantitative arguments are provided both for an agent's decision whether to engage in a favor and to evaluate the global benefits of exploiting the favor relation. We will give examples how agents reason about plan coordination and how they coordinate their actions by modifying their plans.

5.2.1 Favor Detection

The favor detection algorithm has to find refinements, such that a favor action can be transferred. An action can be added to a plan, if the plan contains a preparing action set for it. The search space for favor detection is given by the possible refinements of the actions in plans for which a favor is checked.

A coordination mechanism, which either resides at a central agency or locally at each agent, gets as input two plans p_1 and p_2 of two agents. The basic algorithm for detecting the favor relation is as follows:

Find a pair of successive refinements of p_1 and p_2, leading to p_1' and p_2' (i.e. Do for all refinements until (i) or (ii) are fulfilled):

For all favor actions a in p_2':

If either

(i) a preparing action set for a is contained in p_1',

or

(ii) is it possible to add a set of actions to p_1' such that this set together with other actions in p_1' are a preparing set for a.

Then a favor relation exists.

5.2.2 Plan Modifications

To exploit the favor relation a coordination reasoner suggests that the two plans p_1 and p_2 will be modified in the following manner. If the agents agree (negotiation phase) to expand their plans as it was suggested, the favor action is added to p_1'. In p_2', the action a and the preparing actions can be removed unless required by another action.

These modifications may be *suggested* by a coordination agent. There may be further plan modifications possible of which a coordination reasoner does not know because he has only limited knowledge of the agents plans (only parts of the plans are transmitted), and he may not know anything about the planning agents' goals and intentions. The agents themselves will decide whether and how they adapt their plans[1]. For instance, in addition to the removal of the preparing actions it may be possible to remove follow-up or subsequent actions of a favor action which are not required any more because they were only used to "clear" the effects of a favor action's preparing actions. To deal with this, an agent may have local information such as Follow-up$(a_4, A1, A2)$ denoting that the set of actions $A2$ is a follow-up set of action for an action a, with respect to the preparing action set $A1$.

In addition to the plan modification operator *refine* (see 3.4.1) we need operators to add and remove actions from plans. Let $\mathbb{P}$ be the set of all plans of a given domain.

Definition:

The operator **add** is a partial mapping from $\mathbb{P}$ into $\mathbb{P}$ with

add(af, as): $\mathbb{P} \longrightarrow \mathbb{P}$

with $p = (A, SUB)$ and $p' = $ add$(af, as)(p)$, $p' = (A', SUB')$, $A' = A \cup \{as\}$ and $SUB' = SUB \cup \{(af, as)\}$.

add is applicable if $af \in A$ and $as \notin A$. The "f" in af is standing for father and "s" for son.

Definition:

The operator **remove** is a partial mapping from $\mathbb{P}$ into $\mathbb{P}$ with

remove(af, as): $\mathbb{P} \longrightarrow \mathbb{P}$

with $p' = $ remove$(af, as)(p)$, $p' = (A', SUB')$, $A' = A \backslash \{as\}$ and $SUB' = SUB \backslash \{(af, as)\}$.

remove is applicable if $(af, as) \in SUB$.

Assume that a favor of agent(a_1) for agent(a_2) is possible, i.e. Favor(p_1, p_2) is true with refinements in p_1 $A_{1,1}$...., $A_{1,m}$ of a_{11},...., a_{1m} and refinements in p_2 $A_{2,1}$...., $A_{2,n}$ of a_{21},...., a_{2n}, favor action a and, if need be, an additional preparing set $A2$. An application of the following operators is suggested:

---

[1] The agents are autonomous and intelligent problem solvers and capable of their own decisions and are *not* controlled by an omniscient central coordination agent. A coordination agent, which in fact may be one of the planning agents, has to support coordination and cooperation and is not allowed to enforce it.

$\forall i=1,...,m \; pl_{i+1} := \text{refine}(a_{1i}, A_{1i})(p_{1i})$, with $p_{11} = p_1, p_1' := p_{1_{m+1}}$

$\forall i=1,...,n \; p_{2_{i+1}} := \text{refine}(a_{21}, A_{2i})(p_{2i})$, with $p_{21} = p_2, p_2' := p_{2_{n+1}}$

$\text{add}(a_{1,m-1}, a)(p_1')$

$\forall a \in A2 \; \text{add}(a_{1,m-1}, a)(p_1')$

$\text{remove}(a_1, a)(p_2')$ where a_1 is the superior action of the favor action a.

For all a_1 in the preparing set of a and $A2$ in p_2': $\text{remove}(af, a_1)(p_2')$ where af is superior action of a_1.

Coordinated plans. The plans resulting from the modifications are called *coordinated individual plans* with respect to the favor relation and are denoted as *pc1* and *pc2* (c for "coordinated").

5.2.3 Quantitative Aspects of a Favor Relation Driven Cooperation

A favor relation between two different agents' plans includes that one agent's plan can contribute helpfully to the other agent's plan. The utilization of a favor relation should only require minor modifications of the two plans involved, i.e. a favor should fit within the framework of the existing plans of the agents.

However, even if a favor is possible this does not necessarily mean that it is actually granted. The giving agent often considers quantitative aspects when deciding about granting a favor. From a system wide point of view it is desirable that an overall cost reduction is achieved if both agents adapt their plans to utilize the favor relation. Not every potential favor is worthwhile. In addition to the qualitative definition of favors we consider here quantitative aspects of the favor relation. What is the motivation for an agent to engage in a "favor driven" plan relation? An agent may consider the possible advantages produced by the favor, e.g. because he expects to receive a favor in exchange. Or an agent may have received a favor and there exists an implicit obligation to return it. We will not elaborate further on the last two aspects.

When an agent does a favor, this is not only motivated by some benevolence on the side of the giving agent[1], which is called the *benevolence assumption* in DAI [Rosenschein and

---

[1] A *favor* is a benefit that one is glad to receive, but cannot demand or claim, hence always indicating good will or regard on the part of the person by whom it is conferred. [Britannica World Language Dictionary, USA edition, 1959]

132   Chapter 5: Handling Plan Relations

Genesereth 85]. The giving agent often considers quantitative aspects when deciding about a favor. This involves questions such as 'How much additional effort is necessary for the supporting agent to do the favor?' or 'Does it imply an overall cost reduction if both agents adapt their plans to utilize the favor relation?'

5.2.3.1 Costs

In order to estimate the quantitative benefits of coordination "by doing a favor" we need a measure of the cost of plans.

Definition (cost):
For an atomic action a,
$\text{cost}(a) \in \mathbb{R}^+$ denotes the costs associated with the execution of a.

To define the cost of an *abstract* action we differentiate between atomic leaf actions and those that are not. For a given state of planning $p = (A, SUB)$ where all leaf actions are atomic the cost for an *abstract* action $a \in p$ is defined as

Definition (cost for an abstract action): $\quad \text{cost}(a) = \sum_{a_l \in \text{rm}(a,p)} \text{cost}(a_l).$

The agents are not expected or even forced to deliver their plans at an atomic level. Therefore, agents will also have to estimate the costs of *incomplete* plans. For a given plan $p = (A, SUB)$ where not all leaf actions are atomic actions the cost for an *abstract* leaf action $a \in p$ can only be estimated because it is not sure which of the possible atomic refinements[1] will be selected.

Definition (cost for an abstract action in an incomplete plan):

$$\text{cost}(a) = \min_{\text{atomic rm}(a,p)} \sum_{a_l \in \text{rm}(a,p)} \text{cost}(a_l).$$

---

[1] A series of refinements which leads to a state where all subordinate leaf actions are atomic, is called an *atomic refinement*.

Definition (cost of a plan):

For a plan $p = (A, SUB)$ with $A1 = \bigcup_{a \in A} \text{rm}(a, p)$ the cost is now defined as

$$\text{cost}(p) = \sum_{a \in A1} \text{cost}(a).$$

5.2.3.2 Relative Additional Cost

Let a be the favor action of agent(p_1) for agent(p_2). p_1' is agent(p_1)'s refined plan as found during favor detection and the corresponding refined plan of agent(p_2) is p_2'.

We define the additional cost which is incurred for the supporting agent in Favor(p_1, p_2) as the *relative additional cost* of Favor(p_1, p_2). With the refinements resulting from p_1' and p_2', respectively, favor action a, and additional preparing set $A2$ the relative additional is computed as:

$$\text{Definition: } \textbf{rel-add-cost}(p_1, p_1', p_2, p_2', a, A2) = \frac{\text{cost}(p_1') + \text{cost}(a) + \sum_{a1 \in A2} \text{cost}(a1)}{\text{cost}(p_1)}.$$

The dividend consist of costs for the refined plan plus the cost of the favor action plus the cost of the additional preparing action set. The divisor is the cost of the original individual plan. We have $\text{cost}(p_1') \geq \text{cost}(p_1)$, because $\text{cost}(p_1)$ assumes that a minimal refinement has been selected which may differ from p_1'.

An agent which is asked to do a favor may use the rel-add-cost criterion to guide his decision whether to commit to a favor or not. He might apply the following rule of thumb:

"If *rel-add-cost* stays close to 1, e.g. ≤ 1.5, the favor does not require much additional effort for me and I am ready to execute it. "

5.2.3.3 Combined Cost

The combined cost for executing both modified plans should be less than the sum of the original plans. This aspect is especially interesting with respect to the overall costs incurred by the agents' actions. However, plan refinements which were found during favor detection might result in a more expensive overall cost than other cheaper plan refinements where the plan relation does *not* hold. A reasonable coordination mechanism should therefore consider the combined cost before suggesting plan modifications.

There are two plans p_1 and p_2 given with Favor(p_1, p_2). If the plans are modified as suggested in Section 5.2.2 with resulting plans *pc1* and *pc2*, the *combined cost* is defined as follows:

Definition: comb-cost$(pc1, pc2) = \text{cost}(pc1) + \text{cost}(pc2)$.

The combined cost has to be compared with the sum of cost(p_1) and cost(p_2), which may be cheaper because there may exist cheaper refinements than required for the favor relation, although by exploiting the favor relation some actions are saved.

A coordination of plans with respect to an existing favor relation should therefore only be proposed if the estimated cost of the original individual plans is higher than the combined cost of the modified plans, i.e.

comb-cost$(pc1, pc2) < \text{cost}(p_1) + \text{cost}(p_2)$.

5.2.3.4 Bidirectional Favor Relation

It is conceivable that a favor is possible for both agents (*bidirectional* favor). The question is how to decide 'who serves whom?'.

Let's assume that both Favor(p_1, p_2) and Favor(p_2, p_1) are true. The decision who supports whom might be based on the additional cost which the helping agent has to spend in order to do the favor:

(rule-1) If *rel-add-cost* of agent(p_1) in Favor(p_1, p_2) is less than *rel-add-cost* of agent(p_2) in Favor(p_2, p_1), then prefer Favor(p_1, p_2).

An alternative rule might be:

(rule-2) If *rel-add-cost* of agent$(p1)$ is less than threshold and *comb-cost* for Favor(p_1, p_2) is less than comb-cost for Favor(p_2, p_1), then prefer a favor of agent(p_1) for agent(p_2).

Rule-1 stresses more the *local* aspects of doing a favor by checking how much additional effort is necessary for an agent to support another agent, whereas rule-2 focuses on the saved cost from a *global* point of view and only requires that local costs do not increase too much (threshold).

5.2.4 Example for Favor Relation Detection and Exploitation

A simple example, which needs only a one-step refinement, should illustrate a favor relation and the corresponding plan modifications. A system for the detection of favor relations and execution of the corresponding plan modifications will be presented in Chapter 8.

Agent-1 has plan $p_1 = (A1, SUB_{p1})$. $A1 = \{a_1,...,a_7\}$
Agent-2 has plan $p_2 = (A2, SUB_{p2})$. $A2 = \{ ab_1,...,ab_5\}$
p_1 contains action a_6: buy-stamps-at-the-post-office, executor(a_6) = agent-1
p_2 contains action ab_4: bring-package-to-post-office, executor(b_4) = agent-2

(a) One possible refinement of a_6 is (Fig. 23): a_{61} go-to-post-office, a_{62} buy-stamps, a_{63} go-back-to-work

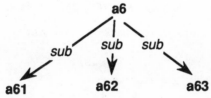

Figure 23: Agent-1's refinement of a_6

(b) A possible refinement of ab_4 consists of (Fig. 24): $ab_{41}(=a_{61})$ go-to-post-office, ab_{42} deliver-package, $ab_{43}(=a_{63})$ go-back-to-work. Pre(deliver-package, {go-to-post-office}).

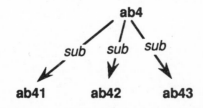

Figure 24: Agent-2's refined plan for ab_6

(c) go-to-post-office in ab_4 is a preparing action for buy-stamps of a_6. buy-stamps is a potential favor action, i.e. Fv-action(buy-stamps) is true.

(d) go-to-post-office in a_6 is a preparing action for deliver-package of b_4. deliver-package is a potential favor action.

Because of (a),(b) and (c), a favor of agent-2 for agent-1 is possible.
Because of (a),(b) and (d), a favor of agent-1 for agent-2 is possible.
That means, that a favor is possible in both directions.

The decision 'who serves whom?' will use the relative additional cost criterion (rule-1). We assume that *cost* for this purpose is defined as distance times weight. A package is heavy and it requires more effort to bring a package than to buy stamps, i.e. the relative additional cost for agent-2 is less than for agent-1. Hence, a favor of agent-2 for agent-1 is proposed. We assume that this proposal is accepted by the agents[1]. Agent-1 knows that in addition to the preparing action go-to-post-office, he can also remove the *follow-up* action go-back-to-work.
As a result we receive the following modified plans:
pc1: A1= {a_1,...,a_5, a_7}. a_6 was removed.
pc2: A2 = {ab_1, ab_2, ab_3, ab_4', ab_5} with ab_4' (Fig. 25): add favor action after preparing action, go-to-post-office, buy-stamps, deliver-package, go-to-work,

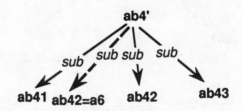

Figure 25: The favor action is added to agent-2's plan

---

[1] The process of negotiating proposals among agents is an important aspect for plan coordination and is discussed in Chapter 6.

5.2.5 Delivery Scenario: The Favor Relation in a Transportation Domain

The following scenario should illustrate the favor relation. The delivery scenario is similar to the Postman Domain which was originally presented by Zlotkin and Rosenschein [Zlotkin and Rosenschein 89b]. However, in addition to their work, our coordination model also considers the formal aspects of plans and plan adaption.

Agencies have to do bring containers from a factory (source) to warehouses (destinations). In order to do the deliveries, agents use trucks. The actions that can be done in this domain are to *drive* a truck to a warehouse, to *load* and *unload* containers on trucks. The containers can only be loaded at the factory. For the aspects considered here it does not matter whether agents are transportation companies (planning agents), which may be represented by their truck drivers (executing agents), or if the trucks are considered as intelligent automated agents themselves. In fact, all alternatives are reasonable.

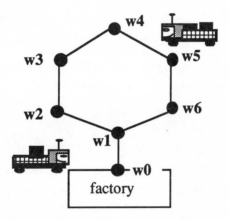

Figure 26: Transportation domain

The topography of the domain is shown in Fig. 26. The nodes in this graph are the factory w_0 and six warehouses $w_1, ..., w_6$ and, the arcs are roads between them.

Agents

The agents are two transportation companies $G = \{g_1, g_2\}$, each of which has its own truck. Although the companies are independent from each other, they sometimes cooperate.

Actions

bring(c,w): bring container c from the factory to the warehouse w.

drive(g,w): agent g drives his truck from the factory to warehouse w.

load(c,g,w): load a container c on agent $g's$ truck at location w.

unload(c,g,w): unload a container c from $g's$ truck at warehouse w

move(g,w_i,w_j): agent g drives his truck from location w_i to w_j with w_i and w_j being neighbor locations.

Atomic actions are load, unload and move.

Preparing actions

Pre(unload(c, g, w), $\{a_1,$ load$(c, g, w_0)\}$) with $a_1 \in \{$move$(g, w_i, w) \mid w_i \neq w\}$.

Pre(load(c, g, w), $\{a_1\}$) with $a_1 \in \{$move$(g, w_i, w) \mid w_i \neq w\}$.

Pre(move(g, w_i, w_j), $\{a\}$) with $a \in \{$move$(g, w, w_i) \mid w_i \neq w \}$

Pre(bring(c, w), $\{$move$(g, w_1, w_0)\}$)

Refinements

Refinement(bring(c,w), $\{$load(c,g,w_0), drive(g,w), unload$(c,g,w)\}$)

Drive actions can be refined to atomic *move* actions. We will not list these refinements here, but some of them will be used in refining the example plans.

Favor actions

Fv-action(bring). An agent is pleased if another agent takes care of his delivery.

Fv-action(unload). If an agent unloads a container instead of another agent, this means in fact that this, i.e. the "unloading", agent, has also done the other actions necessary for unloading.

Costs

cost(load) = 1. cost(unload) = 1. cost(move) = 1.

Individual plans

The first driver g_1 wants to deliver a container c_1 from the factory w_0 to the warehouse w_3. He conveys the plan

$p_{g1} = \{$move(g_1, w_1, w_0), load(c_1, g_1, w_0), drive(g_1, w_3), unload$(c_1, g_1, w_3)\}$.

The second driver g_2 wants to deliver a container c_2 from the factory w_0 to the warehouse w_4 using his truck. He conveys the plan

$p_{g2} = \{$move(g_2, w_1, w_0), load(c_2, g_2, w_0), drive(g_2, w_4), unload$(c_2, g_2, w_4)\}$.

The cost of the plans will be calculated using the following definition for actions

$$\text{cost}(a) = \min_{A} \left\{ \sum_{al \in A} \text{cost}(a_l) \right\}, \text{ where A is an atomic refinement rm}(a,p).$$

This cost definition means that the drivers take the shortest routes.

cost(p_{g1}) = cost(move) + cost(load) + cost(move) + cost(move) + cost(move) +

   cost(unload) = 6.

cost(p_{g2}) = cost(move) + cost(load) + cost(move) + cost(move) + cost(move) +

   cost(move) + cost(unload) = 7.

The combined cost of the *uncoordinated* individual plans is cost(p_{g1}) + cost(p_{g2}) = 13.

Favor detection

We assume that the drivers do not change the direction during a delivery trip and that they stop when they have reached their destinations, i.e. they don't make extra rounds. The actions which can be refined in the agents' plans are the *drive* actions. For each plan there are two possible refinements of the drive action:

g_1: First alternative for drive(g_1, w_3):

Refinement(drive(g_1, w_3), {move(g_1, w_0, w_1), move(g_1, w_1, w_2), move(g_1, w_2, w_3)}).

g_1: Second alternative for drive(g_1, w_3):

Refinement(drive(g_1, w_3), {move(g_1, w_0, w_1), move(g_1, w_1, w_6),

   move(g_1, w_6, w_5), move(g_1, w_5, w_4), move(g_1, w_4, w_3)}).

g_2: First alternative for drive(g_2, w_4):

Refinement(drive(g_2, w_4), {move(g_2, w_0, w_1), move(g_2, w_1, w_6),

   move(g_2, w_6, w_5), move(g_2, w_5, w_4)}).

g_2: Second alternative for drive(g_2, w_4):

Refinement(drive(g_2, w_4), {move(g_2, w_0, w_1), move(g_2, w_1, w_2),

   move(g_1, w_2, w_3), move(g_1, w_3, w_4)}).

Favor relations

The following favor relations exist:

(a) Favor(p_{g1}, $g2$).

A favor of g_1 for g_2 using the first refinement (route via w_1, w_2, w_3) with favor action unload($c2$, g, $w4$) and preparing actions move(g_1, w_0,w_1) for the load action and additional preparing actions load(c_2, g_1, w_0).

The additional cost factor for g1 as defined in Section 4.2 concerning this favor is

$$rel\text{-}add\text{-}cost = \frac{\text{cost}(p_{g1}') + \text{cost(unload)} + \text{cost(load)} + \text{cost(move)}}{\text{cost}(p_{g1})} = \frac{6 + 1 + 2}{6} = 1.5.$$

The combined cost for the coordinated plans are
$comb\text{-}cost = \text{cost}(pc_{g1}) + \text{cost}(pc_{g2}) = 9.$

(b) Favor(p_{g1}, p_{g2}).

A favor of g_1 for g_2 using the second possible refinement (route via w_1, w_6, w_5, w_4) with favor action unload($c2$, g, $w4$) and preparing action set {move($g1$, $w5$, $w4$)} and an additional preparing action, which will be added, load(c_2, g_1, w_0)}.

The additional cost factor for g_1 as defined in Section 4.2 concerning this favor is

$$rel\text{-}add\text{-}cost = \frac{\text{cost}(p_{g1}') + \text{cost(unload)} + \text{cost(load)}}{\text{cost}(p_{g1})} = \frac{8+1+1}{6} = 1.66.$$

The combined cost for the coordinated plans are
$comb\text{-}cost = \text{cost}(pc_{g1}) + \text{cost}(pc_{g2}) = 10.$

(c) Favor(p_{g2}, p_{g1}).

A favor of g_2 for g_1 using the first refinement (route via w_1, w_6, w_5, w_4) with favor action unload(c_1, g_1, w_3) and additional preparing action move(g_2, w_4, w_3) for the favor action.
The additional cost factor for g_2 is rel-add-cost $= \frac{7+1+2}{7} = 1.42.$

The combined cost for the coordinated plans are
$comb\text{-}cost = \text{cost}(pc_{g1}) + \text{cost}(pc_{g2}) = 10.$

(d) Favor(p_{g2}, p_{g1}).

A favor of g_2 for g_1 using the second refinement (route via w_1, w_2, w_3, w_4) with favor action unload(c_1, g_1, w_3) and preparing actions move(g_2, w_2, w_3) for the favor action, and an additional preparing action load(c_2, g_2, w_0).

The additional cost factor for g_2 is rel-add-cost $= \frac{7+1+1}{7} = 1.28$.

The combined cost for the coordinated plans are

$comb\text{-}cost = \text{cost}(pc_{g1}) + \text{cost}(pc_{g2}) = 9$.

Favor Resolution

All favors are worthwhile from a global point of view, because they lead to a reduced cost compared with the cost for the agents' original plans.

The overall cost are minimal for the cases (c) and (d). The relative additional cost is less in case (d), therefore an impartial coordination agent would suggest that driver g_2 does the favor for agent g_1.

The resulting coordinated plans are:

$pc_{g1} = \varnothing$.

$pc_{g2} = \{\text{move}(g_2, w_1, w_0), \text{load}(c_2, g_2, w_0), \text{load}(c_1, g_2, w_0), \text{move}(g_2, w_0, w_1), \text{move}(g_2, w_1, w_2), \text{move}(g_2, w_2, w_3), \text{unload}(c_1, g_2, w_3), \text{move}(g_2, w_3, w_4), \text{unload}(c_2, g_2, w_4)\}$.

Further examples

We will outline a few more examples and indicate how detection of the favor relation can be handled if plans are specified at varying levels of detail. It is clear that if actions are specified at a high level of abstraction, there is, on the one hand, a high degree of freedom to coordinate them, but on the other hand, more computational effort is necessary to reason about the alternatives.

The agents' plans are basically the same as in the first example. They may differ in their detail of specification and what they communicated to each other. We assume that the agents are at the factory while they exchange their plans and reason about the favor relation, i.e. move(g, w_1, w_0), $g \in \{g_1, g_2\}$, is the last action executed by the agents.

Example 2:

$p_{g1} = \{\text{move}(g_1, w_1, w_0), \text{bring}(c_1, w_3)\}$

$p_{g2} = \{\text{move}(g_2, w_1, w_0), \text{bring}(c_2, w_4)\}$.

These plans are very abstract. A bidirectional favor is possible. In order to estimate the costs they have to be refined using the rule Refinement(bring(c,w), $\{\text{load}(c, g, w_0), \text{drive}(g, w), \text{unload}(c, g, w)\}$). Then the detection proceeds as in the preceding example.

Example 3:

The opposite case is that all plans are already specified at the atomic level, e.g.

p_{g1} = {move(g_1, w_1, w_0), load(c_1, g_1, w_0), move(g_1, w_0, w_1), move(g_1, w_1, w_2),

move(g_1, w_2, w_3), unload(c_1, g_1, w_3)}.

p_{g2} = {move(g_2, w_1, w_0), load(c_2, g_2, w_0), move(g_2, w_0, w_1), move(g_2, w_1, w_6),

move(g_2, w_6, w_5), move(g_2, w_5, w_4), unload(c_2, g_2, w_4)}.

A coordination is possible via the favor relations (a) and (c) as described in the first example. Using rule-1 case (c) will be preferred. However, if rule-2 is applied, case(a) is selected.

Example 4:

One agent delivers a very abstract plan, whereas the other plan is very specific.

p_{g1} = {move(g_1, w_1, w_0), bring(c_1, w_3)}.

p_{g2} = {move(g_2, w_1, w_0), load(c_2, g_2, w_0), move(g_2, w_0, w_1), move(g_2, w_1, w_6),

move(g_2, w_6, w_5), move(g_2, w_5, w_4), unload(c_2, g_2, w_4)}.

Favor relations as in cases (a), (b) and (c).

Example 5:

p_{g1} = {move(g_1, w_1, w_0), load(c_1, g_1, w_0), move(g_1, w_0, w_1), move(g_1, w_1, w_6),

move(g_1, w_6, w_5), move(g_1, w_5, w_4), move(g_1, w_4, w_3), unload(c_1, g_1, w_3)}.

Agent g_1 may have some reason to select this plan which is not cost optimal. May be, he just likes to go a different route.

p_{g2} = {move(g_2, w_1, w_0), load(c_2, g_2, w_0), move(g_2, w_0, w_1), move(g_2, w_1, w_2),

move(g_2, w_2, w_3), move(g_2, w_3, w_4), unload(c_2, g_2, w_4)}.

The alternatives for a favor relation are case (b), but with

rel-add-cost = $\dfrac{8+1+1}{8}$ = 1.25, and case (d). However, deviating from the original example, the relative additional cost for g_1 is less than for g_2; therefore case (b) will be preferred.

Summary of favor handling. The coordination model is applicable when intelligent, autonomous agents act in the same environment and communicate about their plans in advance. Coordination may be triggered by exploiting the favor relation. A method has been outlined for checking whether the favor relation holds between two independently generated plans. The mechanisms described are independent of whether the autonomous agents are assisted by dedicated coordination agents or execute the favor detection procedures locally.

In order to estimate the benefits of exploiting a favor relation we have offered a quantitative model of plans and synchronized plans. Cost considerations may both contribute to the agents' decision whether to engage in a favor and be used as a general measure for the overall benefits of plan coordination.

By providing a crisp description of the environment characterization, the agents' plans and their modifications we have offered an operational foundation to detect and utilize positive relations among different planners. We have implemented a reasoner which detects favor relations between plans and proposes how to take advantage of favor relations (see figures in Chapter 8). This system, called COORS ("Coordination System"), runs on a Symbolics LISP machine. Plans of different agents are displayed as graphs. The reasoning part of the system has been written in Prolog.

Examples for plan coordinations driven by the favor relation were given for a transportation domain. In general, we believe the plan coordination mechanism is applicable in multiagent domains where actions may be basically characterized by the predicates *Atom*, *Refinement*, *Fv-action*, *Pre* and *cost*.

5.3 Relation Handling in General

At the same time there may exist several relations between plans, e.g. both negative and positive relations. This section contains suggestions as to guide decisions of a coordination agent and how to proceed if several relations exist. The idea is to model the agents' decisions, which have to be made during plan coordination, as personal rules.

Selection of a relation. The first aspect considers the decision which has to be made during plan coordination when selecting an unresolved relation. If an agent detects more than one relation he has to decide in which order a solution is anticipated, i.e. in which order a negotiation about resolving a relation is started by sending *proposal* messages to the involved agents. An agent's coordination behavior is guided by his coordination strategy.

A simple strategy to decide which relation to tackle next is:

Strategy1 (negative, then positive relations): First, solve the conflicts (because they prevent plans from being executed as intended).
Then, solve the positive relations (because they "only" improve existing plans).

If there are several *conflicts* a decision has to be made which is to solve next. In Section 5.1.3 we presented aspects which guide such a decision. In Section 5.1.4 we explained how to solve a given conflict. If several *favors* are possible we have given rationales which one to prefer in Section 5.2.

Another strategy which is preferable under real time aspects checks how much time is left to resolve a relation and solves first the relation with an action a which is intended to be executed next, i.e. start(a) is minimal.

Personal rules for relation handling. An agent's decision process about relation resolution can be expressed as rules. If an agent reasons about two actions and he detects that a *multiagent plan relations* holds, he determines a proposal (solution) to handle this relation. This proposal is transferred to the planning agents of the related actions.

A *proposal* may depend on:
- the multiagent plan relation,
- the personal relation between the agents, e.g. hierarchy, benevolence,
- the actions of detecting agent's individual plan which are not part of the relation.

Each agent may have his personal rules how to deal with relations. An example for *conflict resolution* (see also Section 5.1):
Rule: If Ncrc(a_1, a_2) AND Overlaps(a_1, a_2)
AND "is-small" (time-overlap(a_1, a_2))
THEN "propose spread"

5.4 Summary of Plan Modification and Coordination Operators

The graphical overview in the following figure is based on Fig. 9 of Section 4.2 and lists the plan modification operators for plan adaption and relation resolution. Here, we have attached the corresponding resolution operations.

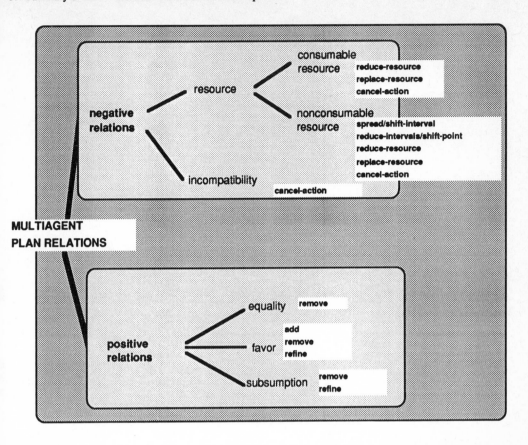

Figure 27: Resolution of plan relations

6 Negotiation for Plan Coordination

Chapters 3, 4 and 5 were concerned with plans, actions and their interactions. It is now time to shift the focus to the agents concerned with creation, execution and coordination of plans. Therefore, this and the next chapter will offer a more general view of coordination and integrate the agents' behavior into the coordination process. Communication is an integral part of distributed planning and it serves two different purposes in our approach:

- The agents communicate about their intended actions ahead of time. Communication occurs first when the agents transfer their plans.
- If there exist (negative or positive) relations among plans, the agents will negotiate about the consequences of these relations trying to prevent negative interferences and utilize positive relations. The function of negotiation can also be seen as binding commitments among agents. Negotiation is considered as a structured interaction by message-passing between the negotiation partners.

6.1 Requirements for Communication

An autonomous agent has its own goals, capabilities and knowledge. In an organization populated by several autonomous agents each of them having potentially diverging goals the reconciliation of their activities is important to ensure a harmonious function of the organization. If there is an equal distribution of control and authority, i.e. no single agent has control over the others, coordination between agents can be achieved by an agreement of the involved agents. Negotiation between these agents is the medium to reach such an agreement.

The need for negotiation is triggered by the existence of negative or positive relations between the actions of different agents' plans. Negative multiagent plan relations are all those relations between plans, which may prevent one or both of the plans from being executed as intended.

The detection of negative relations is crucial for successful plan execution. For instance, in case of a conflict, the goal of the negotiation is to remove a conflict such that the plans of the conflicting agents can be executed without risking a conflict. On the other hand, positive multiagent relations are all those relations between two plans from which some benefit can be derived, for one or both of the agents' plans, by combining them.

Issues. When coordinating the activities of autonomous agents by negotiation, several issues have to be dealt with:

1. What are the agents in the communication network and who communicates with whom?
2. What are the messages exchanged between the communicators?
3. What are the protocols ('when' and 'how') according to which a negotiation takes place?
4. How can the negotiation framework be realized in a technically "sound" manner?

Concerning the first issue, agents in the communication network are autonomous problem solvers. We will differentiate between planning agents and coordination agents, whose task it is to mediate between the negotiating parties. Coordination may take place as a negotiation process between a coordination agent on the one side and a multitude of agents on the other side. There is no dedicated coordination agent determined in advance, i.e. in principle, each agent may initiate a negotiation about plan coordination.

Concerning question 2, we will provide message types both for the exchange of the agents' intentions, i.e. their plans, and for the process of reaching a compromise. The message types reflect the autonomy of the agents by giving them the choice whether to accept, reject, or modify a proposal.

Concerning question 3, we will use a state transition diagram to illustrate the negotiation protocol.

Concerning question 4, we will call protocols "sound" if they guarantee a consistent world view among asynchronously communicating agents and if the danger of deadlocks is suppressed. The design of a "sound" negotiation protocol is realized on two levels: On the application level, an adequate protocol for negotiation is designed, and then, on the analysis and verification level, the protocol is refined in order to make it consistent using a conversation net representation and a simulator.

Basic requirements. Several requirements guided our design of the negotiation protocol. Based on the assumption that negotiation occurs in an *autonomous* agent environment, the protocol should:

- keep communication to a minimum,

- respect the autonomy of the agents,
- allow the exchange of planned actions,
- facilitate the settling of conflicts, and the synchronizing of actions in a beneficial relation,
- support a variety of ways to reach a compromise,
- be usable for human as well as automated agents, i.e. be intuitive and understandable and also formalized enough.

Technical requirements. In addition to the above requirements which reflect the task or specific application of the communication protocol (negotiation between autonomous agents) there are two other requirements on a more technical level which take into account the asynchronous character of communication by message passing and its implementation. Following these requirements

- the protocol should be "sound", i.e. it should ensure a consistent view of the negotiation for both partners,
- its implementation should be simple, i.e. it should use the same (few) concepts and mechanisms of the protocol.

The first of these latter requirements is important because we use an asynchronous message transfer mechanism for negotiation. There is a varying time delay between message dispatch and arrival, and there may be a time delay between the receipt of a message and the dispatch of an answer (no direct feed-back). So, what seems natural in a face-to-face negotiation, the consistent view of the negotiation by both partners, is by no means guaranteed in a computer-mediated negotiation. Messages may even overtake each other, or cross each other traveling in different directions. The result could be inconsistencies or deadlocks in a negotiation, i.e. one partner thinks a compromise has been reached, whereas the other partner sees the negotiation still in a conflict stage, or the negotiation gets stuck because both partners wait for a reaction of the other. If we want to exclude these things to happen, we have to analyze and possibly verify the protocol specification.

The second requirement calls for these same simple concepts and mechanisms to be used in the implementation of the protocol, i.e. we want the protocol *implementation* to directly correspond to the protocol *specification*. In this way, the results of the analysis of the protocol specification can be transferred to the implementation.

These technical problems will be dealt with in Section 6.4.

Flexibility in conversation and planning

Our protocol does not dictate any particular planning paradigm. We do not make any assumptions about the planning stage at which the agents announce their intentions. That implies, for instance, that agents are not forced to transfer only operational, low-level plans or that plans are transferred and synchronized at the same level of abstraction. To cope with this asynchrony, we have developed a flexible mechanism to refine and modify plans (see Chapter 5).

A further degree of freedom is that the agents do not have to transfer complete plans, but only single actions.

Agents do not necessarily conform with other agents' requests. That is, they have the options to reject or counter a proposal. However, the model assumes that agents are not hostile in that agents do not reject a request if they can perform it.

Basic Components

The conversation model basically has three components:

- the *states* a conversation can be in,
- the *message types* which can be exchanged between the conversation partners,
- the *conversation rules* which specify in which states which message types a partner may send or receive.

The negotiation process is seen as a formalized language "game" which follows the rules of the conversation. The negotiation protocol will then be a special conversation type with its own states, message types, and rules within the conversational framework. The message contents do not enter into the negotiation protocol, but rather reflect and determine the course of an individual negotiation within the negotiation "space" delineated by the protocol.

Protocol Development

Negotiation protocol design is not a one-shot process, there are several design stages that require an incremental procedure.

At the beginning of the design of the negotiation protocol we had to decide on the main stages or phases of the negotiation. We identified the opening, the initial negotiation, the re-negotiation, and the termination. The negotiation is opened by a planning agent announcing its intention to execute a certain action. The agent also terminates the negotiation when he considers it no longer necessary. Each agent or a dedicated coordination agent compares the received action with the action messages sent to him by the other agents or with actions of his individual plan. We call an agent whose task it is to check plan relations, and initiate and monitor negotiations about relations resolution, a *coordinator*. After having received the actions and reasoned about relations, an agent may start an initial negotiation phase if necessary. If this phase does not result in a compromise it may be repeated. If a compromise is reached it is tried to be kept stable i.e. a subsequent re-negotiation phase which may be initiated by either agent or coordination agent can only end with a compromise, new or old. If the coordination agent detects that the reason for negotiation has disappeared from his viewpoint (due to some external event), the negotiation returns to the state after the opening.

As a next step in protocol design, we had to select the message types and negotiation states we thought important and necessary for the different stages of the action coordination negotiation. We started with a small set of message types and states, which was gradually extended.

Then we related states and message types. This is done by the conversation rules which specify the state transitions effected by the transmission of certain message types.

The steps, so far, aim at an initial design of a protocol which is adequate for the specific purpose of the negotiation (*application level*). In the last phase (*analysis* and *verification level*) the initial protocol was extended and modified in order to make it consistent with respect to asynchronous communication. This phase relied on a more sophisticated conversation net representation and a simulator tool (see Section 6.4).

6.2 The Protocol: Messages, Agents and Conversation Rules

We will introduce a concept for communication among autonomous agents. Using this *negotiation framework* it will be possible to define the complete model for plan coordination incorporating both agents, their plans, the reasoning about plan relations, the communication about their intentions and the negotiation process for reaching a commitment on how to resolve a relation.

An agent g has a plan p. For each leaf action ai in p there is an internal state cs attached. This state expresses the *conversation state* of ai.

Conversation States

CONV-STATES are the conversation states an agent can be in:
- *initial:* this is the start state.
- *planned:* this is the state when the action is in no conflict or other negotiable relation with other actions.

- *proposed:* an action modification has been proposed by the coordination agent.
- *answered:* a proposal has been answered by the agent.
- *committed:* a compromise has been reached, i.e. a proposed modification has been accepted by the agent, or the action can be executed as planned due to some modifications of other actions (outside this negotiation).
- *unresolved:* a conflict or other reason for negotiation exists and no compromise has been reached yet.
- *re-proposed:* a further action modification has been proposed by the coordination agent (out of an already reached compromise).
- *back-out-requested:* a compromise has been questioned by the agent.
- *re-answered:* a re-proposal has been answered by the agent.
- *executed/withdrawn:* the action has been executed or withdrawn. This is a final state of the conversation.

Roles of agents in negotiations

Agents can have one or two or all of the following *roles* in a conversation:

1. *Planner*: An agent who has established a plan and broadcasted his intention to other agents.
2. *Executor*(affector): The agent who executes an action. This agent does not negotiate about plans. For the purpose of this chapter we assume that executor and planner of an action is the same agent.
3. *Coordinator*: An agent acts as a coordinator of a conversation if he initiates a resolution of a plan relation. If an agent is also the planner of an action which is being negotiated the agent has both roles: planner and coordinator.

When exchanging messages there are two possibilities. The agents can broadcast information about their intended actions to each other (multicast conversation). This may incur a large amount of overhead because more information must be exchanged and because nodes may duplicate each other's reasoning about coordination. Therefore, in our conversation model there is a special kind of agent, called *coordinator*, to which the agents transfer their plans ahead of time. Having a coordinator means that only one agent has to spend its resources on reasoning about coordination and can enforce consistent views.

If an agent is only coordinator of a conversation he acts as a mediator in the process of reaching an agreement. When this agent receives the intended action or whole plans of the other agents he checks whether there are actions which make a negotiation necessary. The coordination agent, acting as an independent mediator, enters in negotiation with each of the parties proposing and modifying compromises until a final agreement is reached. Since the authority resides in the agents, they have to give feedback to the coordination agent about the trade-offs that are acceptable.

Negotiation is originally a multilateral affair between the agents involved in the actions which make a negotiation necessary. However, via a coordination agent, the multilateral negotiation problem is transformed into a set of bilateral negotiations and the coordination agent's coordination strategy. The agents do not interact directly with each other but each agent only communicates with the coordination agent which acts as a mediator.

The concept presented here is not dependent on having a dedicated agent for coordination. We understand the concept of the coordinator as a *role* which agents can hold. How many and which agents in the system act as coordinators (*coordination responsibilities*) is an issue of the system organization in general (*meta-level organization*). An organization depends on the specific application and the number of agents. There is a great range of different organizations possible ranging from having only one dedicated coordinator to each agent being himself both "ordinary" agent and coordinator.

It is a complex task to prepare and monitor a negotiation among autonomous agents. Before a coordinator initiates a negotiation between the agents involved in a negative or positive action relation he has to work out a proposal for a compromise. He then has to take care that the conversation is successful by reaching an agreement in a reasonable amount of time. For the performance of a negotiation the coordination agent may employ a variety of strategies. Strategies may depend on several aspects, of which the most important is the kind of relation between the actions. The problem of finding the right negotiation strategy has been the topic of Chapter 5. The coordinator selects a proposal, which in case of a conflict based on the following factors: temporal relation between the actions, resource type of conflict, relation between duration of action and associated interval, amount of resources needed more than available (a relative value), the preceding proposals (if existing). A proposal contains a suggestion for each agent involved in the conflict.

Message Types

There are several types of messages, called M-TYPES, which can be exchanged between conversation partners:

- *action:* a planning agent announces the details of a planned action to the coordination agent. This message opens the conversation, the action itself will be the topic.

- *proposal:* the coordinator proposes an action modification to the agent in order to reach a compromise with regard to other conflicting or favoring actions.
- *approval/counter/rejection:* possible agent reactions to a proposal.
- *resolution/failure:* positive or negative confirmation of the coordinator; closes the initial negotiation or a re-negotiation phase.
- *disappearance:* announces the reason for the negotiation (e.g. a conflict) to have vanished (caused by a withdrawal of an action in a different negotiation).
- *back-out request/re-proposal:* initiate a re-negotiation of an already reached compromise by either planning agent or coordinator.
- *execution/withdrawal:* the agent announces that the action in question has been executed as agreed (or originally planned), or that he has given up the intention to carry out this action. Both messages terminate the conversation because there is nothing left to negotiate. With respect to the negotiation protocol, both message types can be treated alike, but for the coordinator's overall coordination strategy of course it makes an important difference.

For the concepts presented in this chapter we are only interested in the *type* of a message and not in the *contents* of a message.

Conversation Rules (state transition diagram)

The conversation rules specify the state transitions effected by the transmission of certain message types. These relations can be visualized by state transition diagrams (STD) using the following conventions: states are represented by circles, message transfers are represented by directed arcs connecting the states (Fig. 28). The "color" (grey versus black) of the edges in the STD tells who the originator of the message is. Grey: a message from coordination agent t agent. Black: a message from a planning agent to a coordination agent.

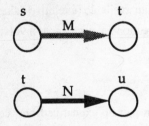

Transmission of message *M* from *A* (agent) to *C* (coordination agent) changes conversation state from *s* to *t*. Transmission of message *N* from *C* to *A* changes conversation state from *t* to *u*.

Figure 28: Two types of edges in the conversation net

This graphical representation of a conversation type is easy to follow through the various moves a partner may take during a negotiation by moving a token around the diagram, or check out how a certain state can be reached, or whether the intended degree of freedom for the negotiation partners is given in the protocol specification.

The state transition diagram of our negotiation protocol is shown in Fig. 29. In order to make the figure not too complicated we have simplified the actual protocol by grouping certain message types into one message type (*execution/withdrawal* into *termination*, and *approval*, *counter*, *rejection* into *answer*) because the differentiation has little or no influence on the further negotiation.

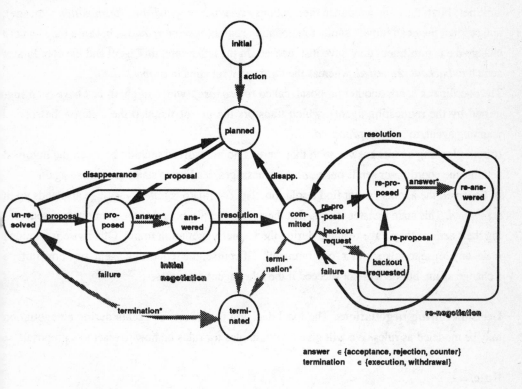

answer ∈ {acceptance, rejection, counter}
termination ∈ {execution, withdrawal}

Figure 29: State transition diagram for action negotiation

A typical path through the protocol commences with a planning agent transmitting an action to another agent, possibly a *coordinator*. In case that the coordinator does not detect any unresolved relation with another action, which he has received earlier, the coordinator remains "quiet", and, if the planning or some executing agent has executed the action, he may receive a termination message (grey arc), which implies that the coordinator removes this action from his stock. If, however, the coordinator detects an uncoordinated relation, he reasons how to resolve this relation (see Chapter 5 for resolution strategies), and then sends a proposal both to the agent who earlier announced his action and(!) to the agent who has announced the other related (e.g., conflicting) action. This means, that all involved agents (the two planning agents and the coordinator) switch their local protocol concerning the "related" actions to state *proposed*.

The coordinator is now waiting for the agents' answers. Answers may be *acceptance*, *rejection* or *counter*. Depending on the *answer* messages (grey arc), the coordinator sends out a *failure* message (black arc), meaning that the relation has not been resolved or he confirms a resolution, which should[1] result in state *committed*. In this state, the planning agents have two possibilities: First, they can announce their actions *execution* or *withdrawal*(*termination* message), and second, they can initiate another negotiation round (*backout request*), because they want to change the commitment they have just reached. In the latter case, this agent and the coordinator switch to *backout requested*, whereas the third agent remains in *committed*.

The coordinator sends another proposal, called *re-proposal* (which might in fact have been suggested by the requesting agent), which transfers the protocols, also the state of the second planning agent, to state *re-proposed*.

If both planning agents answer such that there is no unresolved relation between the involved actions, the coordinator sends out *resolution* messages, leading to states *committed* again.

If, however, the agents cannot find a solution, the coordinator's *failure* message also ends up in *committed*. This state transfer means, that the agents are still bound to the commitment concerning their actions they have reached during the former negotiation round. Otherwise it wouldn't make any sense to talk about a "commitment". Of course, the requesting agent may now initiate a change again, but he will not succeed if the other agent disagrees.

Decision during negotiations. The local decision (behavior) of agents during a negotiation may be modeled as rules. We will give two examples for rules on how to react to a proposal:

Rule:
IF Reason-about(g_1, $\{a_1, a_2\}$) with g_1 = executor (a_1)
AND "proposal" (Rreq, a_1, a_2))
AND "hostility" (planner(a_1), planner(a_2)) ;
THEN "reject" (Rreq, a_1, a_2)

---

[1] We use "should" to express that the communication medium may have problems in correctly and timely transmitting messages. Problems which appear because of the "technical nature" of communication will be dealt with in Section 6.4.

Rule:
IF (reason-about(g_1, $\{a_1, a_2\}$))
AND ("proposal" (Rreq, a_1, a_2))
AND ("master-slave" (planner(a_1), planner(a_2))
      OR "benevolence" (planner(a_1), planner(a_2)))
AND "not busy"
AND "movable" (a_2)
THEN "accept" (Rreq, a_1, a_2)

6.3 A Different Notation for Communication Behavior

As an alternative to the state transition diagram, the communication behavior of an agent can be defined by a 5-tuple of the following form:

$$\text{<CONV-STATES, M-TYPES, receive, send, } s_0 \text{>} \quad \text{with}$$

CONV-STATES: the conversation states an agent can be in (see 6.2).
M-TYPES: message types which can be exchanged between conversation partners (see 6.2).
receive: Conversation rules to specify the conversation states resulting from the reception of message types.
send: Conversation rules to specify the states resulting from the (active) sending of message types.
s_0:   start state.

In our conversation model the reception and sending of messages is directly coupled with a change of an agent's internal conversation states.

An agent's communicative behavior is constrained by two types of *conversation rules* which specify in which state which message types a partner may send or receive. Rules may be nondeterministic and the rule types will be instantiated with values from their domains and ranges. Rules basically relate the states and message types.

$$\text{send}_{\text{roles}} : \text{CONV-STATES} \longrightarrow \text{M-TYPES x CONV-STATES}$$

$$\text{receive}_{\text{roles}} : \text{M-TYPES x M-TYPES} \longrightarrow \text{CONV-STATES}$$

It is feasible to specify rules as axioms. Example for an axiom concerning a *send* rule:

Axiom:

$\text{Equal(role, coordinator)} \wedge \text{eq(conv-state, rejected)} \Rightarrow \text{(send(resolution)} \wedge \text{succ(committed))}$
$\vee \text{(send(failure)} \wedge \text{succ(unresolved))}$

Instead of specifying all the conversation rules as axioms it is more convenient and compact to use the following tables:

Planner	state	input message	output message	successor state
send	initial		action	planned
	planned		termination[1]	terminated
	proposed		acceptance	answered
	proposed		counter	answered
	proposed		rejection	answered
	committed		termination	terminated
	committed		back-out-request	b-o-requested
	re-proposed		acceptance	re-answered
	re-proposed		counter	re-answered
	re-proposal		rejection	re-answered
	unresolved		termination	terminated
receive	planned	proposal		proposed
	answered	failure		unresolved
	answered	resolution		committed
	unresolved	proposal		proposed
	unresolved	disappearance		planned
	committed	disappearance		planned
	committed	re-proposal		re-proposed
	b-o-requested	re-proposal		re-proposed
	b-o-requested	failure		committed
	re-answered	resolution		committed
	re-answered	failure		committed

Table 4: A *planner's* negotiation protocol

---

[1] termination $\in$ {execution, cancellation}

Coordinator	state	Input message	output message	successor state
send	planned		proposal	proposed
	answered		resolution	committed
	answered		failure	unresolved
	unresolved		termination	planned
	unresolved		proposal	proposed
	committed		re-proposal	re-proposed
	committed		disappearance	planned
	b-o-requested		re-proposal	re-proposed
	b-o-requested		failure	committed
receive	initial	action		planned
	planned	termination		terminated
	proposed	acceptance		answered
	proposed	counter		answered
	proposed	rejection		answered
	committed	termination		terminated
	committed	back-out-request		b-o-requested

Table 5: A *coordinator's* negotiation protocol

6.4   Appendix: Technical Problems in Installing a Conversation Protocol

This section deals with aspects of transferring the conversation model of the preceding sections into an implemented version and thus is concerned with the technical problems and not the conceptual problems of designing a protocol.

There are two requirements which take into account the asynchronous character of communication by message passing and its implementation: (i) the protocol should be "sound", i.e. it should ensure a consistent view of the negotiation for both partners, and (ii), its implementation should be simple, i.e. it should use the same (few) concepts and mechanisms of the protocol. The first of these latter requirements is important because we use an asynchronous message transfer mechanism for negotiation. There is a varying time delay between message dispatch and arrival, and there may be a time delay between the receipt of a message and the dispatch of an answer (no direct feed-back). So, what seems natural in a face-to-face negotiation, the consistent view of the negotiation by both partners, is by no means guaranteed in a computer-mediated negotiation. Messages may even overtake each other, or cross each other traveling in different directions. The result could be inconsistencies or deadlocks in a negotiation, i.e. one partner thinks a compromise has been reached, whereas the other partner sees the negotiation still in a conflict stage, or the negotiation gets stuck because both partners wait for a reaction of the other. If we want to exclude these things, we have to analyze and possibly verify the protocol specification. This requests a few but powerful concepts for high-level protocol specification, possibly lending themselves to a formal treatment. The concepts we will use are message types, states of a negotiation, and state changes effected by message exchange between the negotiation partners.

The second requirement calls for these same simple concepts and mechanisms to be used in the implementation of the protocol, i.e. we want the protocol *implementation* to directly correspond to the protocol *specification*. In this way, the results of the analysis of the protocol specification can be transferred to the implementation. The introduction of additional means of dealing with asynchrony (time stamps, message queues) in the implementation *alone* would invalidate the assertions of a protocol verification and is to be avoided. We will show that the development of a sound negotiation protocol is possible without using additional concepts.

Although the STD representation is very suited for application level design purposes, it does not reflect the asynchronous character of the underlying communication: it maintains the notion of a single conversation state. Following the STD model, the negotiation partners move synchronously from state to state when a negotiation message is transmitted. But as we have mentioned above asynchronous communication messages take a usually unpredictable amount of time travelling from sender to receiver, so messages may overtake each other or cross each other travelling in different directions. This can result in inconsistent views of the negotiation or even deadlocks (Figs. 30a and b). In the following, we will analyze such situations in more detail.

As we have seen, a single STD does not properly represent a negotiation based on asynchronous communication. Instead, both negotiation partners have their own state transition diagram, each reflecting its owners view of the negotiation, i.e. these diagrams can and will be differently marked by the token representing the current state.

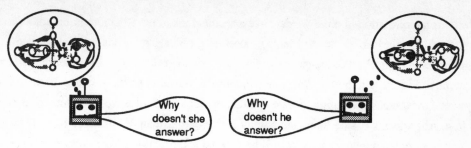

(a) Deadlock due to a difference in the agents' transition diagram

(b) An agent expects a different message

Figure 30: Problems of asynchronous message transfer and different local views

An edge in the STD, originally representing a message transmission, will be interpreted differently according to who is sending the message and who is receiving it. In the following example symbolizing the state transition from s to t effected by the transfer of message M from agent to coordination agent, we have two different interpretations (see Fig. 31).

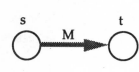

Agent interpretation (active):
If I am in state s, I can decide (possibly among other things) to dispatch message M thereby changing to state t immediately.

Coordination agent interpretation (passive):
If I am in state s, it may happen that I receive message M which would change my state to t.

Figure 31: Different interpretation of a state transition

So, message transmission is split up into two separate events: dispatch and receipt, which are interpreted according to the respective role (sender or receiver).

With this interpretation in mind we can take a second look at the STD representation of a conversation (in general) and try to identify possible problem situations with respect to asynchronous communication (messages overtaking or crossing each other). Consider the following example of Fig. 32 with both partners viewing the conversation being in state s. Partner A may now send message M, changing to state t, and afterwards send message N, thereby changing to state u. At partner's C side, message N may arrive earlier than M. Because there is no state transition associated with s and N, N will be ignored and discarded (remember our simple implementation model: no additional message queues or time stamps). After the eventual arrival of message M, C will change its state to t, with both partners ending up in possibly inconsistent states t and u.

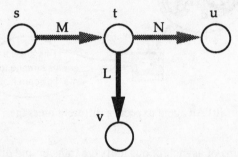

Figure 32: A "problem" node in a conversational diagram

Another problem can also be demonstrated using the above example: Suppose both partners are in state t, then both may simultaneously issue messages N and L, respectively, thereby changing into states u and v. Since the arrival of these messages in the respective states is not specified in the STD a possible deadlock will be the result after the discarding of both messages.

A short inspection of our negotiation protocol of Fig. 28 shows that this is not a purely theoretical problem: If in state *committed* agent A and coordination agent C simultaneously issue a *back-out request* and a *disappearance* message, a deadlock will be the result according to the specification at this stage. Other examples show that this type of problem is usually present in any conversation type of only modest complexity.

At this point in the protocol development three questions arise:
– What types of counter measures can be taken to overcome the above problems in order to make the negotiation protocol "sound", i.e. consistent in the presence of asynchronous communication?
– Can the STD model of a conversation type be enlarged or modified so as to reflect the asynchronies of the communication mechanism?

– Can such an enlarged/modified conversation representation be used to analyze and possibly
verify the negotiation protocol with respect to consistency?

The countermeasures to prevent message overtaking are straightforward: the introduction of acknowledgement messages which are issued immediately upon the receipt of the first message
by the receiver and which have to be waited for before the follow-up message can be sent. In
special cases, where the second message leads to a final state in which the overtaken message
can be safely ignored, of course simpler solutions are possible.
The handling of message crossing is slightly more complex: first one has to settle the priority
question, i.e. which message is more "important", and second one has to see that the messages
crossing each other are not ignored, so that both partners end up in the state indicated by the
message with the higher priority. Figure 33 illustrates these methods at the example we used in
the preceding section (cf. Fig. 32). Note, that message N has priority over message L. The *im-
mediate* dispatch of the acknowledgement messages (without any intermediate state) is indicated
by the bicolored arcs.
Both processes introduce new message types and conversation states which are used only for
synchronization purposes and are not important (and should not be visible) at the application
level. So, by making the negotiation protocol consistent, we introduce a second level of detail
which might be called the analysis/verification level of specification.

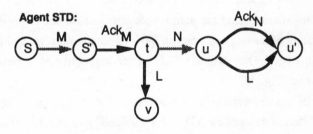

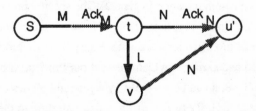

Figure 33: Avoiding conversational inconsistencies by splitting the STD (cf. Fig. 32)

Whereas the remedies for the different synchronization problems might seem straightforward one at a time, our experience shows that the interplay between the protocol modifications in different places may be intricate, which brings us to our second question. There is a need for a more complete conversation model which allows to analyze the consequences of such modifications. As we have seen, the STD representation of a conversation allows to identify possible problem situations (overtaking: edges of the same "color" going into and coming out of a state; crossing: edges of different "colors" coming out of a state). But since we have two states of the conversation representing both partners' views, we cannot represent this aspect of the conversation in a single STD.

For this level of detail we have to tend to the more powerful model of Petri nets [Peterson 81; Reisig 83]. The basic idea is to couple the two STD's (one for each partner) together by a message transfer mechanism. Because this would result in a rather complex structure using elementary Petri nets, we use Pr/T nets, a certain kind of high-level Petri nets [Genrich and Lautenbach 81]. The Pr/T net of our conversation model of negotiations is given in Fig. 34. This conversation net has two places which represent the states of agent and coordination agent. These places carry a token with a value indicating the current state. The other two places of the conversation net represent the communication channels which may carry tokens indicating the messages currently traveling from one partner to the other. The dispatch/receipt transitions "fire" when a permissible state transition is possible; a firing results in the receipt or dispatch of a message and an according state change. Thus, the transitions of the net are "inscribed" (or associated) with tables summarizing the permissible state transitions, respectively. An entry in such a table consisting of the original state, an input or output message, and the successor state corresponds to an edge in the original STD in the respective interpretation of agent or coordination agent (cf. Fig. 30).

The *disadvantage* of this conversation representation is that the graphical quality (clarity) of the STD is lost. The different states of the STD are all "folded" into one state place of the conversation net which carries a token indicating the current state. The graphical structure of the conversation net is that of a bilateral communication in general. The specific properties of a certain negotiation protocol are "hidden" in the associated tables. However, the big *advantage* of this representation is that all protocol modifications made necessary by asynchronous communication can be adequately expressed and *analyzed* which answers our third question. Since the conversation net is an ordinary Pr/T-net it can be analyzed by a general Pr/T-net simulator [Victor and Woetzel 90; Wißkirchen et al. 84]. By tuning this simulator slightly to the special problem of conversation analysis, the simulator will detect all possible inconsistencies: it will indicate when messages are ignored, when deadlocks occur or when the conversation terminates inconsistently.

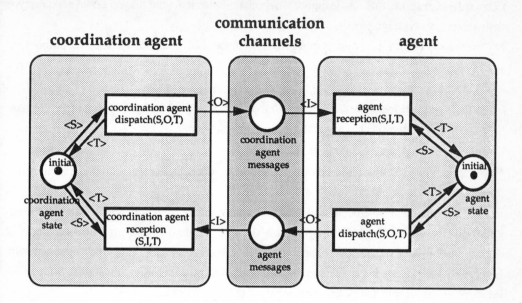

Figure 34: Conversation net

The simulator itself is a 60 line Prolog program, that settles reachability problems for a given Pr/T-net. It will decide whether a given marking can be reached from another marking, which markings can be reached from a given marking, or from which markings a given marking can be reached. All possible solutions of these problems are generated via backtracking by the Prolog system.

With the help of the simulator, we succeeded in extending and modifying the original negotiation protocol of Fig. 28 in order to eliminate all pitfalls of asynchronous communication. This procedure enclosed quite a number of steps in a trial and error fashion. For synchronization purposes, we had to introduce six additional states and four additional message types to the negotiation protocol, resulting in a negotiation with 153 different possible situations, i.e. markings of the respective Pr/T-net. In the end, we have been able to verify by means of *exhaustive* simulation that the resulting protocol is "sound" in the sense that all possible inconsistencies have been excluded.

Summary. We have presented a negotiation framework for the coordination of autonomous agents' activities. Negotiation becomes necessary for agents acting in a common environment, e.g. because of possible conflicts. Our approach integrates both the requirements of the application (negotiation between *autonomous* agents) and the requirements of a realization using asynchronous message passing.

Our experience shows that the design of a negotiation protocol (and that of a conversation type in general) is a two stage process:

– *application level*: initial design of a protocol which is adequate for the specific purpose of the negotiation;

STD representation.

– *analysis* and *verification level*: extension/modification of the initial protocol in order to make it consistent with respect to asynchronous communication;

conversation net representation, simulator tool.

Negotiation protocol design is not a one-shot process, both design stages require an incremental procedure.

Parts of our approach have been implemented as conversation monitors which interpret the negotiation protocol and which interface on the one hand to the communication network (electronic mail) and on the other hand to the agents' application programs. The implementation is currently being extended to include the agents' planning and coordination activities for an office application (agents partly acting on behalf of office workers).

Our experience shows that high-level protocol design at the moment calls for a lot of "manual" work and ad hoc decisions. More design support tools (like the simulator) are needed in the future.

Some comments on related work (in addition to Chapter 2): Other researchers have already used a conversation and negotiation oriented approach to coordinate distributed problem solvers. One of the most studied approach is Davis' and Smith's contract net protocol [Davis and Smith 80, 83; Smith 80]. In contrast to our model these papers use negotiation as a means to decompose problems and allocate tasks and not, as we do, to coordinate and synchronize preformed plans.

Durfee et al. did considerable research on how agents can reach an agreement using negotiation [Durfee 88; Durfee and Lesser 87, 88, 89]. We support their suggestion, emphasized in their work on 'partial global planning', that plans are broadcasted or exchanged in order to allow agents greater access to the anticipated future behavior of others.

A system which mediates between conflicting parties is Sycara's PERSUADER program [Sycara 85, 88, 89a, 89b]. But Sycara's focus is on the negotiation between strongly opposing parties for resolving labor disputes whereas negotiation in our system is based on a more cooperative behavior between the agents.

The next chapter will put the communication protocols developed in this chapter in a more comprehensive cooperation framework.

7 A Synthesized Model of Distributed Planning by Autonomous Cooperating Agents

This chapter synthesizes the aspects developed in the preceding four chapters into one coordination and cooperation framework. The model embraces the agents' abilities to *plan*, *communicate* and *modify* their *plans* – all aspects have been shown as having a great importance on the coordination of distributed problem solvers.

In the second part of this chapter, we will show how our model can be applied using two scenarios.

7.1 Environment

We will shortly review the parameters for domain characterization. These terms were motivated and defined in Chapters 3 and 4.

The coordination environment is characterized by

$G = \{g_1, g_2,..., g_k\}$ the set of agents.

$A = \{a_1, a_2,..., a_l\}$ the set of actions

$R = \{r_1, r_2,..., r_m\}$ the set of resources.

For actions a in A, $A_1 \subseteq A$:

Atom(a) a is an action at the finest level of detail.

Refinement(a, A_1, C_1)   refinement relation between actions.

Pre(a, A_1)   is true iff A_1 is the set of preparing actions for a.

Undo(a, A_1) A_1 is the set of "undoing actions" for a.

Exchangeable-agent(a) is true iff the executing agent for a can be exchanged.

Fv-action(a)   is true iff a is suited as a favor action.

cost(a)   the cost associated with the execution of a

For each pair of actions a_1, $a_2 \in A$:

Incompatible(a_1, a_2)   is true iff both actions can not be executed together.

For each resource $r \in R$:

Consumable(r) is true iff r is consumable.

available(r, i) the amount of resource r available during interval i.

A *plan* consists of a set of actions and a relation between these actions, i.e. a plan is a pair $p = (A, SUB)$, $SUB \subseteq A \times A$.

Terms which describe the structure of plans:

Sub(a_1, a_2, p) the action denoted by a_2 is a subaction of a_1 within p

Sub+(a_1, a_2, p) a_2 is a subaction of a_1 or a succeeding descendant

Leaf(a, p) a is an action without any subaction in p

refine$(a, A1)$: $\mathbb{P} \longrightarrow \mathbb{P}$ refinement operator

Refines(p, p') p' results from p by successive refinements

leaves: $\mathbb{P} \longrightarrow \wp(\mathbb{P})$ collects the most operational actions in a plan

7.2 Agent States

How can agents interact to coordinate their activities? What do the agents know about each others' plans and how do they communicate about it?

A state of an agent in the coordination process has to include the agent's own plan progress and his knowledge about other agents' plans. Furthermore, an agent keeps track of the relationships between his and the other agents' plans and the negotiation states in resolving relations.

Formally, an agent's g *coordination state* is a 5-tuple of the following form:

$$S_g = <LP_g, HY_g, EP_g, CS_g, PR_g>$$

with

- *Local plans* $LP_g = \{a \in A \mid \text{Intends}(g, a) \wedge \text{planner}(a) = g\}$. LP_g denotes an agent's intentions, i.e. the actions which agent g intends to execute in the world.

- *History* $\mathbf{HY_g} = \{a \in A \mid \text{Executed}(a)\}$. The agent's knowledge of the history of the actions which have been executed so far in the world. The *state of the world* at any point in time is mainly a record of the events that have occurred and their interrelationships.
- *External plans* $\mathbf{EP_g} = \{a \in A \mid \exists g_1 \text{ Intends}(g_1, a) \wedge \text{planner}(a) \neq g\}$. The intended actions of other agents within the system as far as they are known by agent g. Both LP_g and EP_g contain only *leaf* actions of the agents' plans, i.e. $a \in \text{leaves}(p)$ for the respective actions and plans.
- *Conversation states* $\mathbf{CS_g} = \{(a, c) \mid a \in LP_g \cup EP_g, c \in \text{CONV-STATES}\}$. Pairs of actions and conversation states. For every action in LP_g or EP_g there is a conversation state attached. The conversation state of an action denotes whether an action has been announced to other agents and whether a negotiation concerning this action is being conducted.

  CONV-STATES = {*initial, planned, proposed, answered, committed, unresolved, re-proposed, back-out-requested, re-answered, executed/withdrawn*} Conversation states have been detailed in Chapter 6.

  The negotiation protocol has been represented as a state transition diagram (Fig. 28, Chapter 6). Each agent participating in a conversation keeps record for each action he is currently communicating about using such a diagram.
- *Plan relations* $\mathbf{PR_g} = \{(a_1, a_2, g_2, Relation) \mid a_1 \in LP_g \cup EP_g, a_2 \in EP_g \text{ with planner}(a_2) = g_2 \wedge Relation \in \{Crc, Ncrc, Incomp, Equal, Subsume, Favor. Rreq, Nreq\}\}$. An agent maintains a list of plan relations between his and other agents' plans or relationships only among other agents' plans. The latter case is meaningful for an agent acting as an independent coordinator. Relations were defined in Chapter 4.

The state S_g as described here is applicable both if an agent is planner and coordinator and if an agent is only coordinator. A *pure* coordinator is an agent who coordinates actions which he has not planned. The state components of a pure coordinator may be simplified:

The *local plans* either do not exist or may be neglected in a conversation which is coordinated by this agent, i.e. $LP_g = \varnothing$. This simplifies the conversation states and the plan relations because LP_g can be omitted:

Conversation states $CS_g = \{(a, c) \mid a \in EP_g, c \in \text{CONV-STATES}\}$.

Plan Relationships $PR_g = \{(a_1, a2, g_2, Relation) \mid a_1 \in EP_g, a_2 \in EP_g \text{ with planner}(a_2) = g_2 \wedge Relation \in \{Crc, Ncrc, Incomp, Equal, Subsume, Favor\}\} \cup \{(a_1, -, g_2, Relation) \mid a_1 \in EP_g, (\text{planner}(a_2) = g \text{ if } a_1 \in EP_g), Relation \in \{Rreq, Nreq\}\}$.

State of the world

If the world w is populated by agents $g_1,..., g_n$, with individual states $S_{g1}, S_{g2}, ..., S_{gn}$, respectively, we define the state of the world as an n-tuple of the following form:

$$S_W = <S_{g1}, S_{g2},..., S_{gn}>.$$

Actually, this global state may not be determined because the system is asynchronous and not centrally controlled.

The coordination problem is specified by the agents' intended actions, their initial states, the environment, and the operations to modify actions.

State changing activities

Agents are able to perform these operations:

- *Reasoning*. An agents *reasons* when he plans, checks for plan relationships with other agents' plans or works out solutions how to resolve relationships.
- *Communication*. Communication means message sending and receiving.
- *Execution*. An agent executes actions of a plan.
- *Plan Modification*. Primitive operations on actions and plans are: *remove, add, refine, reduce resource, set start, set end, set amount, cancel*. More complex operations are *spread, reduce-intervals, reduce-resource*, and *replace-resource*. Descriptions can be found in Chapter 5.

7.3 Coordination Process

Input

The initial state for plan coordination is a set of intended actions (plans) for each planning agent in G and the set of actions which have been executed. The input state is given by a tuple $<S_{g1}, S_{g2}, ..., S_{gn}>$, $S_g = <LP_g, HY_g, EP_g, CS_g>$, with $g \in G$ and $\forall\, g \in G\; EP_g = \emptyset, HY_g = \emptyset, CS_g = \{(a, cs) \mid a \in LP_g \wedge cs = initial\,\}$.

For each intended action $a \in LP_g$, $g \in G$, the following is known:

res(a)   the set of resources required by a,

planner(a)   the agent who has established a plan for a,

executor(*a*)	the agent which is to execute *a*,
time(*a*)	the temporal interval (start- and endpoint) of *a*,
dur(*a*)	the duration of *a*,
amount(*r,a*)	the amount of resource r requested by *a*.

Goals

The *global goal* of plan coordination is a *coordinated* set of plans. The *local goal* of each agent is to "make" $PR_g = \emptyset$. This goal is an optimal result which may not be accomplished. Therefore, given a set of individual plans and a set of plan relationships among these plans, coordination tries to *reduce* the number of these relationships rather than completely resolving all of them. Several heuristics for plan relationships processing, i.e. plan coordination, have been described in Chapter 5. A negative relationship is resolved if the involved plans are modified such that a conflict does not occur, and a positive relationship vanishes if the involved plans are modified to exploit the potential synergy effect between the plans.

Phases of Activity Coordination

After the agents have developed their plans autonomously, they transfer these plans to each other or to a blackboard which can be read by all agents or a specific coordinator. In order to reconcile these plans several tasks have to be executed:
- recognize and evaluate the possible relations between the plans,
- work out solutions to deal with these relations,
- initiate and perform negotiations.

As a result of the coordination process the individual plans are reconciled with respect to their negative and positive relations.

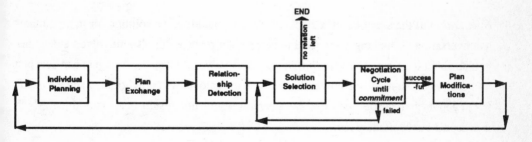

Figure 35: Phases of plan coordination

Coordination consists of several phases (Fig. 35):

1. *Individual Planning.* An agent g_1 has or generates a plan.

2. *Plan Exchange.* He informs another agent g_2, possibly a coordinator, about his plan and, the other agent knows g_1's plan. After agent g_2 has received the intended actions of an agent he updates his knowledge about the other agent's intentions, i.e.
$$\forall g \in G\ EP_g = \{\ LP_{gx} \mid gx \in G \wedge gx \neq g \}.$$

3. *Relationship Detection.* Knowing also his own plans or the plan or further agents, g_2 reasons about these and the just received planned activities with the purpose of detecting multiagent plan relationships. Then, the receiving agent g_2 establishes a set of plan relationships with plans of other agents:
$PR_{g2} = \{(a_1, a_2, g_2, Relation) \mid \exists\ a_1 \in LP_{g2} \cup EP_{g2}\ \exists\ a_2 \in EP_{g2} \wedge Relation(a_1, a_2)$ with
Relation $\in \{Crc, Ncrc, Incomp, Equal, Subsume, Favor\}$
$\vee Relation(a_1, g, g_2)$ with *Relation* $\in \{Rreq\}$
$\vee Relation(a_1, g_2)$ with *Relation* $\in \{Nreq\}\ )\}$

4. *Solution Selection/Internal Relationship Processing.* For each relationship there may be a variety of ways (strategies) possible how to handle (solve) it.
The processing of PR_g is done (initiated) in these principle steps (procedure *process-relations*).
(a) Select a *quadruple* in PR_g. A *quadruple* (a_1, a_2, g_1, g_2) represents an unresolved plan relation between g_1's and g_2's plans.
(b) Determine a *solution* for the quadruple.
(c) Start negotiation to resolve the *quadruple* relation with first proposal *solution*.

5. *Negotiation.* If the agent has detected a relationship and found a solution for it, he initiates a conversation by making a proposal to resolve the relationship. The involved agents negotiate about the proposal (= a *solution* for a *quadruple*, see step 4). An agent can accept a proposal, reject it, modify parameters of it such as 'amount' or 'time' or may suggest a different approach to tackle a conflict. A successful negotiation results in a commitment which is accepted by the participants.

6. *Plan Modification.* The agents modify their plans according to the result of the negotiation.

The 'relationship order' resulting from the strategies in step 4 (Solution Selection) does not necessarily imply that the relations are solved in this order; it only means that solutions are tackled in this order. An agent does not have to wait until a commitment has been reached concerning the resolution of one plan relationship before he starts a negotiation about another relationship. An agent may even negotiate about the solution of all his current plan relationships (contained in PR) in parallel. This means, in fact, that the solutions of relationships may "overtake" each other.

Section 5.3 contained suggestions and assumptions how the agents local decisions during step 4 may be performed.

7.4 Revival of the Art and Bert Example

An example should illustrate how agents interact when coordinating their activities by relationship resolution. All communication among agents follows the protocols defined in Chapter 6. There are two agents, who might be colleagues in an organization and have plans for the same day. This example has been presented already informally in Section 4.1. Justified by the nondeterministic behavior of agents the result of the coordination process differs slightly from the earlier one.

Environment

Agents $G = \{\text{Art, Bert}\}$

Actions $A = \{\text{pick-up, .., go-to-post-office,..}\}$

Resources $R = \{\text{symbolics LM7, ...}\}$

The following predicates are true:

Exchangeable-agent(pick-up)

Fv-action(buy-stamps)

Fv-action(deliver-package)

Refinement(bring-package, {go-to-post-office, deliver-package, go-to-office}, {Before(go-to-post-office, deliver-package}, Before(go-to-post-office, go-to-work)})

Refinement(get-stamps, {go-to-post-office, buy-stamps, go-to-office}, {Before(go-to-post-office, get-stamps}, Before(go-to-post-office, go-to-office)})

Nonconsumable(symbolics LM7)

Furthermore: available(symbolics LM7, 9-25-90)=1.

Initial states

S_{Art} = <LP_{Art}, HY_{Art}, EP_{Art}, CS_{Art}, PR_{Art}> with

LP_{Art} = {pick-up$_{Art}$, produce-video, make-phone-call, answer-mail, get-stamps, give-com-
    ment, copy-papers} with action parameters: res(produce-video)= symbolics LM7. The
    time of the actions are shown in Fig. 36. The *planner* and the *executor* of these actions is
    Art, except for *give-comment*.

HY_{Art} = $\emptyset$

EP_{Art} = $\emptyset$

CS_{Art} = {$(a, cs) \mid a \in LP_{Art} \wedge cs = initial$}

PR_{Art} = $\emptyset$

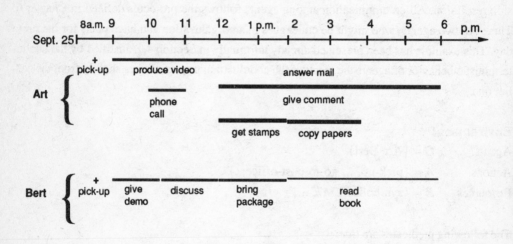

Figure 36: The agents' plans

S_{Bert} = <LP_{Bert}, HY_{Bert}, EP_{Bert}, CS_{Bert}, PR_{Bert}> with

LP_{Bert} = {pick-up$_{Bert}$, give-demo, discuss, bring-package, read-book} with action parame-
    ters: res(give-demo)= symbolics LM7. The *planner* and *executor* of these actions is Bert.

HY_{Bert} = $\emptyset$

$EP_{Bert} = \varnothing$

$CS_{Bert} = \{(a, cs) \mid a \in LP_{Bert} \land cs = initial\}$

$PR_{Bert} = \varnothing$

Coordination process

The coordination framework which has been put forward in this work gives the agents freedom how to coordinate themselves. Hence, the coordination process which will be outlined now is only one out of a variety of possible ones. Degrees of freedom are for instance due to: the number of possible refinements of actions, the way of communication and negotiation (although constrained by protocols), the strategies of conflict resolution and favor relationship exploitation.

After the agents have transferred their intentions to each other (message type *action*), the local states are updated as follows:

$EP_{Art} := LP_{Bert}$

$CS_{Art} = \{(a, cs) \mid a \in LP_{Art} \cup EP_{Art} \land cs = planned\}$

$EP_{Bert} := LP_{Art}$

$CS_{Bert} = \{(a, cs) \mid a \in LP_{Bert} \cup EP_{Bert} \land cs = planned\}$

In this example, there is no coordination agent determined in advance. Both agents may have both roles, i.e. *planner* and *coordinator*. The agents check the relationships between their and the respective other agents' plans. The agent who first launches a proposal message gets the role of a *coordinator* concerning the negotiation for the respective action in addition to his role as *planner*.

$PR_{Art} = \{$ (pick-up$_{Art}$, pick-up$_{Bert}$, Bert, *Equal*),

                   (produce-video, give-demo, Bert, *Ncrc*),

                   (get-stamps, bring-package, Bert, *Favor*),

                   (give-comment, -, Bert, *Rreq*) $\}$

Bert's plan relationship set PR_{Bert} is corresponding.

We will explain the agent's coordination process relation after relation, although, in principle, this process may be done concurrently.

We assume that the agents are highly cooperative, i.e. they agree on a proposal to modify their plans if the plan modification does not endanger the execution of the other actions in their plans. This assumption leads to a simple negotiation process.

Resolving the equality relation. Art sends a *proposal* message to Bert, asking him to commit to pick up Mr. Smith at the station such that he himself can remove the action from his plan. It is important to get the commitment from Bert because thereby it is confirmed that Bert will execute the action. Bert needs Art's agreement to change his plan to pick up Mr. Smith.

Art's conversation state:

CS_{Art} = {(pick-up$_{Bert}$, proposed)} $\cup$ {(a, cs) | $a \neq$ pick-up$_{Bert}$ $\wedge$ $a \in LP_{Art} \cup EP_{Art}$ $\wedge$ $cs =$
    planned}

Bert is in the respective conversation state.

Bert agrees to this proposal by sending an *acceptance* message. Thus, the resolution of the equality resolution is acknowledged by a *resolution* message which results that both agents are in state *committed* concerning *pick-up*$_{Bert}$. Art can remove this action from his set of intended action. He uses a *withdrawal* message to transfer "his" action *pick-up*$_{Art}$ from state *planned* to *terminated*. Now, the agents are in the following states:

S_{Art} = <LP_{Art}, HY_{Art}, EP_{Art}, CS_{Art}, PR_{Art}> with

LP_{Art} = {produce-video, make-phone-call, answer-mail, buy-stamps, give-comment, copy-
    papers}

HY_{Art} = $\varnothing$

EP_{Art} = {pick-up$_{Bert}$, give-demo, discuss, bring-package, read-book}

CS_{Art} = {(a, cs) | $a \neq$ pick-up$_{Bert}$ $\wedge$ $a \in LP_{Art} \cup EP_{Art}$ $\wedge$ cs = *planned*} $\cup$
            {pick-up$_{Bert}$, *committed*} $\cup$ {pick-up$_{Art}$, *terminated*}

PR_{Art} = {   (produce-video, give-demo, Bert, *Ncrc*),

            (get-stamps, bring-package, Bert, *Favor*),

            (give-comment, -, Bert, *Rreq*) }

S_{Bert} = <LP_{Bert}, HY_{Bert}, EP_{Bert}, CS_{Bert}, PR_{Bert}> with

LP_{Bert} = {pick-up$_{Bert}$, give-demo, discuss, bring-package, read-book}

HY_{Bert} = $\varnothing$

EP_{Bert} = {produce-video, make-phone-call, answer-mail, buy-stamps,

$$\text{give-comment, copy-papers}\}$$

$$\text{CS}_{\text{Bert}} = \{(\text{pick-up}_{\text{Bert}}, \textit{committed})\} \cup \{(a,cs) \mid a \in \text{LP}_{\text{Bert}} \cup \text{EP}_{\text{Bert}} \wedge$$
$$a \neq \text{pick-up}_{\text{Bert}} \wedge cs = \textit{planned}\}$$

$$\text{PR}_{\text{Bert}} = \{ \text{ (give-demo, produce-video, Art, } \textit{Ncrc}),$$
$$\text{(bring-package, get-stamps, Art, } \textit{Favor}),$$
$$\text{(give-comment, -, Art, } \textit{Rreq}) \qquad \}$$

Negotiations about the remaining three relations will be explained in less detail.

Resolving the conflict. In an initial negotiation, an agent (coordinator) proposes to resolve the conflict by moving the involved actions, which is not accepted, i.e. intermediate conversation states *un-resolved*. A subsequent negotiation about a reduction of the actions' temporal duration using *reduce-intervals*(produce-video, 60 min, 0 min, give-demo, 0 min, 30 min) as defined in 5.1.1. This negotiation leads to a commitment, i.e. (give-demo, *committed*) and (produce-video, *committed*).

Resolving the favor relation. The result of the negotiation about the favor relation is that Bert does a favor for Art by refining his plan for *bring-package* and integrating the favor action *buy stamps*. In turn, Art can remove the action *get-stamps* from his plan. An example considering a similar type of favor relation was given in Section 5.2.4.

Resolving the request relation. Bert grants Art's request to *give comment* on Art's video film.

Result.
The coordination process finishes with a *coordinated* set of plans:

$$S_{\text{Art}} = <\text{LP}_{\text{Art}}, \text{HY}_{\text{Art}}, \text{EP}_{\text{Art}}, \text{CS}_{\text{Art}}, \text{PR}_{\text{Art}}> \text{ with}$$

$\text{LP}_{\text{Art}} = \{\text{produce-video, make-phone-call, answer-mail, give-comment, copy-papers}\}$

Some parameter values, especially times and durations of actions, differ from the initial values.

$\text{HY}_{\text{Art}} = \varnothing$

$\text{EP}_{\text{Art}} = \{\text{give-demo, discuss, go-to-post-office, deliver-package, buy-stamps, go-to-office,}$
    $\text{read-book}\}$

$\text{CS}_{\text{Art}} = \{(a, cs) \mid a \in \text{EP}_{\text{Art}} \cup \text{LP}_{\text{Art}} \backslash \{\text{copy-papers}\} \wedge cs = \textit{committed}\} \cup$

{copy-papers, *planned*}

$PR_{Art} = \varnothing$. The local goal of coordination has been reached.

$S_{Bert} = <LP_{Bert}, HY_{Bert}, EP_{Bert}, CS_{Bert}, PR_{Bert}>$ with

$LP_{Bert} = \{$pick-up, give-demo, discuss, go-to-post-office, deliver-package,

    buy-stamps, go-to-office, read-book$\}$

$HY_{Bert} = \varnothing$

$EP_{Bert} = \{$produce-video, make-phone-call, answer-mail, give-comment,

    copy-papers$\}$

$CS_{Bert} = \{(a, cs) \mid a \in EP_{Bert} \cup LP_{Bert} \backslash \{$read-book$\} \wedge cs = committed\} \cup$

    {read-book, *planned*}

$PR_{Bert} = \varnothing$.

7.5 Mobile Vehicles as Autonomous Agents

Another scenario which can be used to demonstrate the applicability of our coordination model is *collision avoidance in the traffic domain*. In Section 5.1.2.2 it was indicated how our strategies for conflict resolution can be applied in order to avoid collisions in the traffic domain. In this chapter we will deal with the same domain, but focussing on the states of the agents during their plan reconciliation process.

The following example contains only two vehicles which are in a conflicting situation because they want to cross a single-track intersection during the same or overlapping time periods.

Environment
Agents are *Car1* and *Car2*.
Actions are a variety of types of movements such as drive, overtake, cut in, and speed up.
Resources (see also 5.1.2.2) are the regions on the streets, which may be occupied by vehicles.

The approach of conflicts and their resolution of Chapters 4 and 5 is used to describe potential collisions and avoid them. *Plans* in the traffic domain include the paths the vehicles intend to drive. *Resources* are the locations (sections) which are occupied by the vehicles (*nonconsum-*

able resources). The speed of the cars can be used to compute the time when a vehicle is a certain section (*temporal information*). This means, in terms of plan relations, we know when two agents (vehicle) need the same resource of type location.

Possibilities for *conflicts* exist, if

- two vehicles intend to use the same lane at the same time in opposite direction, e.g. on a narrow road with only one lane.
- two vehicles use the same lane in the same direction. But the second vehicle moves quicker than the first vehicle such that it will reach the other vehicle.
- two vehicles drive on different lanes which cross each other at an intersection.

Collisions can be avoided by:

- *spread intervals*: In order to prevent that vehicles enter the same section at the same time, vehicles may adjust their speed or even stop, which corresponds to *shift intervals* (Section 5.1.1). The speed adjustment will be performed by the conflicting vehicles in opposite direction.
- *reduce-intervals*: If the location (section) of a vehicle is specified only very roughly, e.g. "drive from a to b on road c", there may be some freedom how long a vehicle is in a certain subsection of a section. By influencing the interval (duration) how long a vehicle remains in a region (= requires a resource), conflicts can also be prevented (*reduce-intervals*).
- *replace-resource*: Collisions may be avoided by selecting a different route or lane (pull out, cut in) for one or both conflicting vehicles.

A crossing scenario

We will give an example which shows how agents, acting as autonomous agents, may negotiate and modify their plans to avoid a collision at an intersection (Fig. 37).

The following predicates are true:
Refinement(cross-intersection, {pass-entry-region, pass-crossing-region, pass-exit-region}, {Prior(pass-entry-region, pass-crossing-region), Prior(pass-crossing-region, pass-exit-region)})

Refinement(turn-left-at-intersection, {pass-entry-region, enter-crossing-region, turn-left, leave-crossing-region, pass-exit-region}), {Prior(pass-entry-region, enter-crossing-re-

gion), Prior(enter-crossing-region, turn-left), Prior(turn-left, leave-crossing-region),
Prior(leave-crossing-region, pass-exit-region)})

All regions are *nonconsumable* resources, i.e. Nonconsumable(r).

For all regions r and all temporal intervals i, available$(r, i) = 1$.

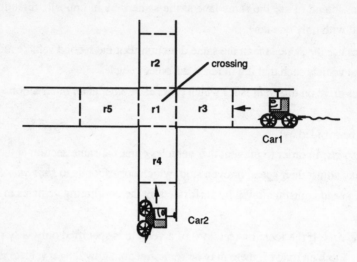

Figure 37: Traffic scenario

Initial states

$S_{Car1} = <LP_{Car1}, HY_{Car1}, EP_{Car1}, CS_{Car1}, PR_{Car1}>$ with

$LP_{Car1} = \{$pass-entry-region, pass-crossing-region, pass-exit-region$\}$

with action parameters:

res(pass-entry-region) = r_3, res(pass-crossing-region) = r_1, res(pass-exit-region) = r_5.

time(pass-entry-region) = i_1, time(pass-crossing-region) = i_2, time(pass-exit-region) = i_3.

The *planner* and *executor* of these actions is Car1.

$HY_{Car1} = \varnothing$

$EP_{Car1} = \varnothing$

$CS_{Car1} = \{(a, cs) \mid a \in LP_{Car1} \wedge cs = initial\}$

$PR_{Car1} = \varnothing$

$S_{Car2} = <LP_{Car2}, HY_{Car2}, EP_{Car2}, CS_{Car2}, PR_{Car2}>$ with

$LP_{Car2} = \{$pass-entry-region, pass-crossing-region, pass-exit-region$\}$

with action parameters:

res(pass-entry-region) = r_4, res(pass-crossing-region) = r_1, res(pass-exit-region) = r_2.

time(pass-entry-region) = i_1, time(pass-crossing-region) = i_2, time(pass-exit-region) = i_3.

The *planner* and *executor* of these actions is Car2.

$IY_{Car2} = \varnothing$

$EP_{Car2} = \varnothing$

$CS_{Car2} = \{(a, cs) \mid a \in LP_{Car2} \wedge cs = initial\}$

$PR_{Car2} = \varnothing$

Plan Relations

There exists a conflict between *Car1's* and *Car2's* plan because they want to cross the intersection at the same time, i.e. a collision were inevitable, if the cars execute their plans as intended. This means formally:

sure-Ncrc(LP_{Car1}, LP_{Car2}) with a_1 = pass-crossing-region and a_2 = pass-crossing-region,
   equal temporal interval i_2,[1] and $r = r_1$. It is a *sure* conflict because the plans do not have to
   be refined in order to detect the conflict.

The agents' pan relations:

$PR_{Car1} = \{(\text{pass-crossing-region, pass-crossing-region, Car2, } Ncrc)\}$

Car2's plan relationship set PR_{Car2} is symmetrical.

Coordination

After the agents have transferred their intentions to each other, the local states are updated as follows:

$EP_{Car1} := LP_{Car2}$

$CS_{Car1} = \{(a, cs) \mid a \in LP_{Car1} \cup EP_{Car1} \wedge cs = planned\}$

$EP_{Car2} := LP_{Car1}$

$CS_{Car2} = \{(a,cs) \mid a \in LP_{Car2} \cup EP_{Car2} \wedge cs = planned\}$

In this example, there is no dedicated coordination agent. Both cars (agents) may have both roles, i.e. *planner* and *coordinator*. They check the relationships between theirs and other plans.

Other interval relations which constitute a conflict are *Overlaps*, *During*, *Starts*, and *Finishes* (as defined in 3.1.).

The agents agree on a proposal to modify their plans if the plan modification does not endanger the execution of other actions in their plans.

Let's assume that at first Car1 receives the plan of Car2. Car1 first considers to accelerate such that it can cross the intersection before Car2 will reach it – which means trying to *shift-interval*(pass-crossing-region, $-d$) with d big enough, such that after the shift it holds, that *Prior*(time(pass-crossing-region of Car1), time(pass-crossing-region of Car2)). Therefore, Car1 proposes that Car2 slows down (decelerate) or stops at the entry-region, such that pass-crossing-region of Car2 will take place after Car1 has left the crossing region. This solution corresponds to a *spread*(pass-crossing-region of Car1, 0, pass-crossing-region, length(i_2)). This conflict resolution might be motivated by the right of way rule "right before left".

Car1 sends a *proposal* message to Car2.

CS_{Car1} = {(pass-crossing-region, *proposed*)} $\cup$ {(a, cs) | a$\neq$pass-crossing-region $\wedge$ a$\in$LP-Car1 $\wedge$ *cs* =*planned*}

Car2 agrees to this proposal and answers by an *acceptance* message. Thus, the resolution of the conflict is acknowledged by a *resolution* message which results that both agents are in state *committed* concerning the action *pass-crossing-region,* respectively.

Result
The coordination process finishes with a *coordinated* set of plans:

S_{Car1} = <LP_{Car1}, HY_{Car1}, EP_{Car1}, CS_{Car1}, PR_{Car1}> with
LP_{Car1} = {pass-entry-region, pass-crossing-region, pass-exit-region}
with action parameters:
res(pass-entry-region) = r_3, res(pass-crossing-region) = r_1, res(pass-exit-region) = r_5.
time(pass-entry-region) = i_1, time(pass-crossing-region) = i_2, time(pass-exit-region) = i_3.
Car1 does not have to modify its plan.
HY_{Car1} = $\emptyset$
EP_{Car1} = $\emptyset$

CS_{Car1} = {(pass-entry-region, *planned*), (pass-crossing-region, *committed*), (pass-exit-region, *planned*)}

PR_{Car1} = ∅

S_{Car2} = <LP_{Car2}, HY_{Car2}, EP_{Car2}, CS_{Car2}, PR_{Car2}> with

LP_{Car2} = {pass-entry-region, pass-crossing-region, pass-exit-region}

with action parameters, part of which has been modified:

res(pass-entry-region) = r_4, res(pass-crossing-region) = r_1, res(pass-exit-region) = r_2.

time(pass-entry-region) = i_1, time(pass-crossing-region) = i_2',

time(pass-exit-region) = i_3'. with Meets(i_2, i_2')

HY_{Car2} = ∅

EP_{Car2} = ∅

CS_{Car2} = {(pass-entry-region, *planned*), (pass-crossing-region, *committed*), (pass-exit-region, *planned*)}

PR_{Car2} = ∅

Summary

We have presented a coordination framework for agents with planning and communicative competence. The aim of plan coordination is, on the one hand, to ensure that the plans do not conflict (negative interactions) and, on the other hand, to exploit chances for beneficial combinations among the agents' plans (positive interactions). The aspects of planning and communication have been synthesized into one coordination and cooperation framework. The framework is defined only by the local states of the agents without any global view. An agent's state consists of the agent's plan, the agent's knowledge about the world history, the agent's knowledge about plans of other agents, the agent's conversation states, and the plan relations between agents' plans. Several examples were provided to illustrate the interactions and state modifications during plan coordination.

The description of our coordination model has been completed now. The next chapter explains the applicability of our approach in a nontechnical domain. Furthermore, it illustrates an implementation of our approach.

8 Plan Coordination for Office Automation and Computer-Supported Cooperative Work

This chapter will shed light on the coordination of distributed planning from a practical (application and realization oriented) point of view.

Our coordination approach will be reviewed under two aspects:

1. Where does the problem of coordinating autonomous planners appear in nontechnical domains? (Section 8.1)

2. What modules do we have to implement in order to support and perform the coordination of distributed activities in organizations (Section 8.2).

A typical domain for DAI approaches is the office environment. Coordination technology may become one key factor in the field of *Computer-Supported Cooperative Work* (CSCW). We will indicate why DAI techniques are appropriate for solving office/CSCW problems. We will then outline how coordination techniques can be utilized in a computer supported work environment for the employees of an organization. We will also describe modules for planning support, for the coordination of plans and for monitoring their execution in an office environment.

8.1 Coordination of Distributed Planning Activities in Organizations

For the last years the support of human cooperative work as for instance in office environments has become a research field of growing interest. This domain differs from usually suggested DAI domains mainly because of its nontechnical nature.

8.1.1 What is the Office and CSCW?

The office can be viewed as an intersection of people, information sources, and information manipulation tools drawn together by common goals, [Ellis and Naffah 87].

Offices are inherently open systems because of the requirement of communication with operational divisions as well as the external world in the task of coordinating the work of the organization, [Hewitt 86]. Open system are not totally in control of their fate. Features of open systems are:

- concurrency,
- asynchrony,
- decentralized control,
- inconsistent information,
- arm's-length relations,
- continuous operation.

Office work is information processing that is done to coordinate all the work that an organization does with the exception of direct manipulation of physical objects [Hewitt 86].

The following characteristics qualify the office as a suitable domain for our model of plan coordination among intelligent autonomous agents:

1. The employees in an office can be seen as *intelligent autonomous agents*.
2. In the office we do not have one single task, but numerous partially interleaved tasks. That is, we need a formalism to express *actions* of multiple agents, whereby the action structure is not restricted to a sequential order.
3. In many cases, office workers perform their tasks based on certain plans. If these plans are executed in the same environment, conflicts between these plans will inevitably arise. Besides there may be chances to utilize beneficial potential between the employees plans. Consequently, we need a model of *plans* and their *relations*, the negative and the positive ones.
4. The employees in an organization can *communicate* freely with each other.

The office as application domain for DAI techniques in general is especially challenging as it has to integrate both human and automated agents (see Fig. 38). Three kinds of interactions have to be considered: among office workers, among machines and between members of the two groups, respectively.

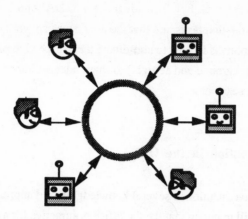

Figure 38: An office model has to cope with a collection of human and automated agents.

Computer-Supported Cooperative Work (CSCW)

Coined by Irene Greif in 1984, the phrase "computer-supported cooperative work" was intended to delineate a new field of research focused on the role of the computer in group work [Greif 88]. The questions being asked relate to all aspects of how large and small groups can collaborate using computer technology: How should people plan to work together to take advantage of this powerful medium? What kind of software should be developed? How will group work be defined and redefined to tap the potential of people and technology? We believe that among the range of disciplines contributing to an answer to these questions Distributed Artificial Intelligence will get a solid standing.

Already many CSCW applications make use of artificial intelligence techniques [Croft 87; Croft and Lefkowitz 87; Fikes 81, 82; Fikes and Henderson 80; Kaye and Karam 87; Kedzierski 88; Lefkowitz and Croft 89; Malone et al. 88; Mukhopadhyay et al. 86; Sathi, Morton and Roth 86; Tsichritzis et al. 87]. By building AI systems that have coordination knowledge we can remove some of the burden from people. Example domains where this is important include intelligent command and control systems and multiuser project coordination [Nirenburg and Lesser 86; Sathi, Morton and Roth 86] and distributed project planning [Goldstein and Roberts 77; Sathi, Fox and Greenberg 85; Sycara et al. 90].

By building a network of "intelligent" automated assistants for the people in an organization[1], we can improve coordination by allowing these assistants to solve (initially routine) coordination problems such as scheduling meetings or routing messages to suitable people [Barber 83; Barber et al. 83; Tsichritzis et al. 87]. The advantages of DAI approaches, besides releasing humans from many coordination tasks, are that the assistants can work in parallel, can dynamically team up to solve problems in how to coordinate their respective people, and can work behind the scenes (in the background and at night) to share relevant information to make decisions and avoid interfering with each other.

8.1.2 Inherent Distribution in the Office

In the last section, we have mentioned several knowledge-based approaches to solve problems in the office. Here, we will maintain that the the office is attractive for a *distributed* approach.

DAI systems reflect many features which are inherently true for the office. In general we can quote Hayes-Roth's statement "All real systems are distributed" [Hayes-Roth 80]. But what does that mean in more specific terms for the office and what speaks in favor of using DAI to solve problems in the office?

– The *fit-to problem* argument. Most of the problems in the office have an inherent distributed structure. It can even complicate the problem-solving process in the office if we reduce it to having a single agent for solving all problems.

– The *hardware* argument. The introduction of a centralized data processing or MIS function in organizations is replaced by a distributed function. Centralization was an economic accident resulting from the large data processing costs. The availability of lower-priced workstations allows the organization to respond to the desire for distribution and autonomy that is present in every organization. DAI is an inevitable consequence of this desire, [Sridharan 87].

---

[1] GMD's institute F3 ("Institute for Applied Information Technology") has just launched a 10 years project called *Assisting Computer*, which aims at the computer as a "personal assistant" for people working in an organization. The result of the project will be an ensemble of integrated support systems for managers researchers, engineers and their supporting clerical staff.

- The *spatial distribution* argument. Almost all applications in the office have a natural spatial distribution of information and processing requirements.

- The *time distribution* argument. Applications in the office have a natural time distribution of processing and processing requirements.

- The *resource distribution* argument: Resources and instruments which are necessary for office work are sometimes centralized. But most of them are found in distributed locations.

- The *information distribution* argument. Information is one of the most important resources in today's offices. Besides having distinguished places where general information is centered as a library there is much information which is only locally available. Information in an organization is often passed by explicit communication between employees.

- The *multiple agents* argument. Viewing office workers as agents, this argument is self-evident. These agents can have different goals for, inconsistent information about and deviating opinions and interpretations about their work and the organization general.

- The *interactive system* argument. Even simple person-machine systems in the office, i.e. one machine and one user can benefit from DAI solutions. In building an interactive AI system, the system ought to be designed using the principles of DAI, [Goodson and Schmidt 87].

- The *natural evolution* argument. Often structures in organizations have developed over many years. For naturally evolved information processing systems decomposition of processing is an absolutely basic strategy for controlling the complexity of computation. Distribution is a natural attribute of evolutionary systems. As the system grows and increases in complexity, a distributed mode provides for replacing a processor with several processors and making mostly local changes in linkage among processors. Adaption to change becomes easier because of mostly local changes (advantages of modularity).

- The *cognitive* argument. Another aspect which speaks in favor of using DAI for office modeling is cognitively motivated. DAI can help us to explore the fundamental aspects of (intelligent) behavior in the office which is the outcome of interaction with others, [Gasser 87].

8.1.3 Distributed Project Planning and Management

If our coordination paradigm is applied to project management, it allows managers or members of a project team to generate their own project plans internally and then synchronize with other parties, both computer-supported. Scheduling and cost reduction can also be integrated into the coordination process because they have been considered within our planning concept. An application may be the design and monitoring of office activities, e.g. the support of a manager who is scheduling a team of employees.

Project Management

Project management is a complex process and is concerned with the management of activities in large projects [Sathi, Fox and Greenberg 1985]. Project management entails the following tasks:

1. *Planning.* Definition of activities and specification of precedence, resource requirements, durations, due dates, and milestones.
2. *Scheduling.* Selection of activities to perform it (if more than one way exists), and the assignment of actual times and resources.
3. *Chronicling.* Monitoring of project performance, detection of deviations from the schedule and the repair of the original schedule.
4. *Analysis.* Evaluation of plans, schedules, and chronicled activities for normal reporting and the detection of extra-ordinary situations.

Managers spend a significant amount of time coordinating project team members and communication plays an important role for project coordination. Plans must be developed through negotiation, tasks assigned and progress monitored. Team members are often involved in task assignments, plan specification, and plan refinement. Some individuals plan their own detailed subprojects and develop task duration estimates in cooperation with the manager. Resource assignment is very much a collaborative issue. Task breakdowns and duration estimates will be negotiated, and team members will thus be directly involved in plan development.

Project Scheduling. We will apply the definitions for "Project Scheduling by PERT-CPM" as used in [Taha 76] and indicate in parentheses (in *italics*) the corresponding notion of our coordination framework.

A project (*individual plan*) defines a combination of interrelated activities (*actions* in our model) that must be executed in a certain order before the entire task (*abstract action*) can be completed. The activities are interrelated in the sense that some activities cannot start until others are completed (predicates *Pre*, *Before* and *Prior*). An activity in a project is usually viewed as a job requiring time (*dur*) and resources (*res*) for its completion. Project scheduling by PERT-CPM consists of three basic phases: planning (*planning*), scheduling (*coordination*) and controlling (*execution*).

Project Planning. The planning phase is initiated by breaking down the project into distinct activities (domain predicates *Refinement* for *abstract* actions lead to *Sub* relations within individual plans). The objective of the scheduling phase is to construct a time chart showing the earliest start (*start*) and latest completion (*end*) times for each activity as well as its relationships to other activities (*Allen's* temporal relations) in the project. In addition, the schedule must pinpoint the temporally critical activities which require special attention if the project is to be completed on time. For the noncritical activities the schedule must show the amount of slack or float times (similar to *inner movableness of actions*) which can be used advantageously when such activities are delayed or when limited resources are to be used effectively. The final phase in project management is project control. This includes the making of periodic progress reports. The schedule may thus be analyzed (*relationship detection*) and, if necessary, a new schedule is determined for the remaining portion of the project (*plan modification*).

Distributed project planning requires the coordination of several project planners. Although the project managers plan their own projects, they belong to the same organization and there might be relations between the projects which should be coordinated. Sometimes a large project may not be handled by a single project manager (*planning agent*) due to a limited planing capacity and knowledge deficits. It is reasonable to break down such a large project into several subprojects and distribute planning to (local) managers or team members (as *planning* and *executing agents*) and then coordinate the resulting plans.

Conflict Resolution in Scheduling. Our scheduling approach may be used to solve scheduling problems in a distributed fashion.

The problem of scheduling a set of actions so that every action has the resources it requires and is finished by its stated deadline is generally considered to be intractable, i.e., belonging to the class of NP-complete problems [Garey and Johnson 78]. We have presented an intelligent decision support approach for tackling resource conflicts (Section 5.1.3). It was provided a comprehensive set of conflict resolution alternatives and a set of rules which can guide the resolution process. The following questions have been answered by our approach: What are possible resolutions for conflicts? In which "conflict situation" is which solution appropriate? In which order will conflicts be solved, if there exist several conflicts?

Summary. As we have seen, the attributes for describing projects correspond to the attributes we have used to describe plans and actions. Provided with the domain knowledge it is therefore feasible to perform coordination of distributed project planning activities using our approach.

8.2 Implementation

In this chapter, we will describe the implementation of a planning and coordination system for the office environment. The diverse components taken together embody a system which applies DAI techniques to the field of Computer-Supported Cooperative Work.

In what environment does coordination take place and how is it principally performed?
The planning agents can be regarded as human beings which work in an office (organization). A coordination agent (coordinator) can be seen as an automated agent. The office workers have workstations which they use for planning. Planning problems in the office are often related to a problem which can only be solved through the cooperation of multiple agents. The output of an office planning process is called an *office procedure*.
The office workers are not restricted in the way they generate their plans. They only have to express them in one common formalism. Basically there are three techniques for office workers to gain plans (office procedures): First, they can directly use a predefined standard plan which is stored in a plan library. Second, they modify an existing, previously executed plan to meet their special requirements. Third, they can synthesize a new plan from scratch.

To avoid conflicts and exploit positive relations between plans it is meaningful to coordinate the intended plans before execution. The office workers may transfer the results of their planning processes to an automated agent. Although communication between the workers is possible and allowed they do not communicate their plans to each other, because it were very expensive to provide a complete global view to each agent in the system. Thus, the strategy of having one coordination agent reduces the cost of communication in the system. It is the automated agent's assignment to promote coordination between the office workers' plans. The computerized agent's task includes evaluating the interactions between plans, making proposals for plan mo-

difications and initiating communication between the workers and moderating their negotiations. It is not allowed to force them to cooperate or modify their plans.

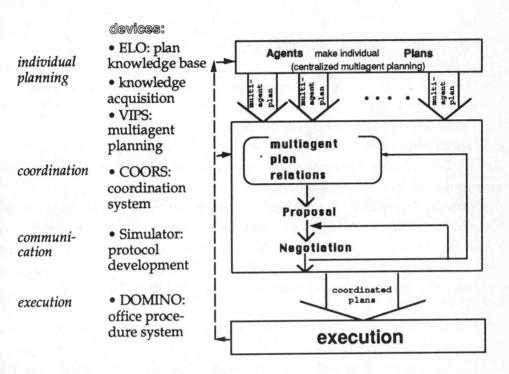

*individual
planning*

devices:

• ELO: plan
knowledge base
• knowledge
acquisition
• VIPS:
multiagent
planning

coordination

• COORS:
coordination
system

*communi-
cation*

• Simulator:
protocol
development

execution

• DOMINO:
office proce-
dure system

Figure 39: Scheme for an office planning, coordination and monitoring support system

The components participating in this overall attempt are (see also Fig. 39):

– a domain knowledge base, called *Electronic Organizational Handbook* (ELO),

– a multiagent planning support system, called *Visual Interactive Planning System* (VIPS),

– a knowledge acquisition tool (PRAGMA),

– a coordination reasoner (COORS),

– a simulator for protocol analysis,

– an office procedure system (DOMINO).

The next section gives an overview about the functionality and realization of these components.

8.2.1 Modules

The Electronic Organizational Handbook (ELO)

The basis of our multifunctional office support system can be a knowledge base which we have called **ELO** standing for *Electronic Organizational Handbook*. Besides general knowledge of our organization, the GMD, the ELO contains a collection of standard plans (*plan library*). We have made a variety of experiments in acquiring knowledge for the ELO [Martial and Victor 88a, 89]. Based on these experiences and experiments we have developed concepts and tools to organize and support knowledge acquisition for a team of knowledge engineers.

The Electronic Organizational Handbook (ELO) is an organizational knowledge base that models aspects of the office world including common sense knowledge. The final handbook should contain all the information of our company. In our case the initial source of knowledge was the organizational manual of our company GMD [GBO 85]. This extensive manual describes on more than 300 pages the structure and organizational rules of GMD.

ELO's functionality. On top of ELO's knowledge base different expert system applications can be build. In order to do so the expertise of various persons in the organization is required. The ELO's functionality for supporting the user's work as described in [Martial and Victor 87] is:

- *Information supply for the user*. The contents of the knowledge base is retrieved without processing it further, e.g. making inferences or deriving new facts. It is also possible to browse graphically through the knowledge base. The result is visualized as a semantic net [Ishii and Martial 88].
- *Advising*. The system advises the user either by responding to questions or by selecting an appropriate standard office procedure to get his work done. The user can input his problem in from of keywords using a menu-oriented style of interaction.
- *Planning*. We have developed an interactive planner for synthesizing office procedures [Martial and Victor 88]. Planning problems occur in situations where the appropriate sequence of applicable actions is unknown. The plan generated is a system which models concurrency, conflicts and causal dependencies between actions. There is a graphical interface which shows the current state of the plan.

Procedural Knowledge. The procedural knowledge of the ELO is used to assemble actions and partially synthesized procedures to more complex ones. Our knowledge base uses four categories of procedural knowledge:

- *Input and output behavior for actions*. The effect of an action can be described by the specification of its input and output behavior. This might include, for instance, what resources it needs to be activated and what objects it produces as result of its execution.

- *Preconditions*. Actions might have conditions that must be fulfilled before starting their execution. For this reason, the knowledge base includes constraints that are checked before executing actions. An example for a precondition is the integration of a necessary predecessor action into the current procedure.

- *Subnets*. How are activities aggregated? It is not sufficient to present a procedure as an intricate network of single actions. Complex procedures which describe, for example, routine tasks always carried out in the same manner, are therefore specified as sub-net. These subnets are used in the synthesizing phase of the planning process. They allow the user a choice between seeing portions of a procedure in detail and gaining an overview over the whole procedure through a more abstract presentation.

- *Dependencies*. We distinguish two dependency relations between actions: *concurrency* and *alternatives*. A concurrency relation between actions expresses that the involved actions can be executed in an arbitrary sequence. This is used in the planning process to resolve conflicts. An alternative situation specifies that the involved actions are mutually exclusive. This is useful to model certain classes of actions, for instance those expressing decisions or permissions.

For the purpose of our model, an action is an object with the following attributes:

Starting condition $pre(a)$:	\<events and conditions for the start of an action\>
Starting date $start(a)$:	\<scheduled point of time for the start\>
Deadline $end(a)$:	\<specified deadline for the execution\>
Duration $dur(a)$:	\<time interval needed for the action\>
Resources $res(a)$:	\<resources needed for the action, e.g. documents, rooms, machines, personnel, ...\>

Result *result*(a):	<result of an action, e.g. documents, software modules, or granted permission>
Actor *actor*(a):	<person> <group of persons>
Refinement *refinable*(a):	<can a be refined by a subnet or a dependency relation>

Not all attributes of an action need to be filled in. There may be actions which have, e.g., no starting conditions or durations or need no resources. If no starting condition and no starting date is given, this means that the action may be started at any time, provided that no implicit restrictions exist with regard to resources or causal dependencies.

In our current implementation, actions are displayed in a simplified form, i.e. the internal action parameters do not appear on the surface. A plan net is displayed on the screen and reflects the causal (dependency) structure of actions.

Multiagent planning (VIPS[1])

Employees create plans to achieve their goals. Plans which are executed by several agents (both human and automated) are called multiagent plans. See Section 2.2.1. for a definition of *centralized multiagent planning*.

The user might utilize a plan support system which we have developed especially for office planning. This system is called **VIPS** (Visual Interactive Planning System"). Vips is called
- "visual" because the planning process is performed via a graphical interface,
- "interactive" because planning is carried out as a process with initiatives both from the user and the system, i.e. user and system cooperate during planning,
- a "planning" system because the result of the problem solving process is a plan consisting of action and with attributes such as actors and precedence relations among actions.

VIPS has been implemented on a Symbolics Lisp machine using Lisp and Prolog.

Knowledge acquisition (PRAGMA)

What is an appropriate way of gathering data or knowledge that can be employed by a planning system? [Martial and Victor 89; Sommer, Martial and Victor 91]. We have developed a compo-

---

[1] VIPS is described in more detail in Section 8.2.2.

nent for supporting the acquisition of action and plan knowledge. Knowledge acquisition is performed via visual design interface and monitored on the basis of an underlying knowledge base, the current state of the plan on screen, and the performed user actions. The acquired procedural knowledge can then serve as a knowledge base for an interactive planning and scheduling system. A special difficulty concerning to the acquisition of planning knowledge is that the target representation is *procedural knowledge*. The central question addressed with respect to acquiring planning knowledge is: How can the user be supported in a most adequate way in formulating and establishing new planning knowledge? Types of knowledge for planning and scheduling covered by the knowledge acquisition component are required activities, activity precedence, aggregations and abstractions of activities, and resources required for activities.

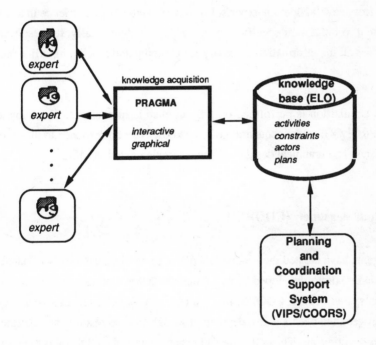

Figure 40: Knowledge acquisition by multiple experts

Our approach is based on a combination of two basic features:

– *visual design*. A visual interface facilitates the capturing of procedural knowledge. An easy to understand graphical language is used to express and manipulate procedures.

– *active system participation*. The system actively supports the user in capturing and fixating new knowledge by asking questions and making suggestions on the basis of an underlying knowledge base, the current state of the procedure on screen, and the performed user actions.

These two features are realized in interleaved phases. During the design of a plan via an interactive graphical component, the system analyzes the current plan, poses questions concerning its structure and clarifies what kind of new knowledge is to be inserted into the knowledge base.

Within an organization there is a need for office procedures in several special domains (for instance accounting, business trip preparation). PRAGMA has been designed for gathering knowledge from several domain experts. Employees who have experience in a certain domain use the system to input their specific procedural knowledge. Ideally, the resulting knowledge base comprises all the information necessary for planning and scheduling office procedures (see Fig. 40).

Knowledge acquisition is performed on a Symbolics Lisp machine. The knowledge base is realized in PROLOG, so the acquisition of new knowledge corresponds to the assertion of new PROLOG facts. The graphical design interface is implemented in LISP.

Coordination reasoner (COORS[1])

After the agents have created their individual plans, these plans can be coordinated. For coordination the plan relations developed by us are the key factor. Coordination can be supported by a coordination system, called COORS. It is the task of COORS to recognize and evaluate relationships between the agents plans, develop proposals how to resolve the relations and initiate and perform negotiations. The detection and proposal part of COORS have been implemented on a Symbolics Lisp machine using Lisp and Prolog. The communication of plans and the negotiation about plan reconciliation can then be performed within a negotiation framework.

---

[1] COORS is presented in more detail in Section 8.2.3.

Protocol development (Simulator)

The simulator is a tool which detects potential inconsistencies and deadlocks in a negotiation. In Section 6.4. we have described how the development of our negotiation framework was supported by this tool. The core of this tool is a *simulator*.

The simulator has been implemented in Prolog on a SUN workstation. It decides whether a given marking can be reached from another marking, which markings can be reached from a given marking, or from which markings a given marking can be reached. All possible solutions of these problems are generated via backtracking by the Prolog system.

With the help of the simulator, we succeeded in extending and modifying negotiation protocols in order to eliminate all pitfalls of asynchronous communication. This procedure enclosed quite a number of steps in a trial and error fashion. We have been able to verify by means of exhaustive simulation that "our" negotiation protocol is sound in the sense that all possible inconsistencies have been excluded.

Office procedure execution (DOMINO)

After the employees have reached an agreement on how to synchronize their plans by relationship resolution the plans are ready to be executed. Concerning the execution it is desirable to have a means of reminding the agents of the actions they have promised to execute, i.e. to bind agents to the commitments they have made for plan reconciliation. This task can be fulfilled by the system DOMINO which has been implemented by our group. DOMINO is implemented in C on UNIX and uses standard electronic mail for communication. DOMINO monitors the execution of office procedures.

The user can delegate the execution of predefined standard office procedures to the office procedure system DOMINO [Kreifelts et al. 84, Kreifelts and Woetzel 87]. DOMINO monitors office processes involving a group of persons where each person is responsible for a certain action or certain actions in the procedure.

DOMINO is a tool for the specification and automation of well-structured and fairly formalized cooperative office processes. It can handle different types of coordination procedures which are described in a specification language and are then translated into an executable control program. When a coordination procedure has been started, DOMINO controls its performance by notifying users about actions due to be performed and by routing the results of such actions the users who need them for subsequent actions. The state of a running procedure may be checked at any time and an activity log is produced upon termination of a procedure.

The main features of DOMINO are the following: DOMINO is a fairly small system, which concentrates on the essential coordination function of an office procedure system, it integrates the usual electronic mail with the procedure system communication and it is implemented on UNIX.

Recently, the DOMINO system has been reimplemented on a network of Apple Macintoshes[1] employing a Hypercard[2] interface. Currently, DOMINO is being beta-tested to automate the procurement process in our institute.

After this overview about the components participating in our coordination approach, the following two sections will consider in more detail the *planning* modules.

8.2.2 A Multiagent Planning Support System

How do employees in an organization acquire their plans? One way is to use VIPS. VIPS ("visual interactive planning system") is a system, which has been developed to support its user in creating multiagent plans. The *agents* are the employees of an organization, and the resulting multiagent *plans* are office procedures.

If the set of actions, its dependency structure and resources are not completely known, then the problem solution involves *planning*. VIPS provides planning support by supplying the user with feasible actions and required resources. It also has knowledge about the dependency structure between actions. VIPS is an *interactive* planning system meaning that both user and system contribute to the development of plans.

Our approach, realized in the system VIPS differs both from traditional AI planners and from netplanning systems. In traditional *AI planners*, see e.g. [Fikes and Nilsson 71; Sacerdoti 88; Tate 85; Winston 77], the planning process is goal oriented and fully automated, i.e. the user has no possibility to interact with the planner. A fully automated approach makes sense in domains with an underlying *closed world assumption*, where the knowledge representing objects and actions is not very rich, e.g. the blocks world domain. This assumption is not true in office

---

[1] Apple is a registered trademark and the name Macintosh is a trademark of Apple Computer, Inc.

[2] Hypercard is a product of Apple.

environments. Therefore, our planner is based on the paradigm of *supporting* the planning process rather than automating it. Goals are not explicitly inserted into the system. Our approach also differs from *project planning* tools, see e.g. [Archibald and Villoria 67; Taha 76], because the system uses knowledge to actively participate in the planning process.

A difficult problem is the description of goals in dynamic, *open* systems. In many planners the goals have to be specified by predicate calculus expressions. But this formalism is too difficult to be handled by the user. Another approach is to specify goals in natural language. Because the semantics of office objects and actions is inherently unclear and vague for people working in that domain, the realization of a natural language planning component seems to be too difficult. In our approach, the planning process is not goal-driven, but rather an interactive construction process.

Planning Phases

A typical planning session with VIPS consists of the following phases:
1. *Initialization.* The user describes his planning problem by selecting a problem domain. The system shows a high-level plan to solve the user's problem.
2. *Cycle of cooperative planning.* User and system interact to refine and modify the initial plan. This cycle terminates if the user is satisfied with the generated plan.
3. *Simulation.* During this phase the user can analyze and verify the established plan. The user has the possibility to supply different initial states. Then the system generates all possible execution sequences of the plan. If the plan turns out to be incorrect or incomplete phase 2 can be executed again (backtracking).
4. *Execution.* One possible sequence of the plan is performed.

The planning process is terminated by the user, when he decides that the synthesized plan describes and solves his problem, i.e. the planning context and the level of abstraction is determined by the user. In [March and Simon 69] this method is called the principle of "satisfying solutions". This may imply that in general a search for information in an organization will return an adequate, rather than the best answer.

User and System Activities. During the process of planning there may be several activities on the user and the system side.

The user can be prompted by the system to choose between several actions. He accepts or rejects the system's proposal for plan refinement or modification. He can ask the system for refinement of actions, determination of agents and places. The user may initiate more complex operations like conflict resolution and the resolution of decisions. The user may also graphically modify the plan, delete parts of it or add something new to it.

After the user has selected a part of the plan for refinement, the system tries to give more details of the selected part. This can mean both to expand an action into a subnet, i.e. to decompose an action into less abstract actions and to find out which agent is responsible for a role.

Sometimes the system is not capable of making a decision on its own either because of lack of information or because a decision is dependent on the agent's preferences. In these cases the user is asked by the system to give the information needed.

Often the system makes proposals to extend a given plan. The motivation to extend a plan is inferred by three different mechanisms:

- The system finds out whether parts (places, transitions) of the net match predefined atomic nets. A matching net can be integrated into an already existing plan.
- Constraints between actions or classes of actions may result in establishing new causal restrictions (arcs) between existing places or actions.
- The application of rules can lead to the insertion of new actions or places into the plan.

The functionality of VIPS includes edit functions (draw-place, draw-arc, connect, delete, etc.), history manipulation (undo, redo, plan history, etc), but most important are the planning functions such as search-forms, check-forms, auto-expand and refine.

An Example

The field of application is the purchasing activity of an organization. We demonstrate the planner by showing snapshots of the interaction between the user and the system. All figures are excerpts of screencopies taken during a session on a Symbolics Lisp machine.

Problem situation: An employee of a big organization wants to purchase a workstation. He doesn't know how to reach his goal.

He consults VIPS. First he specifies his problem situation as a purchase action. This is performed by clicking on the initial box "problem_domain" and then selecting the desired domain in a menu (Fig. 41).

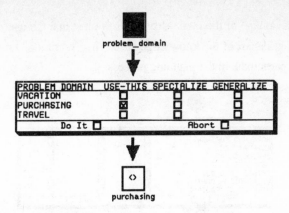

Figure 41: The user selects a problem domain

Now VIPS knows in which context the planning has to be carried out. The very abstract action "purchasing" is displayed. The user asks for a refinement of this action. VIPS specifies "purchasing" as a sequence of two operations, one to demand the purchase object ("demand") and the reception of it ("get_good"). It shows a skeleton of the plan in the form of a net (Fig. 42).

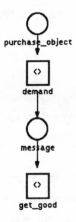

Figure 42: Skeletal plan for purchasing

In the current net, the desired purchase object is not specified. The user wants to inform the system that he wants to acquire a workstation. This can be achieved in two ways: He either directly inserts "workstation" as value of "purchase_object" or VIPS offers a sequence of menus to classify the purchase object (Fig. 43). The user decides in favor of the second alternative, and using via a "help" function and a series of menus, which are dynamically constructed because of the information in the underlying knowledge base, the user finally selects "workstation". An advantage of the menu-driven insertion is that the user selects a term which is known by VIPS, i.e. is part of the knowledge base. This "common" knowledge is important for VIPS to actively participate in the planning process.

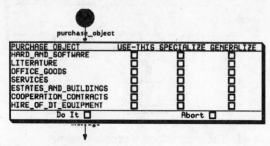

Figure 43: "purchase_object" is replaced by an object of the knowledge base

The user may then initialize some planning steps by initiating "Search Forms" and "Check Preconditions" (subsumed as "Auto Expand").

"Search Forms" causes the place "message" to be replaced by "hard_software_form". This action is the result of several retrieval and inference steps in the underlying knowledge base (ELO). The object "workstation" is a subframe of "IT" (information technology). "IT" is a subframe of "hard_and_software". In this frame there is a slot "form" with value "hard_software_-form" which is inherited by "workstation". Then, this value replaces "message".

There exists a rule which says that a form modelled as output place of an action must also occur as an input for that action. Thus, triggered by calling "Check Forms", an additional input "hard_software_form" is produced for "demand".

Another rule in the knowledge base states that in the context purchasing and the purchase object is hardware then "get_good" has a precondition slot "check_requirements". The corresponding transition is inserted between "order" and "get_good" (*figure 44*).

The user enters his name "Mr. Smith" as actor of "demand". It is specified as the constraint that the roles of "demand" and "get-good" in this plan have to be carried out by the same actor. Thus, the actor variable of " get-good" is automatically replaced by the user's name.

At this stage the user and VIPS have cooperatively gathered the following information:
- The object "workstation" is part of the knowledge base.
- The procurement of a workstation requires a special form.

- The procurement process consists of three sequential steps, namely the demanding of the purchase object, the check of requirements and the reception of the purchase object.

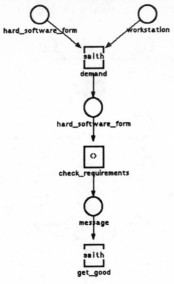

Figure 44: Plan after first steps

If the user is satisfied with the current information, i.e. he knows how to execute the plan, he can stop the planning process. Otherwise he can trigger further refinements. The user wants to know which requirements have to be checked and he selects "check_requirements" to be refined. VIPS knows that this transition can be decomposed in two independent, concurrent actions "check_budget" and "permit" (Fig. 45).

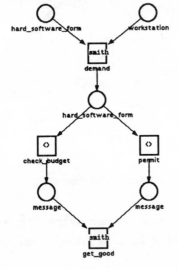

Figure 45: Plan after refining "check_requirements"

When simulating the executability of the current plan, VIPS detects that "check_budget" and "permit" attempt to consume the same form. VIPS can resolve this conflict ("Resolve Conflict") by duplicating the "hard_software_form" as shown in Fig. 46.

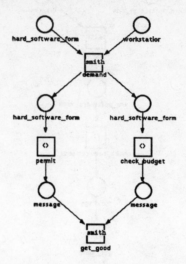

Figure 46: Duplication of a form as a means of conflict resolution

The user wants to get to know details of the action "permit" and asks VIPS to refine it, which results in two branches "permit_yes" and "permit_no" (Fig. 47).

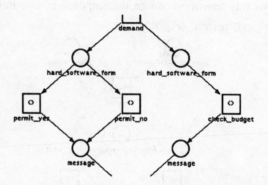

Figure 47: After refinement of "permit"

Both results of the decision result in the same output "message". This does not reflect adequately the ambivalent nature of decision. As a consequence, the decision situation concerning

the permission has to be taken care of by further plan modifications. In case of a negative decision, the user receives a rejection message. A positive decision is a precondition   for
"get_good" (Fig. 48).

In general, a decision situation arises after a refinement operation and involves a place in a plan
with several incoming arcs, e.g. "message" with "permit_yes" and "permit_no".
The user can initiate an investigation and resolution of a decision situation by calling "Resolve
Decision". Applied to "message" VIPS recognizes that the two alternative (yes/no) decisions
have to end in alternative exits. The alternative branches are, based on information in the
knowledge base, constructed and integrated in the existing plan.

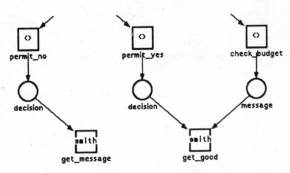

Figure 48: A decision situation has been resolved in two alternative branches

Now, the user wants the action "check_budget" to be refined. A subnet, which is contained in
the knowledge base, is integrated in the current plan (Fig. 49).

Now, the "decide" operation in the plan is refined into two alternatives, and then integrated in
the plan ("Resolve Decision"). The decision situation concerning the budget check is resolved
using the same mechanisms as already described for the permission situation. The planning
state is shown in Fig. 50.

At this point the user stops the process of cooperative planning because he has received enough
information and thinks that the plan is executable.
The user may call "Search Actors". Then VIPS tries to replace empty actor (=executing agents)
positions (<>) by the respective agents or roles.

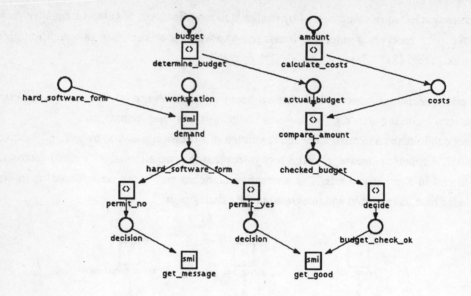

Figure 49: After refinement of "check_budget"

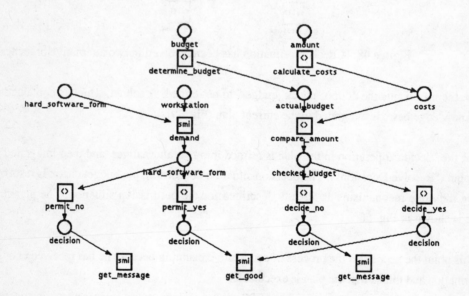

Figure 50: Final plan

Office Procedure Design (Execution monitoring). A plan designed by VIPS can be transformed automatically into the office procedure specification used by the DOMINO system [Victor & Sommer 89; Victor et al. 89]. Using VIPS for the generation of office procedures has, besides offering active planning support, the advantage that it is simpler and more intuitive to formulate an office procedure visually with VIPS than to write code in a specification language. The graphical representation offers a general view of the structure of the plan at every point in the design process. The knowledge base supports the designer of an office procedure by providing access to the rules and regulations of his organization.

This section showed how agents may be assisted by performing their individual planning (phase 1 of Fig. 35 in Chapter 7). The next section will deal with automating the support of co-ordination.

8.2.3 Plan Synchronizer

Agents may have constructed multiagent plans with the help of VIPS. Further steps of plan co-ordination are supported by a tool called COORS ("Coordination System"). COORS gets as input two plans. COORS is implemented on a Symbolics Lisp machine using Lisp and Prolog.

The functionality of COORS covers the following phases of our coordination model (see Fig. 35): *relationship detection* (phase 3), *solution selection* (phase 4) and *plan modification* (phase 6).

COORS will be illustrated with the help of two plans between which a *favor relation* exists. The screencopies may be seen as corresponding to information of a *coordinator*, who is trying to mediate between the related parties. Excerpts of screendumps will be shown during the handling of a favor relation.

Input are two plans created by two different planners (Fig. 52). Actions of the plans are displayed as boxes. The inscriptions of the boxes indicate the executor of the corresponding action. COORS is asked whether favor relationships between these plans exist (function "Detect Favor"). The system's knowledge base contains possible refinements for the actions "send_pa-ckage" and "get_stamps". When it applies these refinements, it detects that a favor of Art for Bert is possible, because Art can buy the stamps instead of Bert. The reason is that Art needs, in order to fulfill his own plan, to go to the post office. The action "move_to_post_office" is however also a preparing action also for Bert's buy stamps. Thus, according to our definition of the favor relation, the favor action "buy_stamps" can smoothly be integrated in Art's plan.

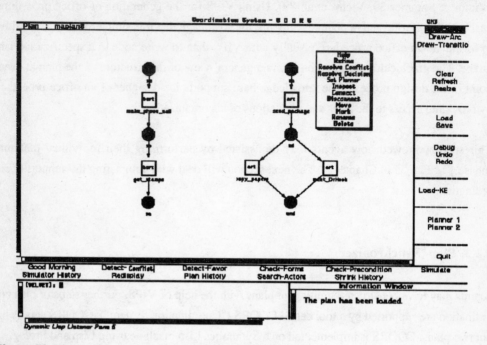

Figure 51: The interface of the coordination system COORS

The user (coordinator) is notified of this detection in the information window (Fig. 53). At the same time the two actions for which the favor relation holds are highlighted.

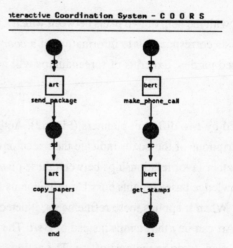

Figure 52: Plans delivered for coordination

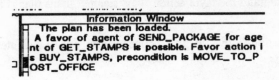

Figure 53:   COORS detects a favor relation and displays a message in the information
window.

After a favor has been detected, the user (or the planning agents) has to give his consent that the
favor will be executed. That means, that the two plans will be modified in order to exploit the
favor relation. First, the plans will be refined as already indicated during the detection of the favor relation (Fig. 54). These refinements are notified in the information window by "A subnet
has been substituted".

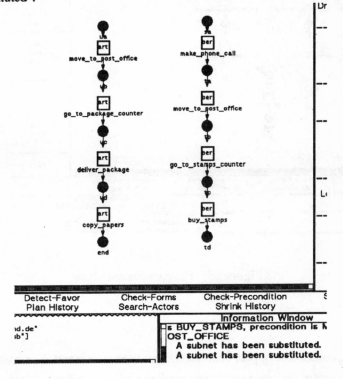

Figure 54: First step of exploiting the favor relation: The two actions are refined.

After the plans have been refined Bert can remove the favor action and the preparing action from his plan. Art integrates the favor action "buy_stamps" in his plan (Fig. 55).

Now the preparing action "move_to_post_office" has only to be executed once, and, thus, the overall cost is reduced.

We hope that the reader got by this simple example an idea of how to implement the transformation of an initially uncoordinated set of plans into a coordinated set of plans.

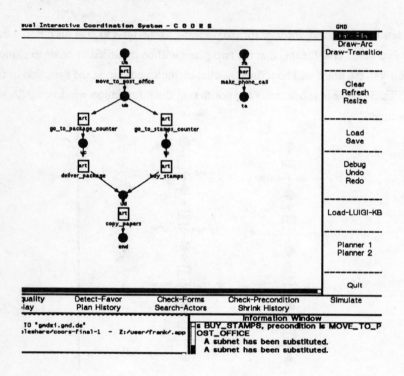

Figure 55: The *coordinated* plans

Summary.
In this chapter, our scheme of plan coordination has been transferred, on a conceptual level, to an application domain, and, on a realization level, to a an implemented system. We have shown how our plan approach (including action/plan representation and the planning process) may be interpreted as plan concepts how they are common in project planning and scheduling. As a consequence, it is possible to apply our coordination approach in these domains, especially to problems involved with distributed project management and planning.

An implementation consisting of an ensemble of modules has been presented in the second half of this chapter. The whole system embraces an ensemble of modules which support employees of organizations in the process of creating, coordinating and executing plans. Concrete examples were given both for the creation of a multiagent plan and for the coordination of plans.

Conclusions

This work has dealt with the coordination of distributed agents which have planning and communicative competence. The agents intend to execute actions within a common environment and coordinate their activities by modifying their intentions. The agents' intentions are expressed as plans.

The agents are intelligent, autonomous problem solvers. An autonomous agent has its own goals, intentions, capabilities, and knowledge. There is an equal distribution of control and authority. The agents broadcast or exchange their plans before execution in order to allow other agents greater access to their anticipated future behavior. The agents have a cordial relationship and tell the truth concerning their plans.

The actions of plans require resources. Plans may contain concurrent or overlapping actions. Agents may exchange plans which are still vague and incomplete. The problem of dealing with vague and incomplete information is taken care in our approach by allowing agents to transfer only parts of their plans and by handling actions at different levels of detail.

The approach put forward in this book belongs to the field of *distributed artificial intelligence* with special area *multiagent planning*. We are primarily interested in the *coordination* of pre-existing plans, this should not be confused with the pure *creation* of plans (planning).

We are less concerned with the problem of distributing tasks among agents, but rather with the problem of coordinating the activities of these agents after task distribution has been performed. There is no overall planning task which has to be solved in close cooperation. Each agent wants to solve its individual problem, i.e. the agents are not originally constrained to cooperate, a situation which occurs quite often in real world settings (inherent distribution of planning activities). The agents are, however, interested in exploiting the potential for cooperation and coordination between their plans.

9.1 Research Issues and Contributions

The interactions which intelligent agents may exhibit when they coordinate their activities hav
been examined at two different levels:
- On the *indirect* interaction level, the agents interact indirectly through the plans they intend
  to execute in the same environment. We have shown how information in the agents' plans
  can be used to work towards a coordinated system.
- On the *direct* interaction level, the agents interact directly by communicating with each
  other. By communication agents announce their intended action or plans, and by communication agents may reach an agreement on how to coordinate their plans.

This section reviews this book´s key issues.

1. Exploration and structuring of multiagent planning
We have worked out a detailed overview of DAI, its related fields, its motivations, principle
and history. *Multiagent planning* was embedded in the general field of DAI. We have defined
taxonomy of planning disciplines, covering both single and multiagent approaches. The problem of plan coordination has been reviewed from several perspectives.

2. A notion of action and plans in multiagent domains as basis for a planning process and plan modifications
How to model plans and their interactions in distributed systems? What plan modification op
erators are necessary for coordination? We have explored the appropriate requirements for plan
in multiagent domains and have used these requirements to develop a concept of distributed
planning. Some of the features captured by our action and plan model are: the expression o
concurrent, overlapping actions, the handling of temporal relations between actions, the inte
gration of refinement operations.

3. A coordination model based on the agents' local states
How to enable individual agents to represent and reason about the actions, plans, and knowl
edge of other agents in order to coordinate with them? How to enable agents to act coherently
Our model integrates both the agents knowledge about each other, their planning process an

ommunication. We have shown how agents can transfer their intended actions (plans), how
hey can use this knowledge to coordinate themselves and how this is connected with communi-
ation. The coordination model allows agents to plan dynamically and modify their plans. The
spects of planning *and* communication have been synthesized into one coherent coordination
nd cooperation framework.

he agents reason about the actions and plans of other agents by trying to detect the relations
etween their plans. Relation detection is straightforward using the corresponding definitions.
Coordination is tightly connected with the question of coherence. In our coordination frame-
vork, the agents act coherently if all existing plan relations have been resolved.

. A taxonomy of relations among plans covering both negative and positive nteractions

*low to recognize and reconcile conflicting intentions among a collection of agents, and how to
ecognize and take advantage of beneficial intentions?* These aspects are covered by the multia-
ent plan relations and by the strategies how to handle them (resolve or exploit). Often, coher-
nce and coordination are only defined via the regulation of resources. Although the require-
ents for resources and resolving conflicts pose an important concept of interaction, it is not
e only one. We have developed a concept of multiagent interactions which goes beyond these
stricted approaches. We not only consider remedies to handle conflicts but also deal with
ituations in which beneficial effects can be achieved by reconciling plans. Our approach covers
e whole spectrum from negative to positive relationships between plans.

ased on these relations we could define an important notion in multiagent worlds, namely,
hen activities of agents can be called "coordinated".

. A negotiation framework for coordination

*low to enable agents to communicate and interact: what communication languages or protocols
 use, and what and when to communicate?* Our negotiation framework permits agents to
ommunicate about their intended actions ahead of time and is suited for reaching a reconcilia-
on of plans. We have worked out the messages exchanged between the communicators and
e protocols according to which a negotiation takes place. Communication may take place
synchronously at arbitrary stages of their planning process.

n important and novel feature of the protocol is its sophistication in connecting dialogue states
ith actions.

e have provided message types both for the exchange of the agents' intentions, i.e. their
ans, and for the process of reaching a compromise.

Our protocol does not dictate any particular planning paradigm. It does not make any assump
tions at what planning stage the agents announce their intentions, that implies, for instance, tha
plans do not have to be synchronized at the same level of abstraction. A further degree of free
dom is that the agents do not have to transfer complete plans, but only single actions. Also is
sues of designing, installing and verifying a negotiation protocol have been dealt with.

Although developed as a medium to negotiate about plan reconciliation, we expect the protoco
to be applicable in general for negotiations in cooperative environments.

6. A new coordination paradigm: Coordination as smoothing of multiagent pla relations

Coordination has been defined as a multiagent plan relation handling process. Most of the othe
issues, although interesting in itself, are either preparations or implications of this one.

We have developed a novel approach to coordinate activities of autonomous agents with plan
ning and communicative competence. The coordination of plans is triggered by the relatior
which exist between the actions of different plans. With the help of an explicit model of the pla
relationships a powerful approach for coordination is realized. No other approach to multiage
planning is based on an explicit taxonomy of such relationships. The overall handling of pla
relations covers both the operations for conflict resolution and for the utilization of favorable re
lations and the way agents can interact about their relations, i.e. the negotiation framework.

9.2 Future Work

The approach described in this book can be carried on in several directions. Some of them wi
be mentioned here.

Direct interactions among more than two agents. It would be interesting to know i
how far n-party interactions (n>2) may fit into our relationship driven coordination approac
Currently, this aspect has only been dealt with implicitly in our approach by splitting up mult
lateral interactions into a set of bilateral interactions. This is performed by a coordination age
(mediator), who is "equipped" with a set of heuristics. Another approach were to directly defi
relations involving more than two participants.

Constraints among different relations. How does the exploitation or prevention of on
relation affect other relations? Does it create new relations? Is it possible to make general stat

ents about the influence of relations on each other? Or can such questions only be answered with fixed underlying application domains? Currently, the influence of relations on each other an be checked by applying the relationship detection after a relationship has been successfully rocessed (resolved). A question is whether meta-mechanisms can be constructed to handle sets f relations in one go.

ifferent organizations. How many and which agents in the system act as coordinators *coordination responsibilities*) is an issue of the system organization in general (*meta-level or-anization*). An organization depends on the specific application and the number of agents. here is a great range of different organizations possible ranging from having only one dedi-ated coordinator to each agent being himself both "ordinary" agent and coordinator. he concept presented here is not dependent on having a dedicated coordination agent. An or-anization depends on the specific application and the number of agents. It is a meaningful un-ertaking to vary the parameters of the problems and evaluate its impact on the form of organi-ation.

elf organization. Tightly related with the last issue is the question of self organization. lthough it may be useful to have specialized fixed organizations, these organizations may not e useful for all possible situations. It is desirable to have flexible organizations, where the or-anizing process is automated, i.e. performed by the agents themselves and not defined from utside. An organization states which role (planner or coordinator) an agent plays for coordina-on in a current situation. Our model can serve as a basis for self organization as it already de-nes the relevant roles for coordination.

xtended simulation. Currently, only restricted aspects of our coordination framework have een simulated, namely the communication protocol involving the conversation states of the gents. In order to understand and model the actual behavior of such systems we also would ave to deal with actual concurrency. We need a more detailed model of the internal processing f the agents. A more comprehensive simulation would have to include not only communication perators, but also plan modification operators, and in a further extension, the execution of ac-ons. This model can only be constructed with a specific application in mind. The conceptual oundations for these simulations have been given by our model.

npact on Application domains. We believe that our coordination paradigm might be use-l in many domains. The impact of our research may range from very technical, automated omains such as distributed traffic control, manufacturing and scheduling or cooperating robots

to domains where cooperation among humans is of primary interest (computer-supported coop
erative work). We have underpined this statement by giving examples from a variety of do
mains and pointing out the applicability for other domains in general (pursuit game, au
tonomous mobile vehicles, delivery scenario, distributed project planning, creation of offic
procedures, coordination of office plans).

There is great potential for experiments in various application domains. A domain has to be pre
pared in the following way to be amendable to our approach: First define the domain using th
predicates introduced in Chapters 3, 4 and 7, and, second, identify the relations in this domai
Then, agents would have to communicate (interact) as proposed in our model. The heuristic
which have been proposed by us may have to be adjusted but can provide a starting point.

Automated, intelligent agent driven animation. Our model can serve as basis for a
animation system, in which the animation is driven by the agents' intentions (plans) and th
modifications resulting from the agents' encounter in the same scenes. Agents have goal:
which are defined by plans. These plans are provided by humans outside the system. In add
tion, the actors have patterns of interaction and plan modification (communication framework
Thus, they know how to adapt to unforeseen situations (namely by evaluating plan relatio
ships and evaluating them). These unforeseen situations are due to the other actors which als
influence and change the world. Besides opening the doors to new forms of art, intellige
agent driven animation can be employed as a visual check of how agent behavior can b
specified.

References

Adler et al. 89] M. R. Adler, A. B. Davis, R. Weihmeyer, R. W. Worrest: Conflict-resolution strategies for non-hierarchical distributed agents. In: L. Gasser, M. N. Huhns (eds.), Distributed Artificial Intelligence, Vol. II, pp. 139-161, London: Pitman, 1989

Allen 83] J. F. Allen: Maintaining knowledge about temporal intervals. Communications of the ACM, 26(11): 832-843 (November 1983)

Allen 84] J. F. Allen: Towards a general theory of action and time. Artificial Intelligence 23, 123-154 (1984)

Archibald, Villoria 67] R.D. Archibald, R.L. Villoria: Network-Based Management Systems (PERT/CPM). New York: John Wiley, 1967

Barber 83] G. R. Barber. Supporting organizational problem solving with a work station. ACM Transactions on Office Information Systems, 1 (1983)

Barber et al. 83] G. Barber, P. de Jong, C. Hewitt: Semantic support for work in organizations. In: R.E.A. Mason (ed.), Information Processing 83. North-Holland, IFIP, 1983

Benda et al. 86] M. Benda, V. Jaganathan, R. Dodhiawala: On optimal cooperation of knowledge sources. Boeing Advanced Technology Center, Boeing Computer Services, Seattle, WA, September 1986

Benda 89] M. Benda (ed.): Proceedings of the Ninth Workshop on Distributed Artificial Intelligence. AAAI, Boeing, Seattle, WA, September 1989

Bond and Gasser 88] A. H. Bond, L. G. Gasser (eds.): Readings in Distributed Artificial Intelligence. San Mateo, CA: Morgan Kaufmann, 1988

Burmeister and Sundermeyer 90] B. Burmeister, K. Sundermeyer: COSY: Towards a methodology of multiagent systems. Proc. 1st Intern. Conf. on Cooperating Knowledge Based Systems, Keele, UK, 1990

Cammarata, McArthur and Steeb 83] S. Cammarata, D. McArthur, R. Steeb: Strategies of cooperation in distributed problem solving. IJCAI-83, pp. 767-770, 1983

[Chandrasekaran 81] B. Chandrasekaran: Natural and social system metaphors for distribute
problem solving: Introduction to the Issue. IEEE Trans. Systems. on Man, Cybernetic
SMC-11(1):1-5 (January 1981)

[Chang 87] E. Chang: Participant systems. In [Huhns 87], pp. 311-339

[Cohen and Feigenbaum 82] P.R. Cohen, E.A. Feigenbaum (eds.): Planning and proble
solving. The Handbook of Artificial Intelligence, Volume III, pp. 513-562, Londo
Pitman, 1982

[Cohen and Levesque 87] P. R. Cohen, H. J. Levesque: Persistence, intention and commi
ment. TR-CSLI-87-88, Center for the study of language and information, Stanfor
University, Stanford, CA, March 1987

[Cohen and Perrault 79] P. R. Cohen, C. R. Perrault: Elements of a plan-based theory
speech acts. Cognitive Science, 3(3):177-212 (1979)

[Conry, Meyer and Lesser 86] S. E. Conry, R. A. Meyer, V. R. Lesser: Multistage negotiatic
in distributed planning. COINS Technical Report 86-67, Amherst, MA, December 1986

[Conry, Meyer and Pope 89] S. E. Conry, R. A. Meyer, R. P. Pope: Mechanisms for asses
ing nonlocal impact of local decisions in distributed planning. In: [Gasser and Huhr
89], pp. 245-258, 1989

[Corkhill 79] D. D. Corkhill: Hierarchical planning in a distributed environment. IJCAI-7
pp. 168-175, 1979

[Corkhill and Lesser 83] D. D. Corkhill, V. R. Lesser: The use of metalevel control for coord
nation in a distributed problem solving network. IJCAI-83, pp. 748-756, 1983

[Croft 87] W. B. Croft: Representing office work with goals and constraints. Proc. of the IF
WG8.4 Workshop on Office Knowledge, Toronto, Canada, August 1987

[Croft and Lefkowitz 87] W. B. Croft, L. S. Lefkowitz: Knowledge-based support of coope
ative activities. In Proceedings of the 21st Annual Hawaii International Conf. on Systen
Science, Vol. III, pp. 312-318, 1988

[Croft and Lefkowitz 88] W. B. Croft, L. S. Lefkowitz: Using a planner to support office work. Proc. Conf. on Office Information Systems, pp. 55-62, Palo Alto, CA, ACM SIGOIS and IEEECS TC-OA, March 1988

[Davis 80] R. Davis: Report on the workshop on Distributed AI. Sigart Newsletter 73:42-52 (October 1980)

[Davis 82] R. Davis: Report on the second workshop on Distributed AI. Sigart Newsletter 80:13-23 (April 1982)

[Davis and Smith 80] R. Davis, R. G. Smith: Cooperative Problem solving with the contract net. Sigart Newsletter 73:42-52 (October 1980)

[Davis and Smith 83] R. Davis, R. G. Smith: Negotiation as a metaphor for distributed problem solving. Artificial Intelligence, 20:63-109, 1983 (also A.I. Memo No. 624, AI Lab MIT, 1981)

[Dean 86a] T. L. Dean: Temporal Imagery: An Approach to Reasoning about Time for Planning and Problem Solving. PhD thesis, Yale University, 1986

[Dean 86b] T. L. Dean: Decision support for coordinated multiagent planning. ACM-SIGOIS, pp. 81-91, 1986

[Decker 87] K. Decker: Distributed problem-solving techniques: a survey. IEEE Transactions on Systems, Man, and Cybernetics, Vol. SMC-17:729-740 (1987)

[Decker et al. 88] K. S. Decker, E.H. Durfee, V.R. Lesser: Evaluating research in cooperative distributed problem solving. COINS Technical Report 88-89, University of Massachusetts at Amherst, MA, August 1988

[deJong 90] P. de Jong: Structure and action in distributed organizations. In: F. H. Lochovsky, R. B. Allen (eds.), COIS90 – Conference on Office Information Systems, pp. 1-10, MIT-Cambridge, New York: ACM, April 1990

[Demazeau and Müller 90] Y. Demazeau, J.P. Müller (eds.): Decentralized A.I. Amsterdam: North-Holland, 1990

[Demazeau and Müller 91] Y. Demazeau, J.P. Müller (eds.): Decentralized A.I. Vol. II, to appear, Amsterdam: North-Holland, 1991

[Durfee 88] E.H. Durfee: Coordination of Distributed Problem Solvers. 269 pages, Bosto MA: Kluwer Academic, 1988

[Durfee and Lesser 87] E. H. Durfee, V. R. Lesser: Using partial global plans to coordina distributed problem solvers. IJCAI-87, pp. 875-883, 1987

[Durfee and Lesser 88] E. H. Durfee, V. R. Lesser: Predictability versus responsiveness: coo dinating problem solvers in dynamic domains. AAAI-88, 1988

[Durfee and Lesser 89] E. H. Durfee, V. R. Lesser: Negotiating task decomposition and all cation using partial global planning," In [Gasser and Huhns 89], pp. 229-244

[Durfee et al. 89a] E. H. Durfee, V. R. Lesser, D. D. Corkhill: Cooperative distributed prot lem solving. In; Barr, Cohen and Feigenbaum (eds.), The Handbook of Artifici Intelligence Volume IV, pp. 85-147, Addison-Wesley 1989

[Durfee et al. 89b] E. H. Durfee, V. R. Lesser, D. D. Corkhill. Trends in cooperative dis tributed problem solving. IEEE Transactions on Knowledge and Data Engineering 1(1):63- 83 (March 1989)

[Durfee and Montgomery 90] E. H. Durfee, A. Montgomery: A hierarchical protocol for c ordinating multiagent behaviors. In AAAI-90, pp. 86-93, 1990

[Ellis and Naffah 87] C. A. Ellis, N. Naffah: Design of Office Information Systems. 24 pages, Surveys in Computer Science, Berlin: Springer, 1987

[Ellis et al. 91] C. A. Ellis, S. J. Gibbs, G. L. Rein: Groupware – Some issues and experi ences. Communications of the ACM, 34(1):39-58 (January 1991)

[Erman et al. 80] L. D. Erman, F. Hayes-Roth, V. R. Lesser, D. R. Reddy: The Hearsay- speech understanding system: Integrating Knowledge to resolve uncertainty. Computin Surveys, 12(2):213-253 (1980)

[Fehling and Erman 83] M. Fehling and L. Erman: Report on the third annual workshop o distributed artificial intelligence. Sigart Newsletter, 84:3-12 (April 1983)

[Feldman and Ballard 82] J. A. Feldman and D. H. Ballard: Connectionist models and the properties. Cognitive Science, 6(3): 205-254 (1982)

Fikes 81] R. Fikes: Automating the problem solving in procedural office work. Proceedings of the AFIPS Office Automation Conference, Houston, TX, March 1981

Fikes 82] R. Fikes: A Commitment-based framework for describing informal cooperative work. Cognitive Science, 6(4),;331-347 (1982)

Fikes and Henderson 80] R. Fikes, A. Henderson: On supporting the use of procedures in office work. AAAI-80, pp. 202-207, August 1980

Fikes and Nilsson 71] R.E. Fikes, N. Nilsson: STRIPS: a new approach to the application of theorem proving to problem solving. Artificial Intelligence, 3(3-4):189-208 (1971)

Findler and Lo 88] N.V. Findler, R. Lo. An examination of distributed planning in the world of air traffic control. In: [Bond and Gasser 88], pp. 617-627

Fox 80] M.S. Fox: Organization structuring. Sigart Newsletter 73 (October 1980)

Fox 81] M.S. Fox: An organizational view of distributed systems. IEEE Trans. on System Man, Cybernetics, Vol. SMC-11:70-80 (January 1981)

Fraichard and Demazeau 90] T. Fraichard and Y. Demazeau: Motion planning in a multiagent world. In; [Demazeau and Müller 90], pp. 137-154

Garey and Johnson 78] M. R. Garey, D. S. Johnson: Computers and intractability: A guide to the theory of NP-completeness. San Francisco, CA: H. Freeman, 1987

Gasser 87] L. Gasser: The 1985 workshop on Distributed Artificial Intelligence. AI Magazine, 8(2):91-97 (Summer 1987)

Gasser 91] L. Gasser: Social conceptions of knowledge and action: DAI foundations and open systems semantics. Artificial Intelligence, (January 1991)

Gasser and Huhns 89] L. Gasser, M.N. Huhns (eds.): Distributed Artificial Intelligence. Vol.2, London: Pitman, 1989

Gasser et al. 89] L. Gasser, N. Roquette, R. W. Hill, and J. Lieb: Representing and using organizational knowledge in DAI systems. In: [Gasser and Huhns 89], pp. 55-78

[GBO 85] "Geschäfts- und Betriebsordung (GBO) der Gesellschaft für Mathematik und Daten verarbeitung mbH", Sankt Augustin, GMD, 1985

[Genesereth and Rosenschein 83] M. Genesereth, J. Rosenschein: The intelligent agents pro ject. Sigart Newsletter No. 84, (1983)

[Genesereth et al. 84] M. Genesereth, M.L. Ginsberg, J.S. Rosenschein: Cooperation withou communication. Technical Report HPP-84-36, Stanford University, CA, Septembe 1984

[Genrich and Lautenbach 1981] H. J. Genrich, K. Lautenbach: System modeling with high level Petri Nets. Theoretical Computer Science, 13:109-136 (1981)

[Georgeff 83] M. Georgeff: Communication and interaction in multiagent planning. AAAI-83 pp. 125-129, 1983

[Georgeff 84] M. Georgeff: A theory of action for multiagent planning. AAAI-84, pp. 121 125, 1984

[Georgeff 86] M. Georgeff: The representation of events in multiagent domains. AAAI-86, pp 70-75, 1986

[Georgeff 87] M. P. Georgeff: Actions, processes, and causality. In: [Georgeff and Lansky 87], pp. 99-122

[Georgeff and Lansky 87] M. P. Georgeff, A. L. Lansky (eds.): Reasoning about Actions and Plans. Los Altos, CA: Morgan Kaufmann, 1987

[Ginsberg 87] M. L. Ginsberg. Decision procedures. In [Huhns 87], pp. 3-28

[Goldstein and Roberts 77] I. P. Goldstein and R. B. Roberts: NUDGE, A knowledge-based scheduling program. IJCAI-77, pp. 257-263, 1977

[Goodson and Schmidt 87] J. L. Goodson, C.F. Schmidt: A distributed problem solving ap proach to person-machine interaction. AI Magazine (Fall 1987)

[Greif 88] I. Greif: Computer-supported cooperative work: A book of readings. Irene Greif (ed.), San Mateo, CA: Morgan Kaufmann, 1988

Grosz 90] B. F. Grosz: Collaborative planning in discourse. In Proceedings of the ECAI-90, pp.774-775, 1990

Grosz and Sidner 88] B. J. Grosz, C. L. Sidner: Distributed know-how and acting: Research on collaborative planning. Proc. Workshop on Distributed Artificial Intelligence, 1988

Hayes-Roth 80] F. Hayes-Roth: Towards a framework for distributed A.I. In [Davis 80], pp.51-52

Hayes-Roth 85] B. Hayes-Roth: A blackboard architecture for control. Artificial Intelligence, 26:251-321 (October 1985)

Hecking 88] M. Hecking: Towards a belief-oriented theory of plan recognition. Proc. of the AAAI-88 Workshop on Plan Recognition. St. Paul, MN, August 1988

Hecking 90] M. Hecking: The SINIX Consultant - Towards a theoretical treatment of plan recognition. In: Norvig, Wahlster, and Wilensky (eds.), Intelligent Help Systems for UNIX. Berlin: Springer, 1990

Hendler 91] J. Hendler: Multiple approaches to multiple agent problem solving. In [IJCAI-91], pp. 553-554

Hewitt 77] C. Hewitt: Viewing control structures as pattern of passing messages. Artificial Intelligence 8:323-364 (1977)

Hewitt 80] C. Hewitt: Message passing semantics: Sigart Newsletter No. 73 (October 1980)

Hewitt 86] C. Hewitt: Offices are open systems. ACM Transactions on Office Information Systems, 4(3): 271-287 (July 1986)

Hoare 78] C. A. R. Hoare: Communicating sequential processes. CACM 21(8):666-677 (August 1978)

Huhns 87] M. N. Huhns (ed.): Distributed Artificial Intelligence. 390 pages, London: Pitman, 1987

Huhns et al. 85] M. Huhns, R. Bonnel, L. Stephens, U. Mukhopadhyay: The MINDS project: multiple intelligent node document servers. AI Magazine (Fall 1985)

[Huhns 90] M. Huhns (ed.): Proceedings of the 10th International Workshop on Distribute
Artificial Intelligence. MCC Technical Report Number ACT-AI-355-90, Austin, TX
MCC, October 1990

[Hynynen 88] J. Hynynen: A framework for coordination in distributed production manage
ment. 94 pages, Series No. 52, Helsinki: Acta Polytechnica Scandinavica, 1988

[Ishii and Martial 88] H. Ishii, F. v. Martial: View control in a semantic net jungle - An appli
cation to an office knowledge base. Proceedings of the 4th Human Interface Symposium
Tokyo: Japanese Society for Instrument and Control Engineers, November 1988

[Jagannathan and Dodhiawala 87] V. Jagannathan and R. Dodhiawala: Distributed Artificia
Intelligence: An annotated bibliography. In [Huhns 87], pp. 341-390

[Kartram and Wilkins 89] N. A. Kartram, D. E. Wilkins: Toward a foundation for evaluatin
AI planners. SRI Technical Note 471, Stanford University, CA, August 1989

[Katz and Rosenschein 89] M. Katz, J.S. Rosenschein: Plans for multiple agents. In: [Gasse
and Huhns 89], pp. 197-228

[Kautz and Pednault 88] H. A. Kautz, E. P.D. Pednault: Planning and plan recognition. AT&T
Technical Journal, Vol. 67, Issue 1, pp. 25-40, January/February 1988

[Kaye and Karam 87] A.R. Kaye, G.M. Karam: Cooperating knowledge-based assistants fo
the office. ACM Trans. on Office Information Systems, Vol.5, October 1987

[Kedzierski 88] B. Kedzierski: Communication and management support in system develop
ment environments. In: [Greif 88], pp. 253-268

[Konolige and Nilsson 80] K. Konolige, N.J. Nilsson: Multiple-agent planning systems
AAAI-1980, pp. 138-142, 1980

[Koo 88] C. C. Koo: A distributed model for performance systems: Synchronizing plan
among intelligent agents via communication, PhD thesis, Stanford University, Stanford
CA, 1988

[Koo and Wiederhold 88] C. C. Koo, G. Wiederhold: A commitment-based communicatior
model for distributed office environments. Proceedings of the Conference on Office
Information Systems (COIS), pp. 291-298, New York: ACM, 1988

[Kornfeld and Hewitt 81] W.A. Kornfeld, C. Hewitt: The scientific community metaphor. IEEE Trans. on Sys., Man, Cybernetics, Vol SMC-11:24-33 (January 1981)

[Kreifelts and Woetzel 87] Th. Kreifelts, G. Woetzel: Distribution and exception handling in an office procedure system. In: G. Bracchi, D. Tsichritzis (eds.), Office Systems: Methods and Tools. pp. 197-208, Amsterdam: North-Holland, 1987

[Kreifelts et al. 84] Th. Kreifelts, U. Licht, P. Seuffert, G. Woetzel: DOMINO: A system for the specification and automation of cooperative office processes. In: B. Myhrhaug, D. R. Wilson (eds.), Proc. Euromicro '84, pp. 33-41, Amsterdam: North-Holland, 1984

[Kreifelts and Martial 90] Th. Kreifelts, F. v. Martial: A negotiation framework for autonomous agents. Proceedings of the 2nd European Workshop on Modelizing Autonomous Agents and Multi-Agent Worlds, Paris, France, August, 1990, (to appear in [Demazeau and Müller 91])

[Kuwabara and Lesser 89] K. Kuwabara, V.R. Lesser: Extended protocol for multistage negotiation. In: [Benda 89], pp. 129-161

[Lansky 87] A. L. Lansky: A representation of parallel activity based on events, structure and causality. In: [Georgeff and Lansky 87], pp. 123-160

[Lansky 88] A. L. Lansky: Localized event-based reasoning for multiagent domains. Technical Note 423, Stanford University, CA: SRI International, January 1988

[Lefkowitz and Croft 89] L.S. Lefkowitz, W.B. Croft: Planning and execution of tasks in cooperative work environments. IEEE Conference on AI Applications, Miami, March 1989

[Lesser and Corkhill 83] V. R. Lesser, D. D. Corkhill: The distributed vehicle monitoring testbed: A tool for investigating distributed problem solving networks. AI Magazine, pp. 15-33 (Fall 1983)

[Lesser and Corkhill 87] V. Lesser, D. Corkhill: Distributed problem solving. In: S. C. Shapiro and D. Eckroth (eds.), Encyclopedia of Artificial Intelligence, Vol. 2, pp. 245-251, New York: John Wiley, 1987

[Lochbaum, Grosz and Sidner 90] K. E. Lochbaum, B. J. Grosz, C. L. Sidner: Models of plans to support communication: An initial report. AAAI-90, pp. 485-490, 1990

[Malone 85] T.W. Malone: What Can AI Learn From Looking at Human Organizations? AI Magazine 6(3) (Fall 1985)

[Malone 87] T.W. Malone: Modeling coordination in organizations and markets. Management Science, 33(10):1317-1332, 1987

[Malone 88] T. Malone: What is coordination theory? Proceedings of the Workshop on Distributed Artificial Intelligence, 1988

[Malone et al. 88] T. W. Malone, K. Grant, K. Lai, D. Rosenblitt: Semistructured messages are surprisingly useful for computer-supported coordination. In: [Greif 88], pp. 311-313

[March and Simon 1969] J. G. March, H. Simon: Organizations. Jon Wiley, 1969

[Martial 90a] F. v. Martial: A conversation model for resolving conflicts among distributed office activities. In: F. H. Lochovsky, R. B. Allen (eds.): COIS90- Conference on Office Information Systems, pp. 99-108, MIT-Cambridge, New York: ACM, April 1990

[Martial 90b] F. v. Martial: Interactions among autonomous planning agents. In [Demazeau and Müller 90], pp. 105-119

[Martial 90d] F. v. Martial: Coordination of plans in multiagent worlds by taking advantage of the favor relation. In [Huhns 90], Chapter 21

[Martial and Victor 87] F. v. Martial, F. Victor: Das Elektronische Organisationshandbuch: Anforderungen und Spezifikation. WISDOM-Verbundprojekt, FB-GMD-87-16, p. 35, Nurenberg: Triumph-Adler, 1987

[Martial and Victor 88a] Frank v. Martial, Frank Victor: An interactive planner for open systems. Proceedings of the Fourth IEEE Conference on Artificial Intelligence Applications, San Diego, pp. 293-298, CA, IEEE, March 1988

[Martial and Victor 88b] F. v. Martial, F. Victor: Construction of an office knowledge base: Experiences and suggestions. In: J. Boose, B. Gaines, M. Linster (eds.), Proceedings of the 2nd European Knowledge Acquisition for Knowledge Based System Workshop, GMD-Studien Nr.143, pp. 32.1-32.14, Sankt Augustin: GMD, June 19-23, 1988

[Martial and Victor 89] F. v. Martial, F. Victor: Knowledge acquisition for an electronic organizational handbook. Proceedings of the Fifth Australian Conference on Applications of Expert Systems, pp.189-202, Sydney: University of Technology, May 1989

[Martial and Victor 91] F. v. Martial, F. Victor: Interaktive Planung von Bürovorgängen. In: R. Lutze, A. Kohl (Hrsg.), WISDOM - Wissensbasierte Systeme zur Bürokommunikation: Dokumentenbearbeitung, Organisation, Mensch-Computer Kommunikation, pp. 313-324, München: Oldenbourg, 1991,

[Martial et al. 90] F. v. Martial, F. Victor, H. Ishii: A System for knowledge-based information extraction. DEXA-90: Proc. International Conf. on Database and Expert Systems Applications, pp. 495-499, Vienna, Austria, Springer, August 1990

[Maruichi 89] T. Maruichi: Organizational Computation – A framework for distributed cooperative problem-solving using autonomous agents and their groups. PhD thesis, Yokohama: Keio University, 1989

[McArthur et al. 82] D. McArthur, R. Steeb, and S. Cammarata: A framework for distributed problem solving. In Proceedings of the 1982 AAAI Conference, pp. 181-184, 1982

[McCarthy and Hayes 69] J. McCarthy, P. Hayes: Some philosophical problems from the standpoint of artificial intelligence. In: D. Michie and B. Meltzer (eds.), Machine Intelligence 4, pp. 463-502, Edinburgh, Scotland: Edinburgh University Press, 1969

[Moore 88] R. C. Moore: A formal theory of knowledge and action. In: Hobbs and Moore (eds.), Formal Theories of the Commonsense World, pp. 319-358, Norwood, NJ: Ablex Publishing Corporation, 1988

[Morgenstern 86] L. Morgenstern: A first order theory of planning, knowledge, and action. In: J. Y. Halpern (ed.), Proceedings of the 1986 Conference on Reasoning about Knowledge, pp. 99-114, San Mateo, CA: Morgan Kaufmann, March 1986

[Morgenstern 87] L. Morgenstern: Knowledge preconditions for actions and plans. IJCAI-87, pp. 867-874, 1987

[Mukhopadhyay et al. 86] U. Mukhopadhyay, L. Stephens, M. Huhns, R. Bonnel: An intelligent system for document retrieval in distributed office environments. Journal of the American Society for Information Science, 37:123-135, 1986

[Nirenburg and Lesser 86] S. Nirenburg, V. Lesser: Providing intelligent assistance in distributed environments. ACM SIGOIS Providence, Rhode Island, pp. 104-112, 1986

[Paranuk 85] H. V. D. Paranuk: Manufacturing experience with the contract net. Proceedings of the 1985 Distributed Artificial Intelligence Workshop, pp. 67-91, December 1985, (also in [Huhns 87])

[Pednault 87] E. P.D. Pednault: Formulating multiagent, dynamic-world problems in the classical planning framework. In: [Georgeff and Lansky 87], pp. 47-82

[Pelavin 88] R.N. Pelavin: A formal approach to planning with concurrent actions and external events. PhD thesis, TR 254, University of Rochester, 301 pages, New York, 1988

[Pernici and Stuart 89] B. Pernici, A.A. Verrijn-Stuart (eds.): Office Information Systems: The design process, IFIP, Elsevier Science Publishers B.V. (North-Holland), 1989

[Peterson 81] J. L. Peterson: Petri net theory and the modeling of systems. Englewood Cliffs, NJ: Prentice-Hall, 1981

[Reisig 83] W. Reisig Petri Nets: An Introduction, Springer, Berlin 1983.

[Retz-Schmidt 91a] G. Retz-Schmidt: Die Interpretation des Verhaltens mehrerer Akteure in Szenenfolgen. PhD thesis, Universität des Saarlandes, 1991

[Retz-Schmidt 91b] G. Retz-Schmidt: Recognizing Intentions, Interactions, and Causes of Plan Failures. In A. Kobsa (ed.): User modeling and user-adapted interaction, 1:173-205, Kluwer (1991)

[Rosenschein 82] J. S. Rosenschein: Synchronization of multiagent plans. AAAI-82, pp. 115-119, 1982

[Rosenschein and Genesrereth 85] J. S. Rosenschein, M. R. Genesereth: Deals among rational agents. IJCAI-85, pp. 91-99, 1985

[Rosenschein 86] J. S. Rosenschein: Rational Interaction: Cooperation among Intelligent Agents. PhD thesis, Stanford University, CA, 1986

[Sacerdoti 75] E. D. Sacerdoti: Planning in a hierarchy of abstraction spaces. IJCAI-75, 1975

[Sacerdoti 77] E. D. Sacerdoti: A Structure for Plans and Behavior. New York: Elsevier North-Holland, 1977

[Sathi 87] A. Sathi: Constraint directed negotiation among organizational entities: An alternative model of project management. AI Magazine, pp.75-85 (Fall 1987)

[Sathi and Fox 89] A. Sathi, M. Fox: Constraint-directed negotiation of resource reallocations. In: [Gasser and Huhns 89], pp. 163-193

[Sathi, Fox and Greenberg 1985] A. Sathi, M. S. Fox, M. Greenberg: Representation of activity knowledge for project management. IEEE Transactions on Pattern Analysis and Machine Intelligence, PAMI-7,5:531-552 (September 1985)

[Sathi et al. 86] A. Sathi, T. E. Morton, S. Roth. Callisto: An intelligent project management system. AI Magazine, pp. 34-52 (Winter 1986), also In: [Greif 88], pp. 269-310

[Schank 75] R. C. Schank: Conceptual Information Processing. Amsterdam: North-Holland, 1975

[Shapiro and Eckroth 87] S. C. Shapiro, D. Eckroth (eds.): Encyclopedia of Artificial Intelligence, Vol. 2, NY: John Wiley, 1987

[SMC-11 81] IEEE Transactions on Systems, Man, and Cybernetics, Special issue on Distributed Problem Solving and DAI (January 1981)

[Smith 80] R. G. Smith: The Contract Net Protocol: High-level Communication and Control in a Distributed Problem Solver. IEEE Transactions on Computers, C-29(12):1104-1113 (December 1980)

[Smith 83] S. F. Smith: Exploiting Temporal Knowledge to Organize Constraints. CMU-RI-TR-83-12, Carnegie Mellon University, PI, 1983

[Smith 85] R. G. Smith: Report on the 1984 Distributed Artificial Intelligence Workshop. AI Magazine, 6(3):234-243, 1985

[Smith and Davis 81] R. G. Smith, R. Davis: Frameworks for cooperation in distributed problem solving. IEEE Trans. on Sys., Man, Cybernetics, Vol SMC-11:61-70 (January 1981)

[Sommer et al. 90] E. Sommer, F. von Martial, F. Victor: PRAGMA: A system for actively capturing procedural knowledge via a graphical interface. In: L. Aiello (ed.), ECAI-90: Proc. 9th European Conference on Artificial Intelligence, pp. 616-621, London: Pitman, August 1990

[Sridharan 87] N.S. Sridharan: 1986 Workshop on Distributed AI. AI Magazine, pp. 75-85 (Fall 1987)

[Steeb et al. 1981] R. Steeb, S. Cammarata, F. A. Hayes-Roth, P. W. Thorndyke, R. B. Wesson: Distributed intelligence for air fleet control. R-2728-ARPA, The Rand Corporation, 1981, (an excerpt can be found In: [Bond and Gasser 88], pp.90-101)

[Stephens and Merx 90] L. M. Stephens, M. B. Merx: The effect of agent control strategy on the performance of a DAI pursuit problem. In: [Huhns 90], Chapter 14

[Stuart 85] C. Stuart: An implementation of a multiagent plan synchronizer. IJCAI-85, pp. 1031-1033, 1985

[Stuart 88] C. J. Stuart: Branching Regular Expressions and Multi-Agent Plans. In [Georgeff and Lansky 88], pp. 161-188

[Sumner 88] M. Sumner: The impact of electronic mail on managerial and organizational communications. Proc. of the Conf. on Office Information Systems, Palo Alto, CA, pp. 96-109, March 1988

[Suzuki and Lu 89] I. Suzuki, H. Lu: Temporal Petri nets and their applications to modeling and analysis of a handshake daisy chain arbiter. IEEE Transactions on Computers, 38(5) (May 1989)

[Sycara 85] K. Sycara-Cyranski: Arguments of persuasion in labor mediation. IJCAI-85, 1985

[Sycara 88] K. Sycara: Resolving goal conflicts via negotiation. AAAI-88, 1988

[Sycara 89a] K. P. Sycara: Argumentation: Planning Other Agents' Plans. IJCAI-89, pp. 517-523, 1989

[Sycara 89b] K. P. Sycara: Multiagent compromise via negotiation. In [Gasser and Huhns 89] pp.119-138], 1989

[Sycara et al. 90] K. P. Sycara, S. Roth, N. Sadeh, M. S. Fox: Decentralized factory scheduling: Coordinating resource allocation using constraint heuristic search. In: [Huhns 90], Chapter 17

[Taha 76] H. A. Taha: Operations Research. MacMillan Publishing, New York, 1976

[Tate 76] A. Tate: Project planning using a hierarchic non-linear planner. Research Report No.25, Dept. of AI, University of Edinburgh, August 1976

[Tate 77] A. Tate: Generating Project Networks. Proc. IJCAI, Cambridge, USA, August 1977

[Tate 85] A. Tate: A review of knowledge-based planning techniques. in M. Merry (Ed.), The Knowledge Engineering Review, 1(2):4-17, 85 (1985)

[Tenney and Sandell 81] R.R. Tenney, N.R. Sandell: Strategies for distributed decisionmaking. IEEE Transactions on Systems, Man and Cybernetics, SMC-11(8):517-526 (1981)

[Thorndyke et al. 81] P. Thorndyke, D. McArthur, S. Cammarata: Autopilot: A distributed planner for air fleet control. In [IJCAI-81], pp. 171-177, August 1981

[Tokoro and Ishikawa 84] M. Tokoro, Y. Ishikawa: An object-oriented approach to knowledge systems. in Proc. of Fifth Generation Computer Systems (FGCS'84), ICOT, 1984

[Tsichritzis 85] D. Tsichritzis: Office Automation - Concepts and Tools. Springer-Heidelberg, M. Brodie, J. Mylopoulos, J. Schmidt (Series editors), 1985

[Tsichritzis et al. 87] D. Tsichritzis, E. Fiume, S. Gibbs, O. Nierstrasz: KNOs: knowledge acquisition, dissemination and manipulation objects. ACM Trans. on Office Information Systems, January 1987

[Victor and Sommer 89] F. Victor, E. Sommer: Supporting the design of office procedures in the DOMINO system. In Proc. First European Conf. on Computer-Supported Cooperative Work, Gatwick, London, Sept. 1989

[Victor and Woetzel 90] F. Victor, G. Woetzel: A Prolog simulator for Pr/t-nets. Breitenecker, Troch, and Kopaceck (Eds.), 6. Symposium on Techniques for Simulation, pp. 284-289, Vienna, Braunschweig: Vieweg, 1990

[Victor et al. 89] F. Victor, E. Sommer, F. von Martial: Das Planungsunterstützungssystem VIPS: Synthese und Analyse von Vorgängen auf der Basis eines elektronischen Organisationshandbuchs. In: M. Paul (Hrsg.), GI-19. Jahrestagung, Computergestützter Arbeitsplatz, München, Heidelberg: Springer, Oktober 1989

[Werner 90] E. Werner. Distributed cooperation algorithms. In [Demazeau and Müller 90], pp. 17-31

[Werner and Reinefeld 90] E. Werner, A. Reinefeld: Distributed algorithms for cooperating agents. in [Huhns 90], Chapter 27

[Wilensky 83] R. Wilensky: Planning and Understanding. Addison-Wesley, Reading, MA, 1983

[Wilkins 84] D.E. Wilkins: Domain-independent planning: Representation and plan generation. Artificial Intelligence, 22:269-301 (1984)

[Wilkins 88] D.E. Wilkins: Practical Planning - Extending the Classical AI Planning Paradigm. San Mateo, CA: Morgan Kaufmann, 1988

[Wißkirchen et al. 84] P. Wißkirchen, S. Niehuis, F. Victor: Ein rechnergestützter Bürosimulator auf der Basis von Pr/T-Netzen und Prolog. Angewandte Informatik 5/84:181-188, 1984

[Wood 83] S. Wood: Dynamic world simulation for planning with multiple agents. IJCAI-83, pp. 69-71, 1983

[Woetzel and Kreifelts 88] G. Woetzel, Th. Kreifelts: Deadlock Freeness and Consistency in a Conversational System. In: B. Pernici, A.A. Verrijn-Stuart (eds.), Proc. IFIP WG8.4 Conf. on Office Information Systems: The Design Process, Linz, Austria, August 1988

[Woo and Lochovsky 86] C.C. Woo, F.H. Lochovsky: Supporting distributed office problem solving in organizations. ACM Trans. on Office Information Systems, 4:185-204 (July 1986)

[Zlotkin and Rosenschein 89a] G. Zlotkin, J. S. Rosenschein: Negotiation and Task Sharing among autonomous agents in cooperative domains. IJCAI-89, pp. 912-917, 1989

[Zlotkin and Rosenschein 89b] G. Zlotkin, J. S. Rosenschein: Negotiation and task sharing in a non-cooperative domain. Proceedings Ninth Workshop on Distributed AI, AAAI, pp. 307-328, September 1989

[Zlotkin and Rosenschein 90a] G. Zlotkin, J. S. Rosenschein: Negotiation and Conflict Resolution in Non-Cooperative Domains. AAAI-90, pp. 100-105, 1990

[Zlotkin and Rosenschein 90b] G. Zlotkin, J. S. Rosenschein: Negotiation and goal relaxation. Proc. 2nd European Workshop MAAMAW'90, pp. 115-131, August 1990

[Zlotkin and Rosenschein 90c] G. Zlotkin, J. S. Rosenschein: Blocks, lies and postal freight: the nature of deception in negotiation. In: [Huhns 90], Chapter 8

Abbreviations

[AAAI-80]   Proceedings of the First Annual National Conference on Artificial Intelligence,
            Stanford University, 1980. Los Altos, CA: Morgan Kaufmann, 1980
[AAAI-82]   Proceedings of the National Conference on Artificial Intelligence, Pittsburgh,
            PA, 1983. Los Altos, CA: Morgan Kaufmann, 1982
[AAAI-83]   Proceedings of the National Conference on Artificial Intelligence, Washington,
            DC, 1983. Los Altos, CA: Morgan Kaufmann, 1983
[AAAI-84]   Proceedings of the National Conference on Artificial Intelligence, University of
            Texas at Austin, 1984. Los Altos, CA: Morgan Kaufmann, 1984
[AAAI-86]   Proceedings of the Fifth National Conference on Artificial Intelligence,
            University of Pennsylvania, 1986. Los Altos, CA: Morgan Kaufmann, 1986
[AAAI-87]   Proceedings of the Sixth National Conference on Artificial Intelligence, 1987.
            Los Altos, CA: Morgan Kaufmann, 1987
[AAAI-88]   Proceedings of the Seventh National Conference on Artificial Intelligence, 1988.
            Los Altos, CA: Morgan Kaufmann, 1988
[AAAI-90]   Proceedings of the Eighth National Conference on Artificial Intelligence, 1990.
            Los Altos, CA: Morgan Kaufmann, 1990

[ECAI]   European Conference on Artificial Intelligence

[IJCAI-75] Advance Papers from the Fourth International Joint Conference on Artificial
            Intelligence, Tbilisi, Georgia, USSR, Two Volumes, September 1975
[IJCAI-77] Proceedings of the Fifth International Conference on Artificial Intelligence,
            Cambridge, Massachusetts, United States, August 1977
[IJCAI-79] Proceedings of the Sixth International Joint Conference on Artificial Intelligence,
            Vols. I and II, Tokyo, 1979. Los Altos, CA: Morgan Kaufmann, 1979.
[IJCAI-81] Proceedings of the Seventh International Joint Conference on Artificial
            Intelligence, Vols. I and II, Vancouver, BC, 1981. Los Altos, CA: Morgan
            Kaufmann, 1981
[IJCAI-83] Proceedings of the Eighth International Joint Conference on Artificial
            Intelligence, Vols. I and II, Karlsruhe, 1983. Los Altos, CA: Morgan
            Kaufmann, 1983
[IJCAI-85] Proceedings of the Ninth International Joint Conference on Artificial Intelli
            gence, Vols. I and II, Los Angeles, 1985. Los Altos, CA: Morgan Kaufmann,
            1985

[IJCAI-87]   Proceedings of the Tenth International Joint Conference on Artificial Intelli
             gence, Vols. I and II, Milano, Italy, 1987. Los Altos, CA: Morgan Kaufmann,
             1987
[IJCAI-89]   Proceedings of the Eleventh International Joint Conference on Artificial
             Intelligence, Vols. I and II, Detroit, 1989. Los Altos, CA: Morgan Kaufmann,
             1989
[IJCAI-91]   Proceedings of the 12th International Joint Conference on Artificial Intelligence,
             Vols. I and II, Sydney, 1991. San Mateo, CA: Morgan Kaufmann, 1991

List of Figures

List of Tables

Index

Lecture Notes in Artificial Intelligence (LNAI)

Lecture Notes in Computer Science